AspectJ Cookbook™

Other Java™ resources from O'Reilly

Related titles Java™ Extreme Programming Cookbook™

Jakarta Commons Cookbook™

Java™ Cookbook™

Eclipse Cookbook™

Java™ Servlet and JSP Cookbook™

Extreme Programming Pocket Guide

JUnit Pocket Guide

Java Books Resource Center *java.oreilly.com* is a complete catalog of O'Reilly's books on Java and related technologies, including sample chapters and code examples.

OnJava.com is a one-stop resource for enterprise Java developers, featuring news, code recipes, interviews, weblogs, and more.

Conferences O'Reilly brings diverse innovators together to nurture the ideas that spark revolutionary industries. We specialize in documenting the latest tools and systems, translating the innovator's knowledge into useful skills for those in the trenches. Visit *conferences.oreilly.com* for our upcoming events.

Safari Bookshelf (*safari.oreilly.com*) is the premier online reference library for programmers and IT professionals. Conduct searches across more than 1,000 books. Subscribers can zero in on answers to time-critical questions in a matter of seconds. Read the books on your Bookshelf from cover to cover or simply flip to the page you need. Try it today with a free trial.

AspectJ Cookbook™

Russ Miles

O'REILLY®

Beijing · Cambridge · Farnham · Köln · Paris · Sebastopol · Taipei · Tokyo

AspectJ Cookbook™
by Russ Miles

Copyright © 2005 O'Reilly Media, Inc. All rights reserved.
Printed in the United States of America.

Published by O'Reilly Media, Inc., 1005 Gravenstein Highway North, Sebastopol, CA 95472.

O'Reilly books may be purchased for educational, business, or sales promotional use. Online editions are also available for most titles (*safari.oreilly.com*). For more information, contact our corporate/institutional sales department: (800) 998-9938 or *corporate@oreilly.com*.

Editor:	Brett McLaughlin
Production Editor:	Matt Hutchinson
Production Services:	GEX, Inc.
Cover Designer:	Emma Colby
Interior Designer:	David Futato

Printing History:

December 2004:	First Edition.

 This book uses RepKover™ a durable and flexible lay-flat binding.

ISBN: 0-596-00654-3
[M]

To Mike Sines

1976–1999

"Friendship is Forever"

Table of Contents

Preface

This book focuses on getting things done with AspectJ. Aspect-Oriented Software Development (AOSD) is a new branding for some old ideas incorporating an object-oriented twist. This rather complex definition really sums up what is a neat approach to solving some traditional object orientation's problems.

While this book does not get into too much detail on the theory behind aspect orientation, a brief overview is provided to give you a useful foundation to support the code recipes that form the rest of the book. The code recipes will walk you through how to get your system set up for aspect oriented development, building your first small programs, and eventually applying aspect orientation to complex real-world problems.

This book aims to be one of those useful books that sit on your desk and regularly get called upon to "just show me how to do that." You should be able to jump directly to the recipes you need as and when you need them in keeping with the "no fluff, just stuff" approach that is synonymous with the O'Reilly Cookbook series. With this in mind, the topics covered in this book include:

- A brief overview of aspect orientation and AspectJ
- Setting up, getting to grips with, and running AspectJ programs in a range of build and target environments
- A practical examination of each of the AspectJ extensions to the Java™ language
- Applying AspectJ to real-world software development problems that benefit from an aspect-oriented approach

Audience

While it will probably suffice to say that this book is for any person interested in learning about AspectJ and aspect orientation, this book will most benefit people who are fairly experienced with object-oriented design, particularly when implemented in Java. Anyone that is open to a fresh approach to solving some of the problems that traditional object orientation suffers from should find something in this book that encourages them to try AspectJ in their own applications.

About This Book

This book covers the following subjects:

- An overview of the elements of aspect orientation using AspectJ, pointcuts, join points, and advice
- Setting up your environment and getting started with AspectJ development
- Running AspectJ based software in various environments
- Deploying your AspectJ applications to varying target environments
- How to use the various forms of pointcut supported by AspectJ
- How to use the various forms of advice available in AspectJ
- Controlling how aspects are created and destroyed
- Changing the static structure of your software and support tools using AspectJ
- Enhancing existing object-oriented design pattern implementations using AspectJ
- Applying aspects to real-world problems within component, system, and enterprise domains

Rarely is a cookbook read from cover to cover, but an overview of each section's focus is useful in order to understand each chapter's place and what it is building towards. This cookbook is organized into four broad sections, as shown in Figure P-1.

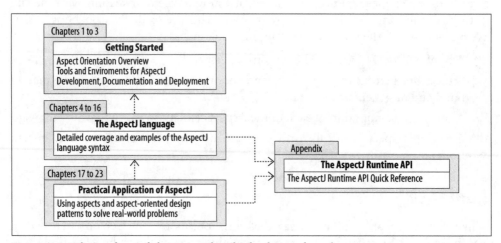

Figure P-1. What each set of chapters within this book intends to show

Chapters 1 through 3 provide a set of recipes to get you started with the tools and environments that support development using AspectJ. These chapters cover how to use command-line tools, Eclipse, even ANT to develop your aspect-oriented applications, and finish up by showing you how to deploy to diverse target environments such as Java Servlets, Java Server Pages, and web services.

Chapters 4 through 16 provide in-depth syntactical examinations of the AspectJ language. These chapters aim to give you a useful and exhaustive reference for how to use the different constructs that the AspectJ language adds to Java.

Chapters 17 through 23 are where AspectJ really gets to showcase its advantages over traditional object-oriented software implementations. In these chapters, Aspects are used to enhance and improve the design of software solutions ranging from design pattern implementations to enterprise applications. Chapter 23 brings this book to a close by introducing some of the aspect-oriented design patterns that are gradually being discovered as tools, such as AspectJ, bringing aspect orientation into the mainstream of software development.

Now that you know what this book is about, it should be explained what this book is not about. As mentioned before, this book is not a theoretical examination of AspectJ. The code is kept at the fore throughout to make sure that every area has a practical focus. There are many great articles online and gradually appearing in the press that examine the more theoretical concerns of AO, so this book does not attempt to deal with these.

This book is also not claiming to be AspectJ in a nutshell. AspectJ is in a very stable state for such a young implementation, but even now extensions to the language and the technologies are being considered, so it is possible that some areas of this book may age faster than others. In an attempt to ensure that this book has the longest life possible, only the most stable areas that were incorporated at the time of writing were included.

Assumptions This Book Makes

The following assumptions are made about your knowledge and experience with the supporting tool, languages, and concepts that accompany aspect-oriented development:

- That you have a reasonably advanced knowledge of the Java language
- That you have an existing Java Source Development Kit (SDK) on your system, at a minimum JSDK 1.2 and preferably 1.4+
- That you have some understanding and experience of Java Server Pages, Java Servlet, and Web Services (specifically Apache Axis) programming
- That you have some knowledge of UML (useful but not essential to understanding the diagrams)

Conventions Used in This Book

The following typographical conventions are used in this book:

Plain text

> Indicates menu titles, menu options, menu buttons, and keyboard accelerators (such as Alt and Ctrl).

Italic

> Indicates new terms, URLs, email addresses, filenames, file extensions, pathnames, directories, and Unix utilities.

`Constant width`

> Indicates commands, options, switches, variables, attributes, keys, functions, types, classes, namespaces, methods, modules, properties, parameters, values, objects, events, event handlers, XML tags, HTML tags, macros, the contents of files, or the output from commands.

`Constant width bold`

> Shows commands or other text that should be typed literally by the user.

`Constant width italic`

> Shows text that should be replaced with user-supplied values.

 This icon signifies a tip, suggestion, or general note.

 This icon indicates a warning or caution.

Using the Code Examples

This book is here to help you get your job done. In general, you may use the code in this book in your programs and documentation. You do not need to contact us for permission unless you're reproducing a significant portion of the code. For example, writing a program that uses several chunks of code from this book does not require permission. Selling or distributing a CD-ROM of examples from O'Reilly books *does* require permission. Answering a question by citing this book and quoting example code does not require permission. Incorporating a significant amount of example code from this book into your product's documentation *does* require permission.

We appreciate, but do not require, attribution. An attribution usually includes the title, author, publisher, and ISBN. For example: "*AspectJ Cookbook* by Russ Miles. Copyright 2005 O'Reilly Media, Inc., 0-596-00654-3."

If you feel your use of code examples falls outside fair use or the permission given above, feel free to contact us at *permissions@oreilly.com*.

We'd Like to Hear from You

We at O'Reilly have done everything to insure that the recipes within this book are tested and verified to the best of the author's ability. However, AspectJ is a fast moving technology and it may be that some features of the supporting toolsets or of the language itself have changed, or that we have simply made mistakes. If so, please address comments and questions concerning this book to the publisher:

O'Reilly Media, Inc.
1005 Gravenstein Highway North
Sebastopol, CA 95472
(800) 998-9938 (in the United States or Canada)
(707) 829-0515 (international or local)
(707) 829-0104 (fax)

We have a web page for this book, where we list errata, examples, and any additional information. You can access this page at:

http://www.oreilly.com/catalog/aspectjckbk

To comment or ask technical questions about this book, send email to:

bookquestions@oreilly.com

For more information about our books, conferences, Resource Centers, and the O'Reilly Network, see our web site at:

http://www.oreilly.com

Safari Enabled

 When you see a Safari® enabled icon on the cover of your favorite technology book, that means the book is available online through the O'Reilly Network Safari Bookshelf.

Safari offers a solution that's better than e-Books. It's a virtual library that lets you easily search thousands of top tech books, cut and paste code samples, download chapters, and find quick answers when you need the most accurate, current information. Try it free at *http://safari.oreilly.com*.

Acknowledgments

Never has so much been owed to so few...or something like that anyway. This book was written by one person but supported by more than I can possibly remember to mention here, so I'll apologize up front if anyone's missed out; I've not forgotten you. It's just that I was trying (but failed) to avoid an Oscar speech.

Here is where I get an opportunity to thank the people that kept me focused and supported me through the writing of my first book. First and foremost in all things has to be my family. Thanks to Mum and Dad, who have seen me through the hardest of times with limitless smiles, warmth, and understanding. Thanks to Bobs, Rich, Ad, and even Aimee, who have always been there to keep me on the straight and narrow. You all helped me get this project complete and keep my feet on the ground when I needed it most, and for that I cannot ever thank you enough, but I'll have fun trying.

Thanks to my editor Brett McLaughlin and all at O'Reilly who saw me through my complete naïveté over the proposal and writing process and for working so hard to get this book out. A heartfelt thanks to Rob Romano for putting up with my "there will only be a small number of figures" optimism at the beginning of the project. Honestly, Rob, I really did think there would only be a few!

Thanks to the true heroes of AspectJ, the AspectJ community. In particular thanks go to Adrian Colyer, George Harley, Matthew Webster, Mik Kersten, and Wes Isberg for making AspectJ such a great implementation. To all involved on the aTrack project headed up by Ron Bodkin for providing so many interesting and useful presentations and such an impressive test bed for many of the concepts expressed in the recipes in this cookbook, and to Ramnivas Laddad for his expert and friendly advice.

Thanks to my team of dedicated, and patient, proofreaders. To Laura Paterson for being so supportive in the very early days when this book was just something I really wanted to do. Without your help and expertise I doubt this project would have gotten past the propsal stage. Also, thanks to Andy (Tiger) Winter, Rob Wilson, and Grant Tarrant-Fisher for being on the receiving end of my enthusiasm on aspect orientation and not going completely nuts. Together, you all make up the best bunch of people I've ever had the pleasure to work with.

Thanks to all in the Oxford University software engineering programme that gave each and every recipe the thorough critique it needed; especially Ganesh Sitamplan for the language input, Peet for the beginners touch, and Jeremy Gibbons for getting the whole process rolling.

Thanks go to my friends who all knew when to be there and when to leave me alone during the long days and nights as I worked and re-worked this book, and that takes real skill from some of the best people I've been fortunate enough to meet. A huge thank you goes to Jo Westcott, Sam and Martin, Jason, and Kerry. Special thanks to Jason for asking, when first told of my aim to write a book, if the book would be made into a film (I truly hope not!).

Finally, I'd like to thank Kim. You have meant so much to me in the past year and you have contributed more than anyone else to this book. Despite my best efforts to completely ruin your grammar skills, you have stuck with me and been the best of friends as well as so much more than that. Thanks alone will never be enough for all the happiness you bring me, and it's a debt I look forward to repaying for many years to come.

Last but not least, a quick catch-all to thank everyone who has helped me out while writing this book. I haven't forgotten your help and I know I owe you all a beer or two!

CHAPTER 1

Aspect Orientation Overview

This chapter gives a brief overview of aspect orientation. What is discussed here is by no means a definitive description of aspect-oriented concepts, but it should present a flavor of these concepts and the related terminology. This provides a reference that will prove useful as you implement the practical recipes throughout the rest of the book.

A Brief History of Aspect Orientation

Aspect orientation is not a completely new approach to writing software. In much the same way as virtual machine systems were not an entirely new concept when Java became recognized and adopted by the software community, there have been tools and development environments for some time that support some of the capabilities that are now being placed under the banner of aspect orientation. Like Java, aspect orientation is becoming a commonly adopted and de facto approach to practicing older ideas that can be traced to almost the beginning of software development.

Development environments and tools that weave code, `pragma` instructions, and even debuggers all contain some of the behavior that underlies the aspect-oriented approach. But the significant difference is in the philosophy behind the approach and how that philosophy drives the technology and tools. Aspect orientation is not about any one of these technologies on its own, though it is a new and more modular implementation of the advantages that these technologies have brought to their own domains in the past.

All that said, the philosophical and conceptual underpinnings of aspect orientation are not a subject for this type of book. If you are interested in finding out more about this side of the technology, it's best to search Google for "Aspect-Oriented Software Development." This book focuses on practical approaches to understanding the technology; it is about getting the job done by harnessing the impressive power of aspect-oriented software development.

AspectJ

It is fair to say that the most significant work to date that is actually labeled under the banner of aspect orientation was completed at that historical wellspring of computing innovation, the Xerox Palo Alto Research Center (PARC). Xerox initially invested in producing special-purpose aspect-oriented languages prior to moving to a general-purpose model in Java. AspectJ was the outcome of this effort and is the core development tool for the recipes found throughout this book.

At the time of this writing, AspectJ is a rapidly maturing aspect-oriented development tool with a wealth of examples available. In 2002, Xerox PARC made the important decision of transferring the development of AspectJ to a more open forum on the eclipse.org web site. Current download figures for AspectJ show that interest in the approach is increasing at an exponential rate, and that the software development community is recognizing that aspect orientation is an extremely important evolution in software development. Now is the time to use this book's real-world, aspect-oriented recipes to add this new and powerful tool to your software development repertoire.

A Definition of Aspect Orientation

Before getting into the actual recipes, it is worth briefly introducing some of the concepts and terms that are used throughout this book.

Cross-Cutting Concerns

The basic premise of aspect-oriented programming is to enable developers to express modular *cross-cutting concerns* in their software. So what does this mean? A cross-cutting concern is behavior, and often data, that is used across the scope of a piece of software. It may be a constraint that is a characteristic of your software or simply behavior that every class must perform.

The most common example of a cross-cutting concern, almost the "Hello World" of the aspect-oriented approach, is that of logging (covered in Chapter 21). Logging is a cross-cutting concern because it affects many areas across the software system and it intrudes on the business logic. Logging is potentially applied across many classes, and it is this form of horizontal application of the logging aspect that gives cross-cutting its name.

Aspects

An *aspect* is another term for a cross-cutting concern. *In aspect orientation, the aspects provide a mechanism by which a cross-cutting concern can be specified in a modular way.*

To fully harness the power of aspects, we need to have some basic concepts in place to allow us to specify and apply aspects in a generic manner. We must be able to:

- Define the aspects in a modular fashion
- Apply aspects dynamically
- Apply aspects according to a set of rules
- Provide a mechanism and a context for specifying the code that will be executed for that particular aspect

The aspect-oriented approach provides a set of semantics and syntactical constructs to meet these demands so that aspects can be applied generically regardless of the type of software being written. These constructs are advice, join points, and pointcuts.

Advice

The code that is executed when an aspect is invoked is called *advice*. Advice contains its own set of rules as to when it is to be invoked in relation to the join point that has been triggered.

 Chapter 13 deals directly with recipes for different forms of advice and shows some of the more advanced features of advice that are available within AspectJ, such as precedence between multiple advices.

Join Points

Join points are simply specific points within the application that may or may not invoke some advice. The specific set of available join points is dependent on the tools being used and the programming language of the application under development. The following join points are supported in AspectJ:

- Join when a method is called
- Join during a method's execution
- Join when a constructor is invoked
- Join during a constructor's execution
- Join during aspect advice execution
- Join before an object is initialized
- Join during object initialization
- Join during static initializer execution
- Join when a class's field is referenced
- Join when a class's field is assigned
- Join when a handler is executed

Pointcuts

Pointcuts are the AspectJ mechanism for declaring an interest in a join point to initiate a piece of advice. They encapsulate the decision-making logic that is evaluated to decide if a particular piece of advice should be invoked when a join point is encountered.

The concept of a pointcut is crucial to the aspect-oriented approach because it provides an abstract mechanism by which to specify an interest in a selection of join points without having to tie to the specifics of what join points are in a particular application.

 How to define and use pointcuts is shown in the recipes found in Chapters 4 though 12.

Putting It All Together

Figure 1-1 shows the relationships between join points, aspects, pointcuts, advice, and your application classes.

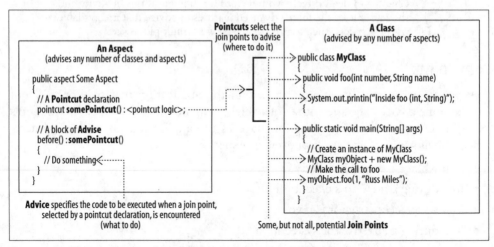

Figure 1-1. The relationships between apects, pointcuts, and advice

Where to Go for More Information

For more detailed information on the concepts and philosophy behind aspect orientation, check out the following web sites:

http://www.parc.xerox.com/research/csl/projects/aspectj/default.html
   The official information on the AspectJ project at Xerox PARC.

http://www.eclipse.org/aspectj
   The official AspectJ development technologies download site with links to support tools.

http://www.eclipse.org/ajdt
   Eclipse has a set of AspectJ Development Tools collected as a downloadable feature using the built-in update site mechanism from the listed web site.

http://sourceforge.net/projects/aspectj4jbuildr/
   A plug-in for Borland JBuilder that allows integration with AspectJ is available at this site.

http://sourceforge.net/projects/aspectj4netbean/
   A plug-in for NetBeans to support AspectJ development is available from this web site.

CHAPTER 2

Getting Started with AspectJ

2.0 Introduction

This chapter contains recipes for getting started in developing your own aspect-oriented code using AspectJ. Beginning with the task of getting a build environment set up and moving through the different types of builds and targets, this chapter provides a tutorial in the basics of AspectJ development.

With an understanding of the fundamental concepts in aspect orientation, this chapter first covers getting your fingers dirty using AspectJ's development environment. At the core of AspectJ is its build support for weaving aspects into your Java code. This is currently done using a compiler, ajc, that interacts with the existing Java compiler, javac. Working within the constraints of the Java compilation process ensures that your aspect-oriented programs produce standard Java classes that can be run by any Java Virtual Machine (JVM). ajc simply automates the mapping of your aspects onto your Java classes.

The ajc tool is used for compile-time weaving of aspects either from the command line or within an IDE or other build tool, but there is also an alternative weaving method supported in AspectJ, load-time weaving. As its title suggests, load-time weaving supports the weaving of aspects into your application at the time when the Java class loader is loading the application into the JVM. This is a fairly new feature of AspectJ and is briefly described in this chapter with the caveat that the current methods by which load-time weaving is achieved using AspectJ may change in the future as this facility matures.

Once you have got the hang of using the ajc command-line compiler then it's time to move on to installing and using some of the capabilities available to the AspectJ developer within the Eclipse development environment. These include how to set up an Eclipse project with an AspectJ Nature using the new project creation wizards and using Eclipse to vary the aspects that are actually built into a single project using AspectJ build configuration files.

Finally, AspectJ project housekeeping tasks such as documentation generation from AspectJ code and building using Ant are covered in this chapter demonstrating just how rich, powerful, and supported the AspectJ development tools are.

2.1 Installing AspectJ

Problem

You want to set up an AspectJ build environment.

Solution

At its simplest, AspectJ installation is a four-step process:

1. Download the AspectJ tools from *http://www.aspectj.org*.
2. Install the downloaded JAR files by double-clicking on them. This will create an *aspectj1.2* directory on your machine.
3. Test your environment with the following command:

```
> ajc
AspectJ Compiler

        Usage: <options> <source file | @argfile>..

AspectJ-specific options:
        ... Listed compiler options


1 fail|abort
```

Don't worry about the 1 fail | abort message here; if you get the output shown above, then the AspectJ tools have been successfully installed and located and are available for use.

4. Copy *aspectj1.2/lib/aspectjrt.jar* to a library directory of your JRE. Typical locations for this directory are *%JAVA_HOME%\jre\lib\ext* for Windows and */Library/Java/Extensions* for Mac OS X.

Discussion

The first step in preparing to develop using aspects is to download the appropriate support tools for your environment. In the case of AspectJ, this involves downloading the AspectJ libraries and tools. These tools can be obtained by accessing *http://www.aspectj.org* and following the links to *Downloads*.

Once the appropriate *AspectJ* development kits have been downloaded, they can be installed by *double-clicking* on the downloaded *.jar* file. After installation, you will find a directory named *aspectj1.2* (if the default installation options were accepted).

The AspectJ installer specifies some important instructions at the end of the installation process. These instructions include setting up your search path so that the AspectJ tools are available from the command line and adding the AspectJ Java libraries to your Java classpath. It's worth taking care to follow those instructions to make things as easy as possible when setting up your AspectJ development environment.

In the *%MY_HOME_DIRECTORY%/aspectj1.2/bin* directory, you will see that AspectJ comes with three tools:

ajc *(ajc.bat on Windows)*
> The AspectJ compiler.

ajbrowser *(ajbrowser.bat on Windows)*
> The AspectJ tools test environment that can be used to develop AspectJ projects.

ajdoc *(ajdoc.bat on Windows)*
> The AspectJ documentation tool.

ajc and ajdoc are the AspectJ equivalents of javac and javadoc from the standard Java Development Kit. In fact, both of the AspectJ tools use the standard Java tools to do their job, providing enhancements to cater to the additional AspectJ syntax and structure.

It is worth taking a look around the AspectJ installation, particularly within the *%MY_HOME_DIRECTORY/aspectj1.2/doc/index.html* directory as a wealth of support documentation is provided, including:

%MY_HOME_DIRECTORY%/aspectj1.2/doc/progguide/
> The AspectJ Programming Guide for all users of AspectJ.

%MY_HOME_DIRECTORY%/aspectj1.2/doc/devguide/
> The AspectJ Developers Guide for anyone who wants to build and contribute to AspectJ.

%MY_HOME_DIRECTORY%/aspectj1.2/doc/api/
> The AspectJ runtime API, also summarized in the appendix.

%MY_HOME_DIRECTORY%/aspectj1.2/examples/
> A collection of useful and interesting AspectJ coding examples to get you started.

You have now set up the environment on your machine for development of aspect-oriented software using *AspectJ*.

It's a good idea to check the AspectJ web site regularly at *http://www.eclipse.org/aspectj* for information on the newest updates to the toolset. You can also register yourself on the AspectJ users mailing list to get notifications of changes to the tools and news on how the AspectJ tools are being employed throughout the software industry.

A set of easy installers to get you up and running as quickly and simply as possible using AspectJ are available at *http://www. aspectjcookbook.com*. These installers install and configure an entire AspectJ build environment including AspectJ, the Eclipse IDE, and the AspectJ plug-in for Eclipse. While the versions contained in these installers are not guaranteed to be the latest that are available from the individual sources at *www.eclipse.org*, *www.eclipse.org/aspectj*, and *www.eclipse.org/ajdt*, they do provide everything you need in an easy to install package.

See Also

The next stage in getting familiar with AspectJ is to start coding your first aspect as shown in Recipe 2.2; the ajdoc tool is examined in some detail in Recipe 2.6; the AspectJ Development Environment Guide available at *http://www.eclipse.org/aspectj* provides more details on the runtime options and flags that the AspectJ tools support; the other recipes in this chapter show how to take things further by compiling more complex AspectJ projects within Eclipse and using the Ant* build tool.

2.2 Developing a Simple Aspect

Problem

You want to write a simple aspect.

Solution

First, write your business logic classes, as shown in Example 2-1.

Example 2-1. A simple business logic Java class

```
package com.oreilly.aspectjcookbook;

public class MyClass
{
    public void foo(int number, String name)
    {
        System.out.println("Inside foo (int, String)");
    }

    public static void main(String[] args)
    {
        // Create an instance of MyClass
        MyClass myObject = new MyClass();
```

---

* Ant, which stands for Another Neato Tool, is a pure Java build tool that is controlled using XML build configuration files, and offers a nice alternative to the more traditional and cryptic Make files.

Example 2-1. A simple business logic Java class (continued)

```
        // Make the call to foo
        myObject.foo(1, "Russ Miles");
    }
}
```

Define an aspect that will be applied to this class. The aspect in Example 2-2 parodies the traditional "Hello World" for AspectJ by providing an aspect that captures all calls to the void foo(int, String) method in the MyClass class.

Example 2-2. A simple HelloWorld aspect in AspectJ

```
package com.oreilly.aspectjcookbook;

public aspect HelloWorld
{
    pointcut callPointcut( ) :
        call(void com.oreilly.aspectjcookbook.MyClass.foo(int, String));

    before() : callPointcut( )
    {
        System.out.println(
            "Hello World");
        System.out.println(
            "In the advice attached to the call pointcut");
    }
}
```

Save this file in the same directory as your business logic class as *HelloWorld.aj* or *HelloWorld.java*. Run the ajc command to compile this simple application and produce the byte code *.class* files for both the aspect and the class:

```
> ajc -classpath %MY_CLASSPATH% -d %MY_DESTINATION_DIRECTORY% com/oreilly/
aspectjcookbook/MyClass.java com/oreilly/aspectjcookbook/HelloWorld.java
```

If you get the following message then you will need to add the *aspectjrt.jar* to your classpath:

```
warning couldn't find aspectjrt.jar on classpath, checked:

error can't find type org.aspectj.lang.JoinPoint


1 error, 1 warning
```

To add the *aspectjrt.jar* to your classpath just for this compilation, type the following command to invoke the ajc compiler (Use ; instead of : to separate the components of the classpath on Windows):

```
> ajc -classpath %MY_CLASSPATH%:%ASPECTJ_INSTALLATION_DIRRECTORY%/lib/aspectjrt.jar
-d %MY_DESTINATION_DIRECTORY% com/oreilly/aspectjcookbook/MyClass.java com/oreilly/
aspectjcookbook/HelloWorld.java
```

The ajc compiler will produce two .class files; *MyClass.class* and *HelloWorld.class*. AspectJ 1.2 produces regular Java byte code that can be run on any 1.2 JVM and above, so you can now use the normal java command to run this application:

```
> java -classpath %MY_CLASSPATH% com.oreilly.aspectjcookbook.MyClass
Hello World
In the advice attached to the call point cut
Inside foo (int, String)
```

Congratulations! You have now compiled and run your first aspect-oriented application using AspectJ.

Discussion

This recipe has shown you your first example of an aspect and how AspectJ extends the Java language. At first, the new syntax can appear a little strange and a good portion of this book is dedicated to examining the ways the new language constructs can be used to create your aspects. To demystify some of this syntax up front, Example 2-3 briefly examines what each line of the aspect from this recipe specifies.

Example 2-3. A simple example of the new AspectJ syntax

```
1   package com.oreilly.aspectjcookbook;
2
3   public aspect HelloWorld
4   {
5       pointcut callPointcut() :
6           call(void com.oreilly.aspectjcookbook.MyClass.foo(int, String));
7
8       before() : callPointcut()
9       {
10          System.out.println(
11              "Hello World");
12          System.out.println(
13              "In the advice attached to the call pointcut");
14      }
15  }
```

Line 3 declares that this is an aspect.

Lines 5 and 6 declare the logic for a single named pointcut. The pointcut logic specifies that any join points in your application where a call is made to the void MyClass.foo(int, String) method will be caught. The pointcut is named callPointcut() so that it can be referred to elsewhere within the aspect's scope.

Lines 7 through 13 declare a single advice block. The before() advice simply states that it will execute before any join points that are matched by the callPointcut() pointcut. When a join point is matched the advice simply outputs a couple of messages to the system to inform you that the advice has been executed.

This recipe provides a good mechanism for testing a development environment to ensure that things are working as they should before performing any customization to the development tools.

 AspectJ aspects can be saved with the *.aj* or *.java* extension. The ajc tool compiles the file supplied, regardless of the extension. The different extensions, *.aj* and *.java*, are largely a matter of personal preference.

The compilation of the aspect and the Java class produces only *.class* files. This is a very important feature of AspectJ; aspects are treated as objects in their own right. Because of this treatment, they can be encoded as class files; this ensures that when the application is run, the Java Runtime Environment (JRE) does not need to understand any additional aspect-specific file formats. With the inclusion of the *aspectjrt.jar* support library in your JRE class path, an aspect-oriented software application can be deployed to any JRE on any platform in keeping with the "Write Once, Run Anywhere" philosophy of Java.

See Also

Prior to using this recipe, it is necessary to get the AspectJ tools and prepare a simple command-line build environment as covered in Recipe 2.1; pointcuts are described in Chapters 4 through 12 and specifically the call(Signature) pointcut is examined in Recipe 4.1; the within(TypePattern) pointcut is described in Recipe 9.1; the NOT (!) operator used in relation to pointcuts is described in Recipe 12.4; the before( ) form of advice can be found in Recipe 13.3.

2.3   Compiling an Aspect and Multiple Java Files

Problem

You want to conveniently compile a selection of aspects that are to be applied to multiple Java classes.

Solution

Create an AspectJ build configuration file titled *<appname>.lst* containing the names of all of the class files and aspects to be included in the compilation, similar to the example *.lst* file in Example 2-4.

Example 2-4. The contents of an example AspectJ build configuration .lst file

```
// File files.lst
com/oreilly/aspectjcookbook/MyClass.java
com/oreilly/aspectjcookbook/MyAspect.java
com/oreilly/aspectjcookbook/AnotherClass.java
com/oreilly/aspectjcookbook/AnotherAspect.java
```

Use the following command to instruct the ajc compiler to apply the aspects to the classes:

```
> ajc -argfile files.lst -classpath %MY_CLASSPATH% -d %MY_DESTINATION_DIRECTORY%
```

Discussion

The process by which the ajc tool completes the compilation of aspects and classes is largely transparent to the developer and can be treated as a black box. You shouldn't really worry about the interim steps that may be taking place inside the AspectJ compiler, short of a desire to get into development work on ajc itself.

It is important to consider the inputs to the build process; this is handled through the creation of the *.lst* build configuration file. The ajc compiler does not search the source or class path for files to compile; it must be told which files are to be involved in the compilation. This means that all of your source that is to be compiled with *aspects* must be fed directly to the ajc compiler. There are three ways to supply the files to be compiled to the ajc compiler (two of which are semantically equivalent):

The -argfile *option*
> You can supply all the files within a *.lst* file by specifying the filename on the ajc command line with this option.

The @ *option*
> This option is equivalent to the —argfiles option.

Directly list the files
> You can simply specify the files on the command line when the ajc compiler is invoked.

See Also

Recipe 2.1 shows how to prepare a simple command-line build area for development using AspectJ; the AspectJ Development Environment Guide is available at *http://www.eclipse.org/aspectj* and provides more details on the runtime options and flags that the ajdoc tool supports; a full description of the AspectJ compiler process is available at *http://hugunin.net/papers/aosd-2004-cameraReady.pdf*; Recipe 2.8 shows how the *.lst* file can be used to vary the aspects that are woven for a particular build configuration.

2.4   Weaving Aspects into Jars

Problem

Your want to weave your aspects into code that has already been compiled and collected into a *.jar* file.

Solution

Use the –inpath command-line option when running the ajc command.

Discussion

The ajc command weaves aspects into Java byte code which can reside in *.class* files, within a Java *.jar* library file or a mixture of the two. The following instructions show you how to take the code from Recipe 2.2 and package the MyClass class in a *.jar* file before weaving the HelloWorld aspect into the library:

1. Compile the MyClass class using the traditional javac command:

   ```
   > javac -classpath %MY_CLASSPATH% -d %MY_DESTINATION_DIRECTORY% com/oreilly/
   aspectjcookbook/MyClass.java
   ```

2. Package the generated *MyClass.class* file into a *.jar* file titled *MyApp.jar*:

   ```
   > jar -cvf MyApp.jar com/oreilly/aspectjcookbook/MyClass.class
   ```

3. Compile the *HelloWorld.java* aspect using the ajc command, specifying the new *MyApp.jar* on the command line using the –inpath option:

   ```
   > ajc -classpath %MY_CLASSPATH% -d %MY_DESTINATION_DIRECTORY% -inpath MyApp.jar
   com/oreilly/aspectjcookbook/HelloWorld.java
   ```

   The –inpath option forces the ajc compiler to extract the Java byte code from the supplied *.jar* files into the destination directory as specified by the –d option. The ajc compiler then includes that extracted byte code in the aspect weaving process.

4. If no errors occur during compilation with ajc then you will have successfully woven the classes contained within the *MyApp.jar* file with the HelloWorld aspect. Because the ajc command extracts the classes from the *.jar* files supplied to the –inpath option, they are no longer needed to run the application. However, you can optionally re-package your new application in a *.jar* file of its own using the –outjar option when running the ajc command:

   ```
   > ajc -classpath %MY_CLASSPATH% -d %MY_DESTINATION_DIRECTORY% -inpath MyApp.jar -
   outjar MyAspectOrientedApp.jar com/oreilly/aspectjcookbook/HelloWorld.java
   ```

This produces a MyAspectOrientedApp.jar that contains your application's aspects and classes that can then be run using the traditional java command:

```
> java -classpath MyAspectOrientedApp.jar com.oreilly.aspectjcookbook.MyClass
```

 Before weaving your aspects into a *.jar* library provided by a third party, make sure that the license covering the library allows you to change the contents. If you don't check that it is ok to change the contents of the *.jar* file then you could be infringing on the third party's license agreement. For example, the license covering the Java Standard Libraries usually does not support the weaving of aspects into code that resides in the java or javax packages or their subpackages.

See Also

Setting up your environment in order to compile your AspectJ projects from the command line is covered in Recipe 2.1.

2.5   Weaving Aspects at Load Time

Problem

You want to postpone the decision as to whether an aspect should be applied to a particular application until the application is being loaded into the Java Virtual Machine.

Solution

Use the new load-time weaving features of AspectJ 1.2.

Discussion

Using the code shown in Recipe 2.2, the following instructions show you how to apply the HelloWorld aspect to the MyClass class at load time:

1. Compile the MyClass class using the traditional javac command:

   ```
   > javac -classpath %MY_CLASSPATH% -d %MY_DESTINATION_DIRECTORY% com/oreilly/
   aspectjcookbook/MyClass.java
   ```

   By using the javac command, you are completely avoiding weaving any aspects into your application at compile time. If you have some aspects that you want to include at compile time, you can use the ajc command and list the aspects to be included at that point in the AspectJ build configuration file, not specifying any aspects you intend to only weave at load time.

2. You can now check to ensure that the MyClass class has been compiled without any aspects by running the application using the java command:

   ```
   > java com.oreilly.aspectjcookbook.MyClass
   Inside foo (int, String)
   ```

3. Compile the HelloWorld aspect into an aspect library *.jar* file using the ajc command:

   ```
   > ajc –outjar helloworldlibrary.jar -d %MY_DESTINATION_DIRECTORY% com/oreilly/
   aspectjcookbook/HelloWorld.java
   ```

   You may find that you get the following warning stating that there is no match to the pointcut logic declared in your HelloWorld aspect:

   ```
   warning no match for this type name: com$oreilly$aspectjcookbook$MyClass [Xlint:
   invalidAbsoluteTypeName]
   call(void com.oreilly.aspectjcookbook.MyClass.foo(int, String));
        ^^^^^^^^^^^^^^^^^^^^^^^^^^^^^^^^^^^^^^
   ```

You are not weaving your aspect into the MyClass class at this point, so the warning is expected and can be ignored in this case.

4. You are now all set to run your separately compiled class and aspect, weaving them together at load time. A script is provided in AspectJ 1.2 to help you run the load-time weaver. This script is currently located in the *%MY_HOME_DIRECTORY%/aspectj1.2/doc/examples/ltw* directory and is called *aj* or *aj.bat*. Just as the ajc command is the AspectJ equivalent of the java command, so the aj script can be seen as the foundation for an AspectJ equivalent of the java command.

 In AspectJ 1.2, the aj script is located in an example directory as part of the AspectJ documentation. In future versions of AspectJ, as the load-time weaving facilities mature, it is likely that the aj script will join the more mainstream scripts in the *%ASPECTJ_INSTALL_DIRECTORY%/bin directory*.

5. The aj command relies on three environment variables being set so that it can pick up the relevant aspect libraries and Java classes for your application. You need to set the following variables to the appropriate project and AspectJ installation locations:

    CLASSPATH
    The location of your project's classes and the *aspectjrt.jar* is usually installed to *%MY_HOME_DIRECTORY%/aspectj1.2/lib*.

    ASPECTPATH
    Points to any *.jar* files that contain aspects to be woven at load time. In this example, this variable should point to the *helloworldlibrary.jar* file.

    ASPECTJ_HOME
    Contains the location of your AspectJ installation.

6. You can now run your application using the aj command. The aspects contained in the *helloworldlibrary.jar* are woven at load time into the MyClass class:

```
> %ASPECTJ_INSTALL_DIRECTORY%/doc/examples/ltw/aj com.oreilly.aspectjcookbook.
MyClass
Hello World
In the advice attached to the call point cut
Inside foo (int, String)
```

In addition to the default implementation of load-time weaving supplied with AspectJ 1.2, you can create your own implementation by extending and using the classes provided in the org.aspectj.weaver.tools package. This is an advanced topic for developers who are working with the AspectJ tools and is not covered here.

This recipe shows you how to work with load-time weaving with the current implementation in AspectJ 1.2. Although load-time weaving of aspects is an important addition to the toolset, it is a fairly new feature in AspectJ and the current implementation is likely to change as it matures.

See Also

Setting up your environment in order to compile your AspectJ projects from the command line is covered in Recipe 2.1; the AspectJ Build Configuration file is shown in more detail in Recipe 2.3; another example of load-time weaving is provided by Adrian Colyer at *http://www.jroller.com/comments/colyer/Weblog/load_time_weaving_ with_aspectj*; a full explanation of the load-time weaving facilities in AspectJ 1.2 is available as part of the documentation for AspectJ and is installed to *%ASPECTJ_ INSTALL_DIRECTORY%/doc/README-12.html*.

2.6   Generating Javadoc Documentation

Problem

You want to generate javadoc format documentation for your AspectJ application.

Solution

Use the ajdoc tool from the command line or from within Eclipse.

Discussion

Java developers have used the javadoc tool for generating comprehensive documentation for their Java applications since Java 1.1. The javadoc tool was never designed to handle the new language constructs that AspectJ introduces and is not able to generate documentation for an AspectJ application. To meet this problem, the developers of AspectJ created ajdoc, a tool that extends javadoc so that it can correctly and usefully document the aspect-oriented structures in your application.

Providing your environment has been set up correctly, as shown in Recipe 2.1, the ajdoc tool can be accessed from the command line by typing the following command:

```
> ajdoc -sourcepath <The root location of you code> -d <The directory in which you
want your documentation to be placed> <The file locations of each of the classes
aspects and classes to include in the generated documentation>
```

The ajdoc tool provides the —argfile parameter so that you can provide an explicit AspectJ build configuration *.lst* file, as mentioned in Recipe 2.3. A *.lst* file contains the build configuration for a set of classes and aspects in your application for which documentation should be produced.

Using ajdoc means that you can now document your pointcuts, advice, and aspects as shown in Example 2-5.

Example 2-5. Applying javadoc tags to the aspects, pointcuts, and advice

```
package com.oreilly.aspectjcookbook;

/**
 * A simple aspect to weave in a HelloWorld message when foo(int,name)
 * is called on objects of the MyClass class.
 * @author russellmiles
 * @version 1.0
 *
 */
public aspect HelloWorld
{
    /**
     * Selects join points on calls to the MyClass.foo(int,String) method.
     */
    pointcut callPointCut( ) :
        call(void com.oreilly.aspectjcookbook.MyClass.foo(int, String));

    /**
     * Simple before advice that prints HelloWorld to the standard output.
     */
    before() : callPointCut( )
    {
        System.out.println(
        "Hello World");
        System.out.println(
        "In the advice attached to the call point cut");
    }
}
```

Example 2-5 is the same aspect that was shown in Recipe 2.2 but highlights the documentation that is provided for the ajdoc tool. To produce documentation from the command line for this simple example, you would type the following from the same directory as your source code, making sure that your AspectJ build environment has been set up correctly (also shown in Recipe 2.2) and that the *docs* directory has been created ready to accept your generated documentation:

```
> ajdoc –sourcepath . –d docs com/oreilly/aspectjcookbook/MyClass.java com/oreilly/
aspectjcookbook/HelloWorld.java
```

If the ajdoc tool runs correctly, you should see something like the following lengthy but successful output from the previous command:

```
> Calling ajc...
> Building signature files...
> Calling javadoc...
Loading source file /source/Chapter 2/2.5/ajdocworkingdir/com/oreilly/
aspectjcookbook/MyClass.java...
```

```
Loading source file /source/Chapter 2/2.5/ajdocworkingdir/com/oreilly/
aspectjcookbook/HelloWorld.java...
Constructing Javadoc information...
Standard Doclet version 1.4.2_03
Generating constant-values.html...
Building tree for all the packages and classes...
Building index for all the packages and classes...
Generating overview-tree.html...
Generating index-all.html...
Generating deprecated-list.html...
Building index for all classes...
Generating allclasses-frame.html...
Generating allclasses-noframe.html...
Generating index.html...
Generating packages.html...
Generating com/oreilly/aspectjcookbook/package-frame.html...
Generating com/oreilly/aspectjcookbook/package-summary.html...
Generating com/oreilly/aspectjcookbook/package-tree.html...
Generating com/oreilly/aspectjcookbook/HelloWorld.html...
Generating com/oreilly/aspectjcookbook/MyClass.html...
Generating package-list...
Generating help-doc.html...
Generating stylesheet.css...
> Decorating html files...
> Decorating /source/Chapter 2/2.5/com/oreilly/aspectjcookbook/MyClass.html...
> Decorating /source/Chapter 2/2.5/com/oreilly/aspectjcookbook/HelloWorld.html...
> Removing generated tags (this may take a while)...
> Finished.
```

The ajdoc tool is also available from within the Eclipse IDE when using the AspectJ Development Tools (AJDT) plug-in. To use the ajdoc tool, select your AspectJ project in the Package Explorer panel and click Project → Generate Javadoc....

When Eclipse shows the Generate Javadoc dialog, you will need to change the Javadoc Command to ajdoc. To do this, click on the Configure button and then navigate to the place where the ajdoc tool has been installed; normally, this is *%HOME DIRECTORY%/aspectj1.2/bin*. Select the ajdoc tool and click on OK. The Javadoc Command should then change to point to the ajdoc tool to indicate that it has been configured as the tool to use when generating your projects documentation. Because the ajdoc tool works in almost the same way as the javadoc tool, Eclipse needs to know nothing more to use the new configuration and you can set up the options for your javadoc generation as normal.

 As of Eclipse 3 and AJDT 1.1.11, the process for generating documentation using ajdoc has been simplified. Before, you had to manually set the javadoc generation to the ajdoc tool; with the release of these versions, the ajdoc documentation has its own menu item that can be accessed by clicking on Project → Generate ajdoc....

See Also

Java in a Nutshell by David Flanagan (O'Reilly); *Eclipse* and *Eclipse Cookbook* by Steve Holzner (O'Reilly); the AspectJ Development Environment Guide available at *http://www.eclipse.org/aspectj* provides more details on the runtime options and flags that the ajdoc tool supports; the AspectJ build configuration file is discussed in Recipe 2.3.

2.7   Compiling an AspectJ Project Using Eclipse

Problem

You want to compile your AspectJ project using Eclipse.

Not Using Eclipse or Ant?

If you are not going to use Eclipse or the Ant tool when writing your aspect-oriented software with AspectJ, then it is worth skipping forward to the next chapter to start looking at the common approaches to deploying your AspectJ applications.

Solution

Download and install the AspectJ Development Tools (AJDT) plug-in into Eclipse.

Discussion

AspectJ is run under the same open source collective as the Eclipse project and provides the most advanced *AspectJ plug-in* for an *IDE*. The AspectJ Eclipse plug-in can be downloaded by following the instructions available at *http://www.eclipse.org/ajdt*.

 It's a good rule of thumb to download the latest version of AspectJ, the corresponding latest version of the AJDT, and then download the supported version of Eclipse just in case the Eclipse tool is a step or so ahead of the AspectJ development. If you are ever confused by the options available, there is a compatibility table available on the AJDT downloads page to point you in the right direction.

To check that the plug-in has been correctly installed, click on File → New → Project... on the Eclipse menu bar. When the *New Project dialog* appears, the *AspectJ* project option should be available, as shown in Figure 2-1.

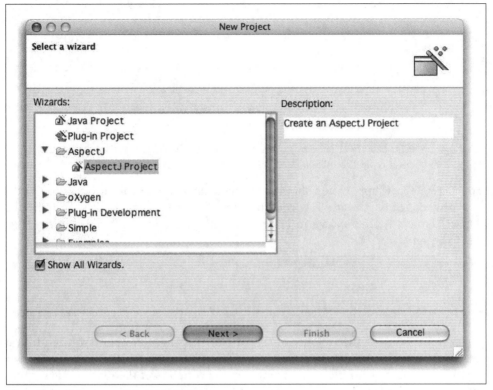

Figure 2-1. Creating a new AspectJ project

By default, early milestone builds of Eclipse 3 hid all additional wizards. To see the New AspectJ Project option, you may have to select the Show All Wizards checkbox.

Highlighting the AspectJ Project option, click on Next in the New Project dialog and complete the next few steps to set up the new AspectJ project.

Once the project wizard has completed, you may be asked to switch to the Java perspective. You may also be asked for some AJDT preferences if this is the very first time that you have used the wizard. It's a good idea to switch to the Java Perspective and accept the default values for the project preferences. Once Eclipse has switched to the Java perspective, your project should look like Figure 2-2.

By default from AJDT 1.1.7 onwards, an AspectJ project will incrementally compile all changes to your aspects and Java classes. This option can be turned off in the Eclipse AspectJ project configuration if the build performance becomes too intrusive.

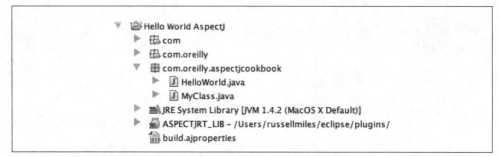

Figure 2-2. AspectJ project sources and jars within the Eclipse Java perspective

Your new AspectJ application should automatically compile with the creation of the new project. If you are at all worried that this hasn't happened, click on the Build AspectJ Project button shown in Figure 2-3. This will force a rebuild of the project just to be sure.

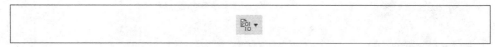

Figure 2-3. Use the Build AspectJ Project button to check that your project has compiled correctly

Your application is now compiled and ready for running, but before you run it, it is interesting to note the enhancements that the AJDT brings to the Java perspective. Perhaps the most obvious enhancement is in the contents of the Outline view which will contain, when an aspect or advised class is selected, new sections indicating where advice has been applied. An example of the additional information available in the Outline view is shown in Figures 2-4 and 2-5.

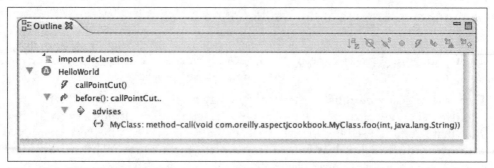

Figure 2-4. Using the Outline View to see on which classes or aspects a specific advice is applied

The AJDT also provides another view of your project that graphically displays an overview of how your aspects are applied to your application, The Aspect Visualization perspective can be opened by selecting Window → Open Perspective → Other... and then enabling the Aspect Visualization perspective. The new perspective on your

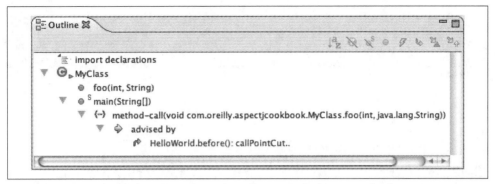

Figure 2-5. *Using the Outline View to see what advice is applied to a specific class*

project will then show a graphical depiction of how the aspects have been applied to the classes as shown in Figure 2-6.

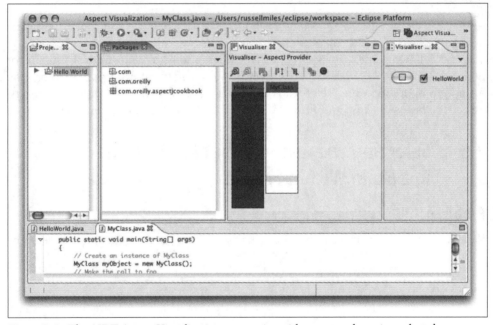

Figure 2-6. *The AJDT Aspect Visualization perspective with an example project selected*

Switching back to the Java perspective, it's time to run your application. In Eclipse, it is as easy to run an AspectJ application as it is to run a traditional Java application. In the Java perspective, click on the class that contains the `public static void main(String[])` method and select Run → Run As → Java Application from the main menu. Eclipse will then search and run the `public static void main(String[])` method in the selected class producing the applications command line output to the Console view as shown in Figure 2-7.

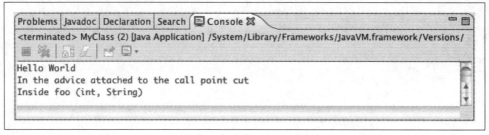

Figure 2-7. The output on the Console view when Recipe 5.1 is run

There are enough features and enhancements supported by the AJDT to fill a chapter in its own right. Take some time to tour the different preferences and features that are available, perhaps while you work with some of the other recipes in this book, to help you get used to what features are most useful to you.

See Also

Recipe 2.9 shows how to automate the build process using the *Ant* tool; a complete user guide for the AJDT plug-in can be accessed by visiting *http://www.eclipse.org/ ajdt* and following the User Resources:Documentation link; an AspectJ plug-in for Borland JBuilder is available at *http://sourceforge.net/projects/aspectj4jbuildr/*; an AspectJ plug-in for Sun's NetBeans is available at *http://sourceforge.net/projects/ aspectj4netbeans/*; *Eclipse* and *Eclipse Cookbook* by Steve Holzner (O'Reilly).

2.8   Selecting the Aspects That Are Woven in a Build Within Eclipse

Problem

You want to vary the aspects that are woven into your application when developing in Eclipse.

Solution

Create a separate AspectJ build configuration for each different selection of aspects that you want to weave into your application. Eclipse then allows you to select the current build configuration it will use to build your AspectJ project so you can easily select the set of aspects you want to apply for a particular build.

Discussion

Recipe 2.3 showed that the AspectJ compiler can use a build confiuguration *.lst* file to select the classes and aspects it will include in its aspect weaving. By default, an AspectJ project in Eclipse has a single *.lst* file, naturally called *default.lst*, that lists all the of the files in your project. Using this default, the AspectJ compile will apply all the aspects to all of classes where indicated by the pointcut logic in those aspects.

For many applications, this default behavior is fine but there are times when you may want to vary the aspects that are applied to a particular application depending on such things as deployment target or feature selection. AspectJ provides a neat way of varying the selection of aspects to be applied using a custom build configuration .*lst* file that excludes or includes the aspects you wish to apply.

Eclipse provides the means by which a custom AspectJ build configuration can be created and used for a particular project.

When the project created in Recipe 2.7 is run, the output produced on the Console in Eclipse is:

```
MyAspect before( ) advice
In the advice attached to the call point cut
Inside foo (int, String)
```

The following steps create a new build configuration that will exclude the single MyAspect aspect in the project from the build and therefore change the behavior of the application as shown by the amended output on the Console.

As of Eclipse 3.0, with the AJDT Version 1.1.11 or later installed, the following steps have changed when creating a new AspectJ build configuration file. There is also now a new format for build configuration files used by the Eclipse AJDT plug-in, the .*ajproperties* file.

You can create a new build configuration in Eclipse 3.0 by clicking on Project → Active Build Configuration → Save as... , entering a new name for your build configuration, and then by following step 8 onwards. This will create a new .*ajproperties* file as opposed to the more traditional .*lst* file.

You can also convert an existing .*lst* file to the newer .*ajproperties* format by right-clicking on the .*lst* file and selecting Save as .*ajproperties* file. If you need to go back to the .*lst* format, you can right-click on a .*ajproperties* file and select Save as .*lst* file.

1. Ensure that your AspectJ project is selected in the Package Explorer view.
2. Click on File → New → Other....
3. In the New dialog, select the AspectJ Build Configuration File and click on Next, as shown in Figure 2-8.
4. The New AspectJ Build Configuration File dialog will appear, as shown in Figure 2-9.
5. Check that the correct project is selected and enter a name for the new build configuration file, for this example use the name *excludeAspects.lst*.
6. Deselect the Include all source files from project checkbox and click on Finish.

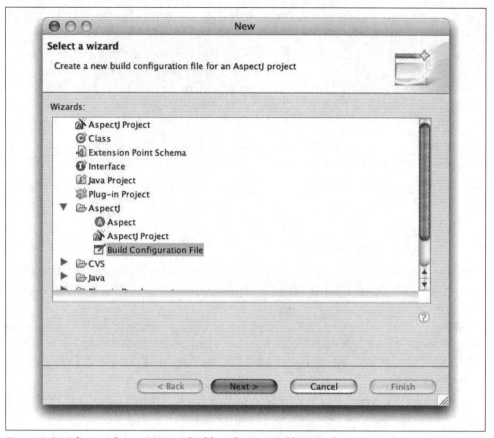

Figure 2-8. Selecting the new AspectJ build configuration file wizard

7. The new *excludeAspects.lst* file will be added to your project and opened in the file editor.

8. Select the files you want to include in this build configuration, as shown in Figure 2-10. In this example, you want to build only the classes and exclude all of the aspects so only the *MyClass.java* file is selected.

9. Save your changes to the build configuration file.

10. You need to tell the AspectJ compiler to switch to your configuration for this project. Find the Build AspectJ Project/Select Configuration button on the Eclipse toolbar, as shown in Figure 2-11.

11. Click on the small down triangle to the right of the button to pop up a list of the available build configurations for this project, as shown in Figure 2-12.

12. Select the new build configuration and the AspectJ compiler will automatically rebuild your project according to the new settings.

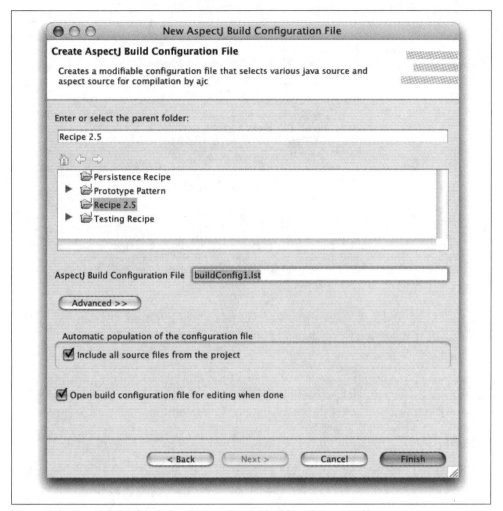

Figure 2-9. Entering the details for the new AspectJ build configuration file

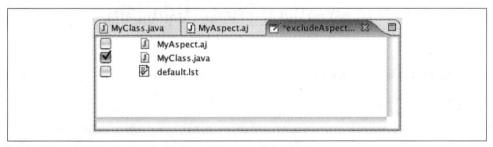

Figure 2-10. Editing the AspectJ build configuration file in Eclipse

Figure 2-11. The Build AspectJ Project/Select Configuration button in Eclipse

Figure 2-12. Selecting the new excludeAspects.lst AspectJ build configuration

 In Eclipse 3.0 with AJDT 1.1.11 or later, you can quickly exclude or include a single source file from the current active configuration; then, you can right-click on the source file and click on Exclude from "%CURRENT_CONFIGURATION%" or Include from "%CURRENT_ CONFIGURATION%" if the file is already excluded.

After building under the new excludeAspects.lst configuration, the Console output will show the following when the application is run again:

```
Inside foo (int, String)
```

The aspects have been removed from your application when building with this configuration. To switch back to the full default build configuration, click on the Selecting down triangle and select the <all project files> option.

See Also

Eclipse and *Eclipse Cookbook* by Steve Holzner (O'Reilly); Recipe 2.9 shows how to use the Ant AspectJ tasks to vary the aspects applied to a specific build of your application.

2.9   Building an AspectJ Project Using Ant

Problem

You want to compile an AspectJ project using Ant.

Solution

Use the tasks included in the AspectJ toolkit to build your project using Ant.

Discussion

The *Ant build.xml* configuration file in Example 2-6 shows an example for how to call upon the additional AspectJ Ant tasks.

Example 2-6. An Ant configuration file that uses the AspectJ tasks

```xml
<?xml version="1.0" encoding="UTF-8"?>
<project basedir="." default="compile" name="test">
    <property name="src" value="src"/>
    <property name="build" value="build"/>
    <taskdef resource="org/aspectj/tools/ant/taskdefs/aspectjTaskdefs.properties">
        <classpath>
            <pathelement location="%ASPECTJ_INSTALLATION%/lib/aspectjtools.jar"/>
        </classpath>
    </taskdef>
    <target name="compile">
        <mkdir dir="${build}"/>
        <iajc destdir="${build}" sourceroots="${src}">
            <classpath>
                <pathelement location="%ASPECTJ_INSTALLATION%/lib/aspectjrt.jar"/>
            </classpath>
        </iajc>
    </target>
</project>
```

Here is what Example 2-6 does:

1. Defines a new task using the AspectJ task properties

2. Specifies the location of the *aspectjtools.jar*

3. Declares a build target that compiles the project using the iajc task that in turn relies upon the *aspectjrt.jar* to execute

See Also

Ant: The Definitive Guide by Jesse Tilly and Eric M. Burke (O'Reilly); the Jakarta Ant online manual at *http://jakarta.apache.org/ant/manual/index.html*.

CHAPTER 3

Deploying AspectJ Applications

3.0   Introduction

Whatever the applications are that you develop with AspectJ, you will usually want to deploy your application to a target environment so it can be made available to your users. Java application deployment can range from being as complex as providing context-specific runtime wrappers and scripts to run your application, or as simple as providing a double-clickable *.jar* or executable. So, deployment can often be a real headache for developers.

To add to this mix, AspectJ adds some additional requirements to your application deployment. The recipes in this chapter describe in detail those additional requirements that an AspectJ application imposes on a traditional Java application and some of the tools support that you have at your disposal to help you in the deployment process.

AspectJ is definitely not limited to just regular Java applications. You can deploy AspectJ applications into many different target runtime environments including Java Servlets and Java Server Pages inside Tomcat and Axis Web Services. These more complicated deployment environments often offer several different ways of deploying the same application. Some of these options are better suited to AspectJ than others and so this chapter focuses on describing the easiest routes to application deployment to these target environments.

As you work through the recipes in this chapter, it's worth remembering that many of the manual steps could be automated using Apache Ant or even command-line scripts and batch files. However, the recipes here deliberately walk you through all of the manual steps required to deploy into the various target environments to keep you in touch with what is going on at all times.

3.1   Deploying a Command-Line AspectJ Application

Problem

You want to deploy a simple AspectJ application to be deployed and then run from the command line.

Solution

A straightforward Java application usually requires nothing more than a Java Runtime Environment on the target machine and the classes of your application added to the Java classpath before you can run your application.

AspectJ requires that the Java Runtime Environment be at Version 1.1 or later, and it needs the additional *aspectjrt.jar* library added to the classpath to support the aspect-oriented features of your AspectJ application.

Discussion

Using the simple application developed in Recipe 2.2, the following steps create a directory containing all of the necessary deployment files needed to run your AspectJ application:

1. Create a new directory to contain your runtime deployment that is separate from your source directories. For this example, name the directory *deployment*.
2. Create a subdirectory of the top-level deployment directory and name it *classes*.
3. Place all of your application's compiled *.class* files in the *classes* directory, taking care to maintain your package directory structure. For this example, the code from Recipe 2.2 is being used, so the directory structure should look like Figure 3-1.

   You can perform this by either manually copying each of the packages of *.class* files or by building your application with the ajc tool with the destination flag, -d, set to the *classes* directory:

   ```
   > ajc -classpath %MY_CLASSPATH% -d %PROJECT_ROOT_DIRECTORY%/deployment/classes
   com/oreilly/aspectjcookbook/MyClass.java com/oreilly/aspectjcookbook/HelloWorld.
   java
   ```

   If you get an error that states that *aspectjrt.jar* cannot be found, then check out Recipe 2.2 where the instructions on how to use the ajc command explain how to overcome this problem.
4. Create a subdirectory beneath the top level *deployment* directory called *lib*.
5. Copy the *%ASPECTJ_INSTALLATION_DIRECTORY%/lib/aspectjrt.jar* file to the new *lib* directory.

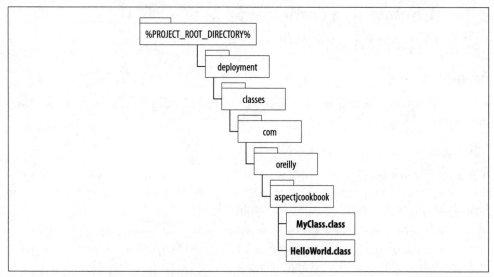

Figure 3-1. The directory structure after you have placed the .class files within your deployment area

6. Your final deployment setup should look something like that shown in Figure 3-2.

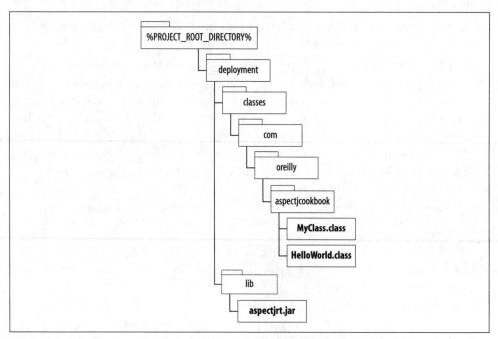

Figure 3-2. The directory structure after the runtime AspectJ library has been added

7. You can copy the *deployment* directory to any target machine with a compatible Java Runtime Environment correctly installed and you should be able to run your application using the java command:

```
java -classpath %MY_CLASSPATH% com.oreilly.aspectjcookbook.MyClass
```

The classpath on your target machines must contain *aspectjrt.jar* within the *deployment/lib* directory and point to the *classes* directory. For example if you are running the java command from within the deployment directory then your classpath content would be something like `classes/.:lib/aspectjrt.jar` remembering to replace : with ; on Windows.

See Also

Recipe 2.2 covers the basics of how to use the `ajc` command to compile your AspectJ applications; *Java in a Nutshell* by David Flanagan (O'Reilly) provides detailed information on the entire set of Java command-line tools including java.

3.2   Deploying an AspectJ Application as a Fully Contained Executable JAR File

Problem

You want to deploy an AspectJ application to be run as an executable JAR file.

Solution

Unpack the contents of the *aspectjrt.jar* file and then repack the AspectJ classes with your own application's classes into a single JAR file. To make the single JAR file executable, an appropriate manifest file should be included that lists the class that contains the standard `public static void main(String[])` method entry point for running Java applications.

Discussion

Creating an executable JAR file is a popular way of deploying conventional Java applications. The JAR file format, by default, contains all of the necessary classes for a software component, and it has the potential to be configured as a packaged Java application that can be run simply by double-clicking on the file within most popular operating systems.

The following steps manually create an executable JAR file for the application shown in Recipe 2.2:

1. Take a copy of the *deployment* directory as it was created in Recipe 2.1.
2. Unjar the contents of the *aspectjrt.jar* that is stored in the *deployment/lib* directory using the jar tool from the command line:

```
jar -xvf aspectjrt.jar
```

3. After the jar extraction has completed, you will find that two folders have been extracted within the *deployment/lib* directory, *META-INF* and *org*. The *META-INF* directory contains a *MANIFEST.MF* file containing the manifest information for the *aspectjrt.jar*. The *org* directory contains the *.class* files needed by the aspect-oriented mechanisms within your application to run when it is deployed.

4. Copy the *deployment/lib/org* directory and all of its contents into the *deployment/classes* directory

5. Create a manifest file called *manifest* in the new *deployment* directory, using a text editor, that contains similar information as that presented in Example 3-1.

Example 3-1. An example of the contents of an executable .jar files manifest

```
Manifest-Version: 1.0

Name: com/oreilly/aspectjcookbook/
Specification-Title: My simple AspectJ Application
Specification-Version: 1.0
Specification-Vendor: Russ Miles
Implementation-Title: com.oreilly.aspectjcookbook
Implementation-Version: 1.0
Implementation-Vendor: Russ Miles
Main-Class: com.oreilly.aspectjcookbook.MyClass
```

It is important that the `Main-Class` information in the manifest file correctly points to the class that contains the `public void main(String[])` method that starts up your application.

6. Once you have created and saved the manifest file to the *deployment* directory the directory structure of *deployment* and *deployment/classes* directories should look like that shown in Figure 3-3.

7. Create a subdirectory of the *deployment* directory called *build*.

8. Run the following jar command from within the *deployment* directory to create the executable *myapplication.jar* file in the *deployment/build* directory:

```
jar -cfm build/myapplication.jar manifest -C classes/
```

9. To run the executable *.jar* file, remembering that this example application is a console application and so has no GUI, you can either run the java command from the *build* directory using the –jar option as shown below or double-click on the *myapplication.jar* file.

```
java –jar myapplication.jar
```

10. If you are using Mac OS X and decide you are going to double-click the *myapplication.jar*, then you could run the Console application first, located in the */Applications/utilities* directory, to see the output of your application running as shown in Figure 3-4.

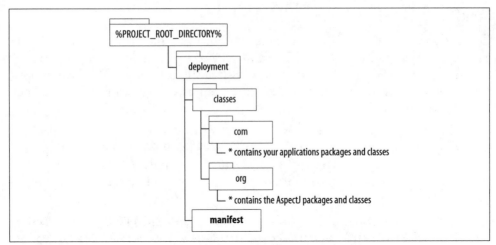

Figure 3-3. The content of the deployment and classes directories once you have copied over the org directory, which contains the AspectJ classes and creates a new manifest file

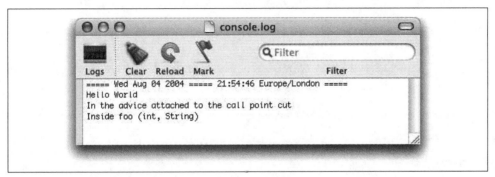

Figure 3-4. The Console application in Mac OS X showing the output of double-clicking the executable myapplication.jar

See Also

Java in a Nutshell by David Flanagan (O'Reilly) provides detailed information on the entire set of Java command-line tools, including java and jar.

3.3 Deploying a Java Servlet That Uses AspectJ

Problem

You want to deploy a servlet that has been developed using AspectJ into Apache Tomcat.

Solution

Compile your Java Servlet from the command line using the `ajc` command or inside an Eclipse AspectJ project. Under the *webapps* directory inside Apache Tomcat, set up a new web application directory and *WEB-INF* subdirectory. Make the appropriate amendments to the *server.xml* file in the Tomcat configuration to enable your web application.

Copy the compiled Java Servlet *.class* files and corresponding aspect *.class* files into the *webapps/%YOUR_APPLICATION_DIRECTORY%/WEB-INF/classes*. Copy the *aspectjrt.jar* file into the *webapps/%YOUR_APPLICATION_DIRECTORY%/WEB-INF/lib* so the aspect-oriented features of your software can find the support components they need.

Amend your web application's *webapps/%YOUR_APPLICATION_DIRECTORY/WEB-INF/web.xml* file to support access to the new Java Servlet. Finally, restart Tomcat to activate your web application.

Discussion

The following steps show how to create, compile, and deploy a simple Java Servlet that uses AspectJ:

1. Create a Java Servlet and corresponding aspect similar to the ones shown in Examples 3-2 and 3-3.

   Example 3-2. A simple HelloWorld Java Servlet

   ```
   package com.oreilly.aspectjcookbook;

   import java.io.IOException;

   import javax.servlet.ServletException;
   import javax.servlet.ServletOutputStream;
   import javax.servlet.http.HttpServlet;
   import javax.servlet.http.HttpServletRequest;
   import javax.servlet.http.HttpServletResponse;

   public class AOHelloWorldServlet extends HttpServlet
   {
       public void doGet (HttpServletRequest request, HttpServletResponse response)
           throws ServletException, IOException
       {
           ServletOutputStream out = response.getOutputStream( );
           out.println("<h1>Hello World from an aspect-oriented Servlet!</h1>");
       }

       public String getServletInfo( )
       {
           return "Create a page that says <i>Hello World</i> and send it back";
   ```

· Example 3-2. A simple HelloWorld Java Servlet (continued)

```
    }
}
```

Example 3-3. An aspect that advises the doGet(..) method on the AOHelloWorldServlet class

```
package com.oreilly.aspectjcookbook;

import java.io.IOException;

import javax.servlet.ServletOutputStream;
import javax.servlet.http.HttpServletRequest;
import javax.servlet.http.HttpServletResponse;

public aspect AddHTMLHeaderAndFooter
{
    public pointcut captureHttpRequest(HttpServletRequest request,
                                       HttpServletResponse response) :
        execution(public void AOHelloWorldServlet.doGet(HttpServletRequest,
                                                        HttpServletResponse)) &&
        args(request, response);

    before(HttpServletRequest request, HttpServletResponse response)
        throws IOException :
        captureHttpRequest(request, response)
    {
        response.setContentType("text/html");
        ServletOutputStream out = response.getOutputStream( );
        out.println("<html>");
        out.println("<head><title>Adding a title using AspectJ!</title></head>");
        out.println("<body>");
    }

    after(HttpServletRequest request, HttpServletResponse response)
        throws IOException :
        captureHttpRequest(request, response)
    {
        ServletOutputStream out = response.getOutputStream( );
        out.println("</body>");
        out.println("</html>");
    }
}
```

2. Compile your Java Servlet and aspect as normal using either the ajc command-line tool or as part of an AspectJ project in Eclipse.

3. Create a new web application directory in Tomcat by creating a subdirectory of *%TOMCAT_INSTALL_DIRECTORY%/webapps* called *mywebapplication*.

4. Create a subdirectory of *mywebapplication* called *WEB-INF* that contains a *classes* and *lib* directory.

5. Create a new file inside *mywebapplication/WEB-INF* called *web.xml* that has the following contents:

```xml
<?xml version="1.0" encoding="ISO-8859-1"?>

<!DOCTYPE web-app
    PUBLIC "-//Sun Microsystems, Inc.//DTD Web Application 2.3//EN"
    "http://java.sun.com/dtd/web-app_2_3.dtd">

<web-app>

  <display-name>MyApplication</display-name>
  <description>
    A simple web application that demonstrates the deployment of Java Servlets
    that have been built using AspectJ.
  </description>

  <servlet>
    <servlet-name>AOHelloWorld</servlet-name>
    <servlet-class>com.oreilly.aspectjcookbook.AOHelloWorldServlet</servlet-class>
  </servlet>

  <servlet-mapping>
    <servlet-name>AOHelloWorld</servlet-name>
    <url-pattern>/AOHelloWorld</url-pattern>
  </servlet-mapping>

</web-app>
```

6. Copy the *.class* files generated from your compilation of the Java Servlet and aspect to the *mywebapplication/WEB-INF/classes* directory remembering to preserve the package directory structure.

7. Copy the *aspectjrt.jar* from *%ASPECTJ_INSTALL_DIRECTORY%/lib* to *mywebapplication/WEB-INF/lib*.

8. For convenience, create a new file inside *mywebapplication* called *index.html* that has the following contents:

```html
<html>
<title>Homepage for MyApplication</title>
<body>
<h1>
Testing hompage for aspect-oriented Java Servlets</h1>
<p>
The purpose of this page is to simply provide a set of links with which
to conveniently access your aspect-oriented Java Servlets.
</p>
<p>
<ul>
  <li>
  <a href="AOHelloWorld">
    The simple HelloWorld aspect-oriented Java Servlet
    </a>
```

9. The directory structure for your deployed web application should be as shown in Figure 3-5.

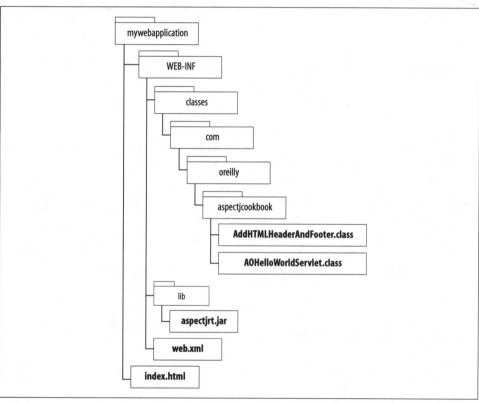

Figure 3-5. The deployed web application directory and file structure

10. Edit the *%TOMCAT_INSTALL_DIRECTORY%/conf/server.xml* and add the following lines to enable your web application inside Tomcat:

```
<Context path="/mywebapplication" docBase="mywebapplication" debug="0"
              reloadable="true" crossContext="true">
</Context>
```

11. Finally, restart Tomcat, and you should be able to access your web application and its Java Servlets using your browser by entering a URL similar to *http://*

<HOSTNAME>:<TOMCAT_PORT>/mywebapplication/index.html, entering the hostname and Tomcat port number for your installation of Tomcat. Figure 3-6 shows the homepage for your web application.

Figure 3-6. Your web applications homepage

12. By clicking on the "The simple HelloWorld aspect-oriented Java Servlet" link on your web applications homepage, your browser should show the output of your Java Servlet, as shown in Figure 3-7.

Figure 3-7. The output from your aspect-oriented Java Servlet

See Also

Compiling using the ajc command-line tool is explained in Recipe 2.2; creating and compiling an AspectJ project in Eclipse is described in Recipe 2.7; the execution(Signature) pointcut is explained in Recipe 4.4; the args([TypePatterns | Identifiers]) pointcut is explained in Recipe 11.3; the before() form of advice is discussed in Recipe 13.3; the after() form of advice is shown in Recipe 13.5; *Java Servlet & JSP Cookbook* by Bruce W. Perry (O'Reilly) contains examples of how to configure and deploy your Java Servlets in Tomcat and other containers; *Tomcat: The Definitive Guide* by Jason Brittain and Ian Darwin (O'Reilly).

3.4   Deploying a JSP That Uses AspectJ

Problem

You want to build and deploy a JSP that uses AspectJ into Apache Tomcat.

Solution

Create a Java Servlet from your JSP using the tools supplied with Tomcat. Compile your Java Servlet from the command line using the ajc command or inside an Eclipse AspectJ project.

Set up a directory structure from which to deploy your complete JSP application, including the *aspectjrt.jar* support library and the *.class* files that were compiled by the ajc command-line tool.

Copy the deployment directory entirely to the *%TOMCAT_INSTALL_DIREC-TORY%/webapps* directory. Make the appropriate amendments to the *server.xml* file in the Tomcat configuration to enable your web application. Finally, restart Tomcat to activate your web application.

Discussion

Java Server Pages are trickier than Java Servlets when it comes to using a custom compiler such as AspectJ because a JSP is traditionally compiled into a Java Servlet transparently by the Servlet containers like Apache Tomcat.

The following steps describe how to build and deploy a simple JSP that uses AspectJ into Apache Tomcat:

1. Create a directory in your project area called *jsp*.

2. Create a file in the *jsp* directory called *simple.jsp* that has the following contents:

    ```
    <html>
    <body bgcolor="white">
    <h1> Request Information </h1>
    <font size="4">
    JSP Request Method: <%= request.getMethod() %>
    <br>
    Request URI: <%= request.getRequestURI() %>
    <br>
    Request Protocol: <%= request.getProtocol() %>
    <br>
    Servlet path: <%= request.getServletPath() %>
    <br>
    </font>
    </body>
    </html>
    ```

3. Create a directory in your project area called *source* to hold your aspect and pre-processed JSP source code.

4. Create a directory in your project area called myjspapplication and a subdirectory called WEB-INF to hold your finished web application when it is ready for deployment to Tomcat. Also add classes and lib subdirectories to the WEB-INF directory. Once you've completed these changes your directory structure should look something like what is shown in Figure 3-8.

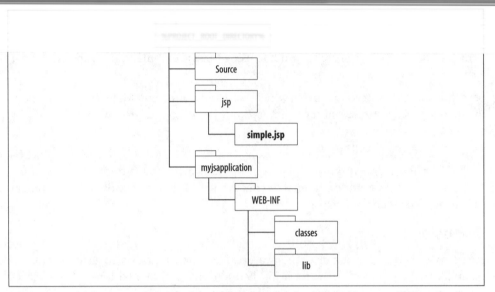

Figure 3-8. The directory structure after you have created the myjspapplication deployment directory, the source directory, and one .jsp file in the jsp directory

5. Run the jspc command-line tool that comes with Tomcat from your project area. This will generate the source code Java Servlet that is the first step when precompiling JSPs:

```
jspc -d source/ -webxml myjspapplication/WEB-INF/web.xml -webapp jsp/
```

6. After you have run the jspc command-line tool, you will find a *web.xml* file in the *myjspapplication/WEB-INF* directory and a *simple_jsp.java* file in the source directory.

7. Create a file called *AddCopyrightTomcatJSP.java* in the *source* directory with the code shown in Example 3-4.

Example 3-4. Using an aspect to affect the output of a JSP

```
import javax.servlet.jsp.JspWriter;

public aspect AddCopyrightTomcatJSP
{
    public pointcut captureOutput(String message, JspWriter writer) :
        call(public void JspWriter.write(String) ) &&
        within(simple_jsp) &&
```

Example 3-4. Using an aspect to affect the output of a JSP (continued)

```
      writer.write("<p>Copyleft Russ Miles 2004</p>\n");
    }
    catch (Exception e)
    {
        e.printStackTrace( );
    }
  }
}
```

8. Compile the two files, *simple_jsp.java* and *AddCopyrightTomcatJSP.java*, in your *source* directory using the ajc command-line tool from the project root directory:

   ```
   ajc -classpath %TOMCAT_INSTALL_DIRECTORY%/common/lib/servlet.jar:%TOMCAT_INSTALL_
   DIRECTORY%/common/lib/jasper-runtime.jar -d myjspapplication/WEB-INF/classes
   source/simple_jsp.java source/AddCopyrightTomcatJSP.java
   ```

9. The result of running this ajc command will be that two *.class* files will be generated in the *myjspapplication/META-INF/classes* directory.

10. Copy the *aspectjrt.jar* from *%ASPECTJ_INSTALL_DIRECTORY%/lib* to *mywebapplication/WEB-INF/lib*.

11. For convenience, create a new file inside *mywebapplication* called *index.html* that has the following contents:

    ```
    <html>
    <title>Homepage for MyJSPApplication</title>
    <body>
    <h1>
    Testing hompage for aspect-oriented Java Server Pages</h1>
    <p>
    The purpose of this page is to simply provide a set of links with which
    to conveniently access your aspect-oriented Java Server Pages.
    </p>
    <p>
    <ul>
      <li>
      <a href="simple.jsp">
        The simple aspect-oriented Java Server Page example
        </a>
      </li>
    </ul>
    </p>
    </body>
    </html>
    ```

This is an optional step that provides an HTML page that can be used to access your JSP conveniently from the browser without having to enter its specific URL manually.

12. The final contents of your deployable *myjspapplication* directory are shown in Figure 3-9.

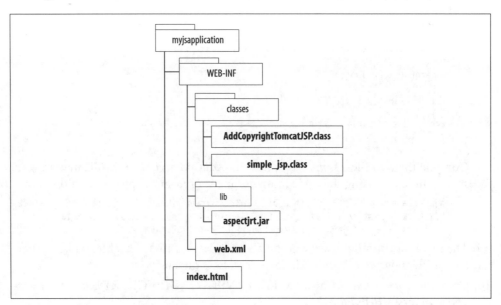

Figure 3-9. The contents of the myjspapplication directory when it is all set for deployment into Tomcat

13. Copy the entire *myjspapplication* directory and all its contents to *%TOMCAT_INSTALL_DIRECTORY%/webapps*.

14. Edit the *%TOMCAT_INSTALL_DIRECTORY%/conf/server.xml* and add the following lines to enable your web application inside Tomcat:

```
<Context path="/myjspapplication" docBase="myjspapplication" debug="0"
         reloadable="true" crossContext="true">
</Context>
```

15. Finally, restart Tomcat and you should be able to access your web application and its Java Servlets using your browser by entering a URL similar to *http://<HOSTNAME>:<TOMCAT_PORT>/myjspapplication/index.html* and entering the hostname and Tomcat port number for your installation of Tomcat. Figure 3-10 shows the homepage of your new JSP web application.

16. By clicking on the "The simple aspect-oriented Java Server Page example" link on your web applications homepage, your browser should show the output of your JSP, as shown in Figure 3-11.

The "Copyleft Russ Miles 2004" message was woven into the output of the JSP using the AddCopyrightJSPTomcat aspect.

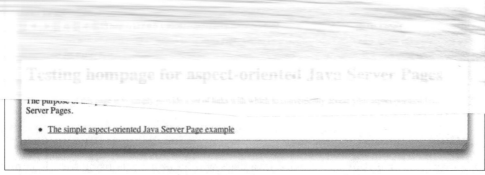

The purpose of ... ... Server Pages.

- The simple aspect-oriented Java Server Page example

Figure 3-10. Your JSP web applications homepage

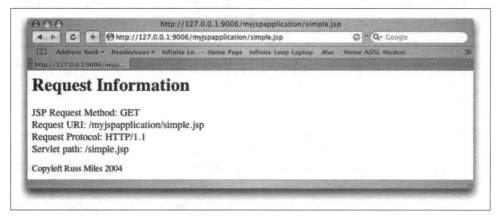

Figure 3-11. The output from your aspect-oriented Java Server Page

See Also

Compiling using the `ajc` command-line tool is explained in Recipe 2.2; creating and compiling an AspectJ project in Eclipse is described in Recipe 2.7; the `call(Signature)` pointcut is explained in Recipe 4.1; the `within(TypePattern)` pointcut is discussed in Recipe 9.1; the `target(TypePattern | Identifier)` pointcut is explained in Recipe 11.2; the `args([TypePatterns | Identifiers])` pointcut is explained in Recipe 11.3; the `if(Expression)` statement is described in Recipe 12.1; the `around( )` form of advice is discussed in Recipe 13.4; *Java Servlet & JSP Cookbook* by Bruce W. Perry (O'Reilly) contains examples of how to configure and deploy your Java Servlets in Tomcat and other containers; *Tomcat: The Definitive Guide* by Jason Brittain and Ian Darwin (O'Reilly).

3.5   Deploying an Axis Web Service That Uses AspectJ

Problem

You want to deploy an aspect-oriented Apache Axis web service that has been created using AspectJ.

Solution

Create and compile your web service Java class with your aspects using the ajc command line tool or in AspectJ project in Eclipse. Copy your application's *.class* files to the *%AXIS_INSTALLATION_IN_TOMCAT%/WEB-INF/classes* directory and the *aspectjrt.jar* to *%AXIS_INSTALLATION_IN_TOMCAT%/WEB-INF/lib*.

Create an Apache Axis deployment configuration file and use the org.apache.axis. client.AdminClient command-line tool to register your new web service with Apache Axis.

Discussion

Apache Axis is rapidly becoming one of the most popular web service implementations for Java developers. Not only is it open source but, thanks to its very active supporting developer base, it also has a high degree of success in interoperability with web services developed using other web service frameworks such as .NET.

Once you have Apache Axis running within Tomcat on your machine, you can use the following steps to compile a simple aspect-oriented web service and deploy it within Apache Axis:

1. Create a directory within your project area called *source*, and within that new directory, create a file called *MyWebService.java* that contains:

   ```
   package com.oreilly.aspectjcookbook;

   public class MyWebService
   {
       public String echo(String message)
       {
           return message;
       }
   }
   ```

2. Create another file in the *source* directory called *AddMessageHeaderAspect.java* that contains:

   ```
   package com.oreilly.aspectjcookbook;

   public aspect AddMessageHeaderAspect
   {
       public pointcut captureEcho(String message) :
   ```

}

3. Create a *classes* directory within your project area.

4. Compile the two files, *MyWebService.java* and *AddMessageHeaderAspect.java*, in your *source* directory using the ajc command-line tool from the project root directory:

```
ajc -classpath %AXIS_INSTALL_DIRECTORY%/lib/axis.jar:%AXIS_INSTALL_DIRECTORY%/
lib/axis.jar -d classes/ source/*.java
```

5. Once you have successfully run the ajc command, the compiled *.class* files and package structure will be generated under the *classes* directory.

6. Create a file called *deploy.wsdd* within the *classes* directory that is going to be used to automatically deploy your web application to Axis. The *deploy.wsdd* should contain the following information:

```
<deployment xmlns="http://xml.apache.org/axis/wsdd/"
            xmlns:java="http://xml.apache.org/axis/wsdd/providers/java">

  <service name="MyWebService" provider="java:RPC">
   <parameter name="className" value="com.oreilly.aspectjcookbook.MyWebService"/>
   <parameter name="allowedMethods" value="*"/>
  </service>

</deployment>
```

7. It is a good practice to create an *undeploy.wsdd* file in the same classes directory as the *deploy.wsdd* to be able to remove your web application from Axis. The *undeploy.wsdd* should contain the following information:

```
<undeployment xmlns="http://xml.apache.org/axis/wsdd/">
 <service name="MyWebService"/>
</undeployment>
```

8. Copy the *%ASPECTJ_INSTALL_DIRECTORY%/lib/aspectjrt.jar* to *%AXIS_INSTALLATION_IN_TOMCAT%/WEB-INF/lib*.

9. Copy your *.class* files located in the *classes* directory, preserving the package directory structure, to *%AXIS_INSTALLATION_IN_TOMCAT%/WEB-INF/classes*.

10. Ensuring that Tomcat is running if you are deploying to Apache Axis running within Tomcat, run the following java command from the *classes* directory to

run the Apache Axis deployment program that registers your new web service with Axis:

```
java -classpath %AXIS_INSTALL_DIRECTORY%/lib/axis.jar: %AXIS_INSTALL_DIRECTORY%/
lib/jaxrpc.jar:%AXIS_INSTALL_DIRECTORY%/lib/log4j-1.2.4.jar:%AXIS_INSTALL_
DIRECTORY%/lib/commons-logging.jar:%AXIS_INSTALL_DIRECTORY%/lib/commons-
discovery.jar:%AXIS_INSTALL_DIRECTORY%/lib/saaj.jar org.apache.axis.client.
AdminClient -h%HOST% -p%PORT% deploy.wsdd
```

11. Restart Tomcat to ensure it has refreshed all of the libraries and applications it manages, including Axis.

12. To test that your web service has been deployed correctly, you can go to *http://<hostname>:<post>/axis/services/MyWebService* in your browser, and you should see the output shown in Figure 3-12.

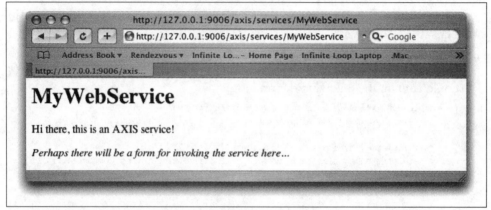

Figure 3-12. The aspect-oriented MyWebService service, initialized and ready for use inside Apache Axis

13. Web service clients can now use your new aspect-oriented web service. For example, the output of a simple AppleScript that uses the MyWebService is shown in Figure 3-13.

See Also

Compiling using the ajc command-line tool is explained in Recipe 2.2; creating and compiling an AspectJ project in Eclipse is described in Recipe 2.7; execution(Signature) pointcut is explained in Recipe 4.4; the args([TypePatterns | Identifiers]) pointcut is explained in Recipe 11.3; *Programming Apache Axis* by Christopher Haddad, Kevin Bedell, and Paul Brown (O'Reilly); *AppleScript in a Nutshell* by Bruce W. Perry (O'Reilly).

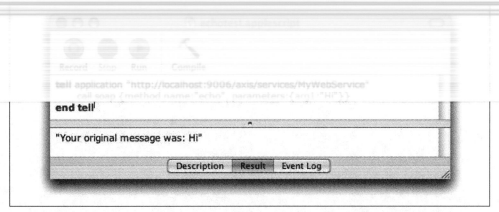

Figure 3-13. An AppleScript web service client using the echo method on the aspect-oriented MyWebService service

CHAPTER 4

Capturing Join Points on Methods

4.0   Introduction

A *join point* is a specific point at which advice can be woven into the code of an application. *Pointcuts* provide logical definitions for picking the join points that will invoke a piece of advice.

The next nine chapters correspond to the types of Java language constructs that contain join points that can be captured using pointcut declarations in AspectJ. This chapter focuses on pointcuts that can capture the selection of join points that are available on Java methods.

The before( ) form of advice is used for most of these pointcut-based recipes that make up the next eight chapters to avoid confusing things by using different types of advice. Where it's unavoidable, other forms of advice may have to be used, so it might be helpful to refer to Chapter 9 to understand the implications that the different forms of advice bring to the solutions provided.

 Once you have grasped the different types of pointcut that AspectJ provides in Chapters 4 through 12, check out Mik Kersten's standard pointcut idioms by going to *http://www.eclipse.org/aspectj* and then by clicking on Documentation → standard pointcut idioms. These reusable pointcut definitions provide some great tools with which to construct your own pointcut logic.

4.1   Capturing a Method Call

Problem

You want to capture when calls are made to methods that match a specific signature.

Solution

Use the call(Signature) pointcut. The syntax of the call(Signature) pointcut is

    pointcut <pointcut name>(<any values to be picked up>)
        call(<optional modifier> <return type> <class> <method>(<parameter types>));

In contrast to Java method parameters, whitespace in the Signature parameter is important as it is used to separate out the different components.

Discussion

The call(Signature) pointcut has two key characteristics:

1. Advice is triggered on a method call; the context is that of the calling class.
2. The Signature can include wildcard characters to select a range of join points on different classes and methods.

Table 4-1 shows some examples of the wildcard options available when using supplying a method Signature to a pointcut declaration.

Table 4-1. Examples of using wildcards within a method Signature

Signature with wildcards	Description
`* void MyClass.foo(int, float)` `void MyClass.foo(int, float)`	Captures join points on a method regardless of the modifier. Can also be achieved by leaving out the visibility entirely.
`* * MyClass.foo(int, float)` `* MyClass.foo(int, float)`	Captures join points on a method regardless of the modifier or return type.
`* * *.foo(int,float)` `* * foo(int,float)`	Captures join points on a method regardless of the modifier, return type, or class.
`* * *.*(int,float)`	Captures join points on a method regardless of the modifier, return type, class, or method.
`* * *.*(*,float)`	Captures join points on a method regardless of the modifier, return type, class, or method where the parameters include anything followed by a float.
`* * *.*(*,..)`	Captures join points on a method regardless of the modifier, return type, class, or method where the parameters include at least a single value followed by any number of parameters.
`* * *.*(..)` `* *(..)`	Captures join points on a method regardless of the modifier, return type, class, or method where there are any number of parameters.
`* mypackage..*.*(..)`	Captures join points on any method within the mypackage package and subpackages.
`* MyClass+.*(..)`	Captures join points on any method on the MyClass class and any sub-classes.

Example 4-1 shows the call(Signature) pointcut being used to declare an interest in all methods that match the signature MyClass.foo(int,String).

Example 4-1. Using the call(Signature) pointcut to catch calls to a specific method signature

```
public aspect CallRecipe
{
    /*
    Specifies calling advice whenever a method
    matching the following rules gets called:

    Class Name: MyClass
    Method Name: foo
    Method Return Type: void
    Method Parameters: an int followed by a String
    */
    pointcut callPointCut() : call(void MyClass.foo(int, String));

    // Advice declaration
    before() : callPointCut()
    {

        System.out.println(
            "------------------- Aspect Advice Logic --------------------");
        System.out.println(
            "In the advice attached to the call point cut");
        System.out.println(
            "Actually executing before the point cut call ...");
        System.out.println("But that's a recipe for Chapter 6!");
        System.out.println(
            "Signature: "
                + thisJoinPoint.getStaticPart().getSignature());
        System.out.println(
            "Source Line: "
                + thisJoinPoint.getStaticPart().getSourceLocation());
        System.out.println(
            "------------------------------------------------------------");

    }
}
```

Figure 4-1 shows how the call(Signature) pointcut is applied to a simple class.

 Be aware that the call(Signature) and execution(Signature) pointcut definitions can result in strange behavior in certain situations when capturing join points on an object's inherited and/or overridden methods, depending on the dynamic and static types of the object.

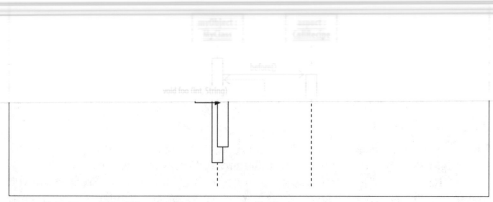

Figure 4-1. How the call(Signature) pointcut is applied

In AspectJ, the call(Signature) pointcuts and execution(Pointcuts) (see Recipe 4.4) can have strange behavior depending on the static and dynamic type of the target of the method. Consider the following:

```
A someObject = new E( );
someObject.foo( );
```

In this simple example, E is a subclass of A; according to the dynamic typing rules in Java, the static type of someObject is A, whereas the dynamic type is E. You can then declare a call(Signature) pointcut to capture the call to someObject.foo( ):

```
call(public void A.foo( ))
```

If the foo( ) method is declared in A and inherited by E, then the pointcut will capture the call to the method. However, if the foo( ) method is overridden in E, then the call(Signature) pointcut will *still* capture the method call join point. This may seem strange at first, but it makes sense if you think of the call(Signature) pointcut as examining the static type of someObject, which is still A.

Now things get a little strange. What if you change the static type of someObject to E, leaving the foo( ) method being overridden in E, and change the code that uses the method to:

```
E someObject = new E( );
someObject.foo( );
```

The static type of the object is the same as its dynamic type, both are E, which is still a subclass of A. foo( ) is overridden in E, then no code in A is invoked nor is the static type A referenced. Using the same pointcut definition as before you would not expect the call to someObject.foo( ) to be caught, but in fact it *is*. In this case you might have expected to be forced to use the + inheritance specifier to capture calls to foo( ), for example:

```
call(public void A+.foo()) // Captures calls to foo() on A and all subclasses
```

Because of the way that the call(Signature) pointcut is implemented in AspectJ, you do not need the + specifier to capture calls to methods that are overridden in a subclass. It appears that even though the static and dynamic type of someObject is declared as E, because foo( ) is a method that exists on A, which is a still a super class of E, then the original call(Signature) pointcut definition still captures the method call. This appears even stranger when you consider the original pointcut definition does not even mention E nor does it use the + inheritance specification to indicate an interest in subclasses of A.

This is just one example of the subtle and sometimes confusing ways the call(Signature) pointcut works with inherited and/or overridden methods depending on the static and dynamic types of an object and the type declared within the Signature. The execution(Signature) pointcut definition has similar but not identical problems because it puts more emphasis on the dynamic type of the object, which is what you'd perhaps expect when capturing join points that are within a method as opposed to on the call to a method.

A complete investigation into these subtleties would require a full report, and one is available at *www.cs.iastate.edu/~leavens/FOAL/papers-2004/barzilay-etal.pdf*. Normal day-to-day use of the call(Signature) and execution(Signature) probably won't result in you encountering these issues; however it is helpful to at least keep them in mind and know of their existence just in case.

See Also

The subtle characteristics of call(Signature) and execution(Signature) pointcuts when capturing join points in inherited or overridden methods are explained in more detail in the report available at *www.cs.iastate.edu/~leavens/FOAL/papers-2004/barzilay-etal.pdf*; how to capture parameters on a join point, in particular on a method call, is shown in Recipe 4.2; Chapter 13 describes the different types of advice available in AspectJ.

4.2   Capturing the Parameter Values Passed on a Method Call

Problem

You want to capture and use the parameters passed on a method call.

Solution

Create a pointcut that specifies the parameters that you want to capture as identifiers in its signature. Use the call(Signature) and args([TypePatterns | Identifiers]) pointcuts to capture the call to the method and then to bind the required identifiers to the values of the method's parameters.

Discussion

Example 4-2 shows the call(Signature) pointcut being used to declare an interest in all methods that match the signature MyClass.foo(int,String). The
captureCallParameters(int,String) pointcut requires an int and a String as specified by the value and name identifiers. Those identifiers are then bound to the
methods parameters by the args([Types | Identifiers]) pointcut.

*Example 4-2. Capturing the int and String values that are passed on a call to the MyClass.foo(..)
method*

```
public aspect CaptureCallParametersRecipe
{
    /*
    Specifies calling advice whenever a method
    matching the following rules gets called:

    Class Name: MyClass
    Method Name: foo
    Method Return Type: void
    Method Parameters: an int followed by a String
    */
    pointcut captureCallParameters(int value, String name) :
        call(void MyClass.foo(int, String)) &&
        args(value, name);

    // Advice declaration
    before(int value, String name) : captureCallParameters(value, name)
    {

        System.out.println(
            "------------------ Aspect Advice Logic -------------------");
        System.out.println(
            "In the advice attached to the call point cut");
        System.out.println("Captured int parameter on method: " + value);
        System.out.println("Captured String parameter on method: " + name);
        System.out.println(
            "----------------------------------------------------------");
    }
}
```

The before( ) advice can access the identifiers declared on the captureCallParame-
ters(int,String) pointcut by including the value and name identifiers in its signature
and then binding those identifiers to the captureCallParameters(int,String) pointcut.

See Also

The call(Signature) pointcut is described in Recipe 4.1; Recipe also 4.1 shows some
of the wildcard variations that can be used in a Signature; Recipe 11.3 discusses the
args([Types | Identifiers]) pointcut; combining pointcut logic using a logical AND

(&&) is shown in Recipe 12.2; the before( ) form of advice is shown in Recipe 13.3; the calling context that is available to advice is covered in Chapter 13.

4.3 Capturing the Target of a Method Call

Problem

You want to capture the object being called as a method is invoked.

Solution

Create a pointcut that specifies a single parameter of the same type as the target of the method call that you want to capture. Use the call(Signature) and target(Type | Identifier) pointcuts to capture the invocation of a method and then to bind the single identifier to the object that the method is being called upon.

Discussion

Example 4-3 shows the call(Signature) pointcut being used to declare an interest in all methods that match the signature MyClass.foo(int,String). The captureCallTarget(MyClass) pointcut requires a MyClass object as specified by the myObject identifier. The myObject identifier is then bound to the object that is being called by the MyClass.foo(int,String) method by the target(Type | Identifier) pointcut.

Example 4-3. Capturing the object upon which the MyClass.foo(..) method is invoked

```
public aspect CaptureCallTargetRecipe
{
    /*
    Specifies calling advice whenever a method
    matching the following rules gets called:

    Class Name: MyClass
    Method Name: foo
    Method Return Type: void
    Method Parameters: an int followed by a String
    */
    pointcut captureCallTarget(MyClass myObject) :
        call(void MyClass.foo(int, String)) &&
        target(myObject);

    // Advice declaration
    before(MyClass myObject) : captureCallTarget(myObject)
    {

        System.out.println(
            "------------------- Aspect Advice Logic --------------------");
        System.out.println(
```

Example 4-3. Capturing the object upon which the MyClass.foo( ) method is invoked (continued).
        "in the advice attached to the call point cut");
    System.out.println("Captured target object for the method call: " + myObject);
    System.out.println(
        "

The before( ) advice can access the single identifier declared on the captureCallTarget(MyClass) pointcut by including the myObject identifier in its signature and then binding that identifier to the captureCallTarget(MyClass) pointcut.

See Also

The call(Signature) pointcut is described in Recipe 4.1; Recipe 4.1 also shows some of the wildcard variations that can be used in a Signature; Recipe 11.2 discusses the target(Type | Identifier) pointcut; combining pointcut logic using a logical AND (&&) is shown in Recipe 12.2; the before( ) form of advice is shown in Recipe 13.3; the calling context that is available to advice is covered in Chapter 13.

4.4   Capturing a Method When It Is Executing

Problem

You want to capture when methods that match a specific signature are executing.

Solution

Use the execution(Signature) pointcut. The syntax of the execution(Signature) pointcut is:

```
pointcut <pointcut name>(<any values to be picked up>) :
    execution((<optional modifier> <return type> <class>.<method>(<paramater types>);
```

Discussion

The execution(Signature) pointcut has two key characteristics:

1. The context of a triggering join point is within the target class method.
2. The Signature can include wildcard characters to select a range of join points on different classes and methods.

Example 4-4 shows the execution(Signature) pointcut being used to declare an interest in method execution join points on any method that matches the signature MyClass.foo(int,String).

Example 4-4. Using the execution(Signature) pointcut to catch join points within the execution of a method

```
public aspect ExecutionRecipe
{
    /*
        Specifies calling advice whenever a method
        matching the following rules enters execution:

        Class Name: MyClass
        Method Name: foo
        Method Return Type: int
        Method Parameters: an int followed by a String
    */
    pointcut executionPointcut() : execution(void MyClass.foo(int, String));

    // Advice declaration
    before() : executionPointcut() && !within(ExecutionRecipe +)
    {
        System.out.println(
            "------------------ Aspect Advice Logic --------------------");
        System.out.println("In the advice picked by ExecutionRecipe");
        System.out.println(
            "Signature: "
                + thisJoinPoint.getStaticPart().getSignature());
        System.out.println(
            "Source Line: "
                + thisJoinPoint.getStaticPart().getSourceLocation());
        System.out.println(
            "-----------------------------------------------------------");
    }
}
```

Figure 4-2 shows how the execution(Signature) pointcut is applied to a simple class.

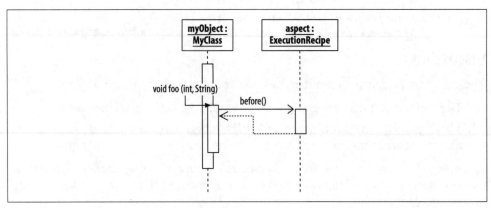

Figure 4-2. How the execution(Signature) pointcut is applied

At first, the execution(Signature) pointcut appears to offer nothing more than the call(Signature) pointcut described in the previous recipe. The important thing to remember with this recipe is *where* the advice is invoked and what is its context.

In the case of the call(Signature) pointcut, the advice is invoked where the method is invoked. The context of the advice invocation is the calling class. The execution(Signature) pointcut is invoked once the method has been entered and therefore the calling context is the method being executed.

Finally, if you haven't already read Recipe 4.1, then it is worth going back a couple of pages to read about the strange behavior that the call(Signature) and execution(Signature) pointcuts can have when capturing join points on an object's methods that are inherited and/or overridden depending on the object's static and dynamic type.

See Also

The subtle characteristics of call(Signature) and execution(Signature) pointcuts when capturing join points in inherited or overridden methods are explained in more detail in the report available at *www.xs.iastate.edu/~leavens/FOAL/papers-2004/ barzilay-etal.pdf*; Recipe 4.1 shows some of the wildcard variations that can be used in a Signature; how to capture parameters on a join point, in particular on a method call, is shown in Recipe 4.2; the calling context that is available to advice is covered in Chapter 13.

4.5   Capturing the Value of the this Reference When a Method Is Executing

Problem

When capturing a method during execution, you want to expose the object pointed to by the Java this reference so it can be used by your advice.

Solution

Create a pointcut that specifies a single parameter of the same type as the this reference you want to capture. Use the execution(Signature) and this(Type | Identifier) pointcuts to capture the execution of a method and then to bind the single identifier to the object that the this reference points to during the method's execution.

Discussion

Example 4-5 shows the execution(Signature) pointcut being used to declare an interest in all methods that match the signature MyClass.foo(int,String). The captureThisDuringExecution(MyClass) pointcut requires a MyClass object as specified by the myObject identifier. The myObject identifier is then bound to the methods this reference by the this(Type | Identifier) pointcut.

Example 4-5. Capturing the this reference during the execution of the MyClass.foo(..) method

```
public aspect CaptureThisReferenceRecipe
{
    /*
    Specifies calling advice whenever a method
    matching the following rules gets executed:

    Class Name: MyClass
    Method Name: foo
    Method Return Type: void
    Method Parameters: an int followed by a String
    */
    pointcut captureThisDuringExecution(MyClass myObject) :
        execution(void MyClass.foo(int, String)) &&
        this(myObject);

    // Advice declaration
    before(MyClass myObject) : captureThisDuringExecution(myObject)
    {

        System.out.println(
            "------------------- Aspect Advice Logic -------------------");
        System.out.println(
            "In the advice attached to the execution point cut");
        System.out.println("Captured this reference: " + myObject);
        System.out.println(
            "-----------------------------------------------------------");
    }
}
```

The before() advice can access the identifier that references the object originally pointed to by this during the method's execution by including the myObject identifier in its signature and then binding that to the captureThisDuringExecution(MyClass) pointcut.

See Also

Recipe 4.1 shows some of the wildcard variations that can be used in a Signature; the execution(Signature) pointcut is shown in Recipe 4.4; how to capture parameters on a join point, in particular on a method call, is shown in Recipe 4.2; Recipe 11.1 discusses the this(Type | Identifier) pointcut; combining pointcut logic using a logical AND (&&) is shown in Recipe 12.2; the before() form of advice is shown in Recipe 13.3.

CHAPTER 5

Capturing Join Points on Exception Handling

5.0   Introduction

This chapter shows how to include exception handling as part of the cross-cutting concerns you are applying to your application using aspects.

When an exception is thrown in Java, it is passed up the call chain until it is either handled by a catch statement as part of a try/catch block or it reaches the Java runtime and causes a messy message on your console. If a Java exception is caught then the exception is passed as an object to the corresponding catch block where the appropriate action can take place to handle the problem.

The aspects you are applying to your applications may find it useful to know when an exception has been handled. It is quite possible that part of the cross-cutting behavior you are implementing, using aspects, requires something to be done in addition to, or instead of, the normal behavior of a catch block.

AspectJ provides the handler(TypePattern) pointcut for use when you want to capture when a catch block has been invoked with a particular type of exception. This chapter shows you some of the ways to use the handler(TypePattern) in your aspects so that they can capture and interact with the exceptions that can be raised by your target application.

5.1   Capturing When an Exception Is Caught

Problem

You want to capture when a particular type of exception is caught.

Solution

Use the `handler(TypePattern)` pointcut. The syntax of the `handler(TypePattern)` pointcut is:

```
pointcut <pointcut name>(<any values to be picked up>) : handler(<class>);
```

Discussion

The `handler(TypePattern)` pointcut has five key characteristics:

1. The `handler(TypePattern)` pointcut picks up join points within the scope of where a exception is caught.
2. The `handler(TypePattern)` pointcut's advice will only be applied where the type pattern specifies `Throwable` or a subclass of `Throwable`.
3. The `TypePattern` declares that whenever the matching type of exception, or a subclass of that exception, is caught, then the corresponding advice is to be applied.
4. Only the `before()` form of advice is supported on `handler(TypePattern)` pointcuts. This means that you cannot override the normal behavior of a catch block using something like `around()` advice.
5. The `TypePattern` can include wildcard characters to select a range of join points on different classes.

Table 5-1 shows some examples of the wildcard options available when using a `TypePattern` to a pointcut declaration.

Table 5-1. Examples of using wildcards within a TypePattern

TypePattern with wildcards	Description
mypackage..*	Captures join points class within the mypackage package and subpackages.
MyClass+	Captures join points within the MyClass class and any subclasses.

Example 5-1 shows the `handler(TypePattern)` pointcut to capture a `MyException` exception being caught.

Example 5-1. Using the handler(TypePattern) pointcut to capture join points when a specific type of exception is caught

```
public aspect HandlerRecipe
{
    /*
        Specifies calling advice when any exception object is caught
        that matches the following rules for its type pattern:

        Type: MyException
    */
    pointcut myExceptionHandlerPointcut() : handler(MyException);
```

Example 5-1. Using the handler(TypePattern) pointcut to capture join points when a specific type of exception is caught (continued)

```
// Advice declaration
before() : myExceptionHandlerPointcut( )
{
    System.out.println(
        "-------------- Aspect Advice Logic ---------------");
    System.out.println(
        "In the advice picked by " + "myExceptionHandlerPointcut( )");
    System.out.println(
        "Signature: "
            + thisJoinPoint.getStaticPart().getSignature( ));
    System.out.println(
        "Source Line: "
            + thisJoinPoint.getStaticPart().getSourceLocation( ));
    System.out.println(
        "-------------------------------------------------");
}
}
```

The handler(TypePattern) pointcut captures join points where an exception is caught, *not* where it is raised.

Figure 5-1 shows how the handler(TypePattern) pointcut is applied to a simple class hierarchy.

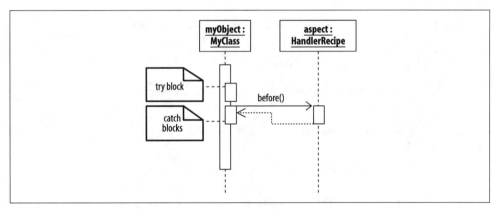

Figure 5-1. How the handler(TypePattern) pointcut is applied

See Also

Chapter 13 describes the different types of advice available in AspectJ.

5.2 Capturing the Thrown Exception

Problem

Within the advice triggered by a join point captured using the handler(TypePattern) pointcut, you want to access the exception that was being caught by the catch block within the corresponding advice.

Solution

Combine the args([Types | Identifiers]) pointcut with the handler(TypePattern) pointcut to expose the caught exception as an identifier on your pointcut that can be passed to the corresponding advice.

Discussion

Example 5-2 shows how the MyException exception is passed to the before() advice as the exception identifier on the myExceptionHandlerPointcut pointcut.

Example 5-2. Accessing the caught MyException exception

```
public aspect AccessThrownException
{
    pointcut myExceptionHandlerPointcut(MyException exception) :
        handler(MyException) &&
        args(exception);

    // Advice declaration
    before(MyException exception) : myExceptionHandlerPointcut(exception)
    {
        System.out.println(
            "-------------- Aspect Advice Logic --------------");
        System.out.println(
            "In the advice picked by " + "myExceptionHandlerPointcut()");
        System.out.println(
            "Signature: "
                + thisJoinPoint.getStaticPart().getSignature());
        System.out.println(
            "Source Line: "
                + thisJoinPoint.getStaticPart().getSourceLocation());

        System.out.println("Exception caught:");
        exception.printStackTrace();

        System.out.println(
            "-------------------------------------------------");
    }
}
```

See Also

The `handler(TypePattern)` poincut's syntax is shown in Recipe 5.1; Recipe 5.1 also shows some of the wildcard variations that can be used in a `TypePattern`; the `args([Types | Identifiers])` pointcut declaration is explained in Recipe 11.3; Chapter 13 describes the different types of advice available in AspectJ.

5.3   Capturing the Object Handling the Exception

Problem

Within the advice triggered by a join point captured using the `handler(TypePattern)` pointcut, you want to access the object that caught the exception and use it within the corresponding advice.

Solution

Combine the `this([Type | Identifier])` pointcut with the `handler(TypePattern)` pointcut to expose the exception handling object as an identifier on your pointcut that can then be passed to the corresponding advice.

Discussion

Example 5-3 shows how the exception handling `MyClass` object is passed to the `before()` advice as the `myObject` identifier on the `myExceptionHandlerPointcut` pointcut.

Example 5-3. Accessing the object that contained the catch block that handled the MyException exception

```
public aspect AccessHandlingObject
{
   pointcut myExceptionHandlerPointcut(MyClass myObject) :
      handler(MyException) &&
      this(myObject);

   // Advice declaration
   before(MyClass myObject) : myExceptionHandlerPointcut(myObject)
   {
      System.out.println(
         "-------------- Aspect Advice Logic --------------");
      System.out.println(
         "In the advice picked by " + "myExceptionHandlerPointcut()");
      System.out.println(
         "Signature: "
            + thisJoinPoint.getStaticPart().getSignature());
      System.out.println(
```

Example 5-3. Accessing the object that contained the catch block that handled the MyException exception (continued)

```
        "Source Line: "
          + thisJoinPoint.getStaticPart().getSourceLocation( ));

    System.out.println("Exception caught by:" + myObject);

    System.out.println(
      "--------------------------------------------------");
  }
}
```

See Also

The handler(TypePattern) pointcut's syntax is shown in Recipe 5.1; Recipe 5.1 also shows some of the wildcard variations that can be used in a TypePattern; the this([Type | Identifier]) pointcut declaration is explained in Recipe 11.1 combining pointcut logic using a logical AND (&&) is shown in Recipe 12.2; Chapter 13 describes the different types of advice available in AspectJ.

CHAPTER 6

Capturing Join Points on Advice

6.0 Introduction

In AspectJ, aspects are first-class language constructs just like classes. Classes and their business logic can be advised by aspects and so can aspects themselves. Although aspects can contain methods and other candidate join points, there is one construct that is specific to aspects that is in need of its own mechanism for capturing its join points. That construct is advice.

This chapter deals with using pointcut definitions that are purely concerned with capturing join points that occur within advice. AspectJ provides the solitary adviceexecution( ) pointcut for this purpose.

Introducing the adviceexecution( ) pointcut's syntax and a simple example of its use, this chapter then shows how the adviceexecution( ) pointcut can provide an especially effective means of working with situations where advice and the behavior it invokes need to be excluded from being advised by the other aspects in your application.

This chapter ends by showing how to use some interesting characteristics of how AspectJ implements advice to access the original join point that triggered the advice that is in turn being advised using the adviceexecution( ) pointcut.

The adviceexecution( ) pointcut is a reasonably new addition to the AspectJ developers toolbox, and this chapter shows how useful this pointcut can be when working with aspects that apply to aspects.

6.1 Capturing When Advice Is Executing

Problem

You want to capture when any piece of advice is executing.

Solution

Use the adviceexecution( ) pointcut. The syntax of the adviceexecution( ) pointcut is:

```
pointcut <pointcut name>() : adviceexecution();
```

Discussion

The adviceexecution( ) pointcut captures the join points where any advice is executed within an application. Example 6-1 uses the adviceexecution( ) pointcut to apply advice when other advice begins execution.

Example 6-1. Using the adviceexecution() pointcut to apply advice

```
public aspect AdviceExecutionRecipe
{
    /*
        Specifies calling advice whenever advice is executed
    */
    pointcut adviceExecutionPointcut() : adviceexecution();

    // Advice declaration
    before() : adviceExecutionPointcut()
        && !within(AdviceExecutionRecipe +)
    {
        System.out.println(
            "------------------- Aspect Advice Logic --------------------");
        System.out.println("In the advice picked by ExecutionRecipe");
        System.out.println(
            "Signature: "
                + thisJoinPoint.getStaticPart().getSignature());
        System.out.println(
            "Source Line: "
                + thisJoinPoint.getStaticPart().getSourceLocation());
        System.out.println(
            "-----------------------------------------------------------");
    }
}
```

Figure 6-1 shows how the adviceexecution( ) pointcut is applied to a simple class.

See Also

Recipe 6.3 protects against code in the aspect being called by using the adviceexecution( ) pointcut combined with the NOT (!) operator; Chapter 9 discusses scope based pointcuts; combining pointcut logic using a logical AND (&&) is shown in Recipe 12.2; the unary NOT (!) operator is shown in Recipe 12.4; Chapter 13 describes the different types of advice available in AspectJ.

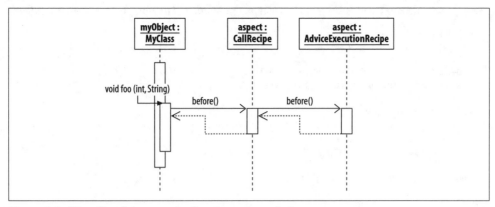

Figure 6-1. How the adviceexecution() pointcut is applied

6.2 Excluding Join Points That Are a Result of Advice Execution

Problem

You want to ignore all join points that are directly triggered within an advice block or as a result of advice execution. This is useful when you want to ignore anything an advice block triggered and just concentrate on join points that are within the control flow of your regular application's code business class's logic.

Solution

Supply the `adviceexecution()` pointcut declaration as the parameter to the `cflow(Pointcut)` pointcut. Use the unary NOT (!) operator to exclude the join points captured by the `cflow(Pointcut)` pointcut.

Discussion

It is sometimes useful to ignore the join points that occur directly within advice execution and those that may be triggered indirectly. If you use the `within()` pointcut with the unary NOT (!) operator alone, you can exclude all join points that occur directly within a particular aspect or aspects. However, any join points triggered indirectly by the advice within those aspects will still be caught.

An example of this problem can be demonstrated by amending the `CallRecipe` aspect from Recipe 4.1 as shown in Example 6-2. The `before()` advice has been enhanced to invoke the `foo()` method on the `AnotherClass` object.

Example 6-2. Making a call to the foo() method on the AnotherClass class from within some advice

```
public aspect CallRecipe
{
    /*
    Specifies calling advice whenever a method
    matching the following rules gets called:

    Class Name: MyClass
    Method Name: foo
    Method Return Type: * (any return type)
    Method Parameters: an int followed by a String
    */
    pointcut callPointCut() : call(void MyClass.foo(int, String));

    // Advice declaration
    before() : callPointCut()
    {

        System.out.println(
            "------------------- Aspect Advice Logic --------------------");
        System.out.println("In the advice attached to the call point cut");

        System.out.println(
                "Signature: " + thisJoinPoint.getStaticPart().getSignature());
        System.out.println(
            "Source Line: "
            + thisJoinPoint.getStaticPart().getSourceLocation());

        AnotherClass anotherClass = new AnotherClass();
        anotherClass.foo();

        System.out.println(
            "------------------------------------------------------------");

    }
}
```

The foo() method on the AnotherClass object in turn makes a call to the bar() method on the same class:

```
public class AnotherClass
{
    public void foo()
    {
        System.out.println("Inside method AnotherClass.foo()");
        this.bar();
    }

    public void bar()
    {
        System.out.println("Inside method AnotherClass.bar()");
    }
}
```

Using the !within(CallRecipe+) pointcut as shown in Example 6-3, the call to foo( ) would be correctly excluded but the indirect call to bar( ) would still be captured by the tracedCalls( ) pointcut.

Example 6-3. Incorrectly protects an aspect from tracing using the within(TypePattern) pointcut and the Boolean NOT (!) operator

```
public aspect TraceCalls
{
    /*
      Specifies calling advice when not within the TraceCalls and CallRecipe aspects
      or any of their subaspects.
    */
    pointcut tracedCalls() : call(* *.*(..)) &&
        !within(TraceCalls+) &&
        !within(CallRecipe+);

    // Advice declaration
    before() : tracedCalls()
    {
        System.out.println(
            "------------------- Aspect Advice Logic --------------------");
        System.out.println("In the advice picked by TraceCalls");

        System.out.println(
            "Signature: "
                + thisJoinPoint.getStaticPart().getSignature());
        System.out.println(
            "Source Line: "
                + thisJoinPoint.getStaticPart().getSourceLocation());
        System.out.println(
            "------------------------------------------------------------");
    }
}
```

The call on the bar( ) method in the AnotherClass class is still caught by the before( ) advice because it does not occur directly in the CallRecipe aspect. However, it does occur within the control flow of the before( ) advice block in that the foo( ) method is called by the advice which, in turn, calls the bar( ) method.

The traceCalls( ) pointcut can be changed by adding a cflow(Pointcut) pointcut, combined with the adviceexecution( ) pointcut, so you can exclude even those join points that occur indirectly within the control flow of an advice block.

```
pointcut tracedCalls() : call(* *.*(..)) &&
    !within(TraceCalls+) &&
    !within(CallRecipe+) &&
    !cflow(adviceexecution());
```

See Also

The call(Signature) pointcut is covered in Recipe 4.1; the cflow(Pointcut) pointcut is explained in Recipe 10.1; combining pointcut logic using a logical AND (&&) is shown in Recipe 12.2; the unary NOT (!) operator is shown in Recipe 12.4; Chapter 13 describes the different types of advice available in AspectJ.

6.3   Exposing the Original Join Point When Advice Is Being Advised

Problem

Where you are advising a piece of advice using the adviceexecution( ) pointcut, you want to access the original join point that triggered the advice block you are, in turn, advising.

Solution

Add the JoinPoint identifier to your pointcut definition. Bind your JoinPoint identifier as the single parameter to an args([Types | Identifiers]) pointcut declaration. Add the JoinPoint identifier to the corresponding advice you wish to expose the original join point to.

Discussion

In Example 6-4, the original join point that triggered the advice being advised is accessed from the AdviceExecution aspect's before( ) advice using the originalJoinPoint identifier.

Example 6-4. Accessing the original triggering join point when advising advice

```
import org.aspectj.lang.JoinPoint;

public aspect AdviceExecutionRecipe
{
    /*
      Specifies calling advice whenever advice is executed
    */
    pointcut adviceExecutionPointcut(JoinPoint originalJoinPoint) :
        adviceexecution( ) &&
        args(originalJoinPoint) &&
        !within(AdviceExecutionRecipe);

    // Advice declaration
    before(JoinPoint originalJoinPoint) : adviceExecutionPointcut(originalJoinPoint)
    {
        System.out.println(
            "------------------- Aspect Advice Logic --------------------");
```

```
      System.out.println("In the advice picked by AdviceExecutionRecipe");
      System.out.println(
         "Signature: "
            + thisJoinPoint.getStaticPart().getSignature( ));
      System.out.println(
         "Source Line: "
            + thisJoinPoint.getStaticPart().getSourceLocation( ));

      System.out.println(
            "Advised Advice's Join Point Signature: "
               + originalJoinPoint.getSignature( ));

      System.out.println(
         "-----------------------------------------------------------");
   }
}
```

> In AspectJ, there is an implicit JoinPoint object passed to every advice block as it is invoked. The single JoinPoint parameter is normally passed transparently to the advice and becomes the value of the thisJoinPoint reference. To populate the thisJoinPoint reference, every advice block, as it is implemented by AspectJ, must include the single JoinPoint argument as part of its signature.

See Also

The syntax of the adviceexecution( ) pointcut is shown in Recipe 6.1; the within(TypePattern) pointcut is described in Recipe 9.1; the args([Types | Identifiers]) pointcut declaration is explained in Recipe 11.3; combining pointcut logic using a logical AND (&&) is shown in Recipe 12.2; the unary NOT (!) operator is shown in Recipe 12.4; Chapter 13 describes the different types of advice available in AspectJ.

CHAPTER 7

Capturing Join Points on Class and Object Construction

7.0   Introduction

There are four initialization and construction stages that Java classes and objects go through before they can be used within your application, ignoring the actual loading of the class into your Java Virtual Machine (JVM) by its class loader.

The first step in the process is the invocation of a constructor using the new keyword. This invocation, if the class has not been previously used by the application, triggers static class initialization for the class of the object being constructed. *Static class initialization* is when the class itself is initialized so that all of its static variables and methods are properly constructed.

Once the class has been statically initialized, and before the constructor method can be executed, the object itself must be initialized. Object initialization first constructs the inheritance hierarchy for the object by executing all of the object's superclass constructors. Finally, once the superclass constructors have returned successfully, the initialized object is all set to complete the execution of its constructor method.

AspectJ provides a specific pointcut for each of the stages involved in a class and object's construction and initialization, and this chapter will walk you through the syntax and key characteristics of each.

7.1   Capturing a Call to a Constructor

Problem

You want to capture when a call to a constructor that matches a specific signature is invoked.

Solution

Use the call(Signature) pointcut with the additional new keyword as part of the signature. The syntax for using the call(Signature) pointcut in relation to constructors is:

```
pointcut <pointcut name>(<any values to be picked up>) :
        call(<optional modifier> <class>.new(<parameter types>));
```

Discussion

The call(Signature) pointcut has three key characteristics when used to capture calls to constructors:

1. The call(Signature) pointcut with the new keyword captures join points when a class is instantiated into an object.
2. By using the around( ) form of advice, the call(Signature) pointcut can override the type of returned object, within the bounds of the normal inheritance rules of Java.
3. The specified Signature is not checked by the compiler to correspond to an actual constructor.

Example 7-1 shows how to use the call(Signature) pointcut to capture calls to the constructor on the MyClass class that takes an int and String as parameters.

Example 7-1. Using the call(Signature) pointcut to capture join points when a constructor is called

```
public aspect CallNewRecipe
{
    /*
        Specifies calling advice when any constructor is called
        that meets the following signature rules:

        Class Name: MyClass
        Method Name: new (This is a keyword indicating the constructor call)
        Method Parameters: int, String
    */
    pointcut myClassConstructorWithIntAndStringPointcut() :
            call(MyClass.new (int, String));

    // Advice declaration
    before() : myClassConstructorWithIntAndStringPointcut()
    {
        System.out.println(
            "-------------- Aspect Advice Logic --------------");
        System.out.println(
            "In the advice picked by "
                + "myClassConstructorWithIntAndOthersPointcut( )");
        System.out.println(
            "The current type of object under construction is: ");
        System.out.println(thisJoinPoint.getThis( ));
        System.out.println(
```

```
        "Signature: "
            + thisJoinPoint.getSignature( ));
    System.out.println(
        "Source Line: "
            + thisJoinPoint.getSourceLocation( ));
    System.out.println(
        "-------------------------------------------------");
    }
}
```

Figure 7-1 shows how the call(Signature) pointcut is applied.

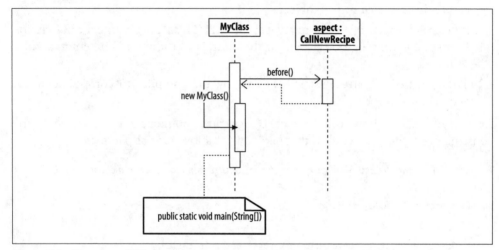

Figure 7-1. How the call(Signature) pointcut is applied to constructors

See Also

The execution(Signature) and call(Signature) pointcuts in Recipes 4.1 and 4.4 respectively deal with attaching advice to methods other than constructors; Recipe 4.1 shows some of the wildcard variations that can be used in a Signature; Chapter 13 deals with the environments available to the advice when picked by the different pointcuts; Recipe 20.2 describes in more detail the use of the around( ) advice, specifically in dealing with overriding constructors to return a different type of object.

7.2 Capturing a Constructor When It Is Executing

Problem

You want to capture a constructor that matches a specific signature when it is executing.

Solution

Use the execution(Signature) pointcut with the additional new keyword as part of the signature. The syntax of the execution(Signature) pointcut when using in relation to constructors is:

```
pointcut <pointcut name>(<any values to be picked up>) :
        execution(<optional modifier> <class>.new(<parameter types>));
```

Discussion

The execution(Signature) pointcut has three key characteristics when it is used to capture the execution of a constructor:

1. The execution(Signature) pointcut with the new keyword triggers join points when a class constructor is executing.

2. The exact point at which the join point is triggered cannot be prior to the class's constructor being invoked. This prevents overriding of the returned object.

3. The implementation, but not the type of object being constructed, of the constructor method can be overridden using around( ) advice.

Example 7-2 shows the execution(Signature) capturing the execution of the MyClass constructor that takes an int and a String as parameters.

Example 7-2. Using the execution(Signature) pointcut to capture join points within a specific constructor

```
public aspect ExecutionNewRecipe
{
    /*
        Specifies calling advice when any constructor executes
        that meets the following signature rules:

        Class Name: MyClass
        Method Name: new (This is a keyword indicating the constructor call)
        Method Parameters: int, String
    */
    pointcut myClassConstructorWithIntAndStringPointcut() :
            execution(MyClass.new (int, String));

    // Advice declaration
    before() : myClassConstructorWithIntAndStringPointcut()
    {
```

Example 7-2. Using the execution(Signature) pointcut to capture join points within a specific constructor (continued)

```
    System.out.println(
        "--------------- Aspect Advice Logic ----------------");
    System.out.println(
        "In the advice picked by "
            + "myClassConstructorWithIntAndOthersPointcut()");
    System.out.println(
        "The current type of object under construction is: ");
    System.out.println(thisJoinPoint.getThis().getClass());
    System.out.println(
        "Signature: " + thisJoinPoint.getSignature());
    System.out.println(
        "Source Line: " + thisJoinPoint.getSourceLocation());
    System.out.println(
        "----------------------------------------------------");
    }
}
```

Figure 7-2 shows how the execution(Signature) pointcut is applied to constructors.

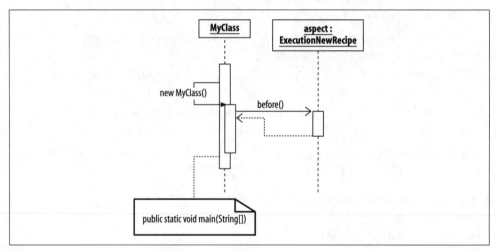

Figure 7-2. How the execution(Signature) pointcut is applied to constructors

See Also

Recipe 4.1 shows some of the wildcard variations that can be used in a Signature; describes how the call(Signature) pointcut is applied to constructors and is similar to this recipe's pointcut, with the exception that the call(Signature) pointcut has the power to override the object that is being constructed; Recipes 4.1 and 4.4 respectively show how to define the call(Signature) and execution(Signature) pointcuts to capture join points from regular methods; Chapter 13 describes the different types of advice available in AspectJ.

7.3   Capturing When an Object Is Initialized

Problem

You want to capture when an object is initialized, invoked by a call to a constructor that matches a specific signature.

Solution

Use the initialization(Signature) pointcut. The syntax of the initialization(Signature) pointcut is:

```
pointcut <pointcut name>(<any values to be picked up>) :
            initialization(<optional modifier> <class>.new(<parameter types>));
```

Discussion

The initialization(Signature) pointcut has five key characteristics:

1. The initialization(Signature) pointcut must contain the new keyword.

2. Join points caught by the initialization(Signature) pointcut occur after the initialization of any super classes and before the return from the constructor method.

3. The Signature must resolve to a constructor, not a simple method, of a particular class.

4. The initialization(Signature) pointcut provides compile-time checking that a constructor is being referenced.

5. Due to a compiler limitation in the AspectJ compiler, the initialization(Signature) pointcut cannot be used when associated with around( ) advice.

Example 7-3 shows the initialization(Signature) capturing the initialization of objects of MyClass when the constructor has the signature MyClass.new(int,*).

Example 7-3. Using the initialization(Signature) pointcut to capture join points when a constructor is executing

```
public aspect InitializationRecipe
{
  /*
      Specifies calling advice when any object
      initializes using a constructor
      that meets the following signature rules:

      Class Name: MyClass
      Method Name: new (This is a keyword indicating the
                        constructor call)
      Method Parameters: int and any others
  */
  pointcut myClassObjectInitializationWithIntAndOthersPointcut() :
            initialization(MyClass.new (int, *));
```

```
// Advice declaration
before() : myClassObjectInitializationWithIntAndOthersPointcut()
{
    System.out.println(
        "------------- Aspect Advice Logic ---------------");
    System.out.println(
        "In the advice picked by "
            + "myClassObjectInitializationWithIntAndOthersPointcut()");
    System.out.println(
        "The current type of object under construction is: ");
    System.out.println(thisJoinPoint.getThis().getClass());
    System.out.println(
        "Signature: "
            + thisJoinPoint.getStaticPart().getSignature());
    System.out.println(
        "Source Line: "
            + thisJoinPoint.getStaticPart().getSourceLocation());
    System.out.println(
        "-------------------------------------------------");
    }
}
```

Figure 7-3 shows how the initialization(Signature) pointcut is applied to pick join points on constructors.

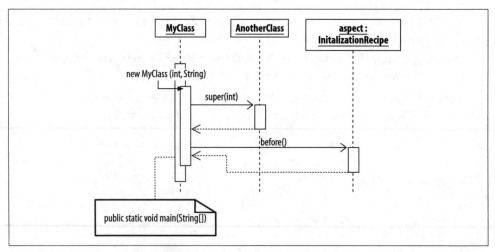

Figure 7-3. How the initialization(Signature) pointcut is applied

The biggest advantage to using the initialization(Signature) pointcut over the execution(Signature) pointcut is in the compile-time checking that occurs to ensure that the signature is actually specifying a constructor.

See Also

Recipe 4.1 shows some of the wildcard variations that can be used in a Signature; Recipe 7.2 shows the execution(Signature) pointcut for a comparison of its similarities to this recipe; Chapter 13 describes the different types of advice available in AspectJ.

7.4 Capturing When an Object Is About to Be Initialized

Problem

You want to capture when an object is about to be initialized using a constructor that matches a specific signature.

Solution

Use the preinitialization(Signature) pointcut. The syntax of the preinitialization(Signature) pointcut is:

```
pointcut <pointcut name>(<any values to be picked up>) :
          preinitialization(<optional modifier> <class>.new(<parameter types>));
```

Discussion

The preinitialization(Signature) pointcut has five key characteristics:

1. The preinitialization(Signature) pointcut must contain the new keyword.
2. Join points caught by the preinitialization(Signature) pointcut occur after the caught constructor is entered and before any super class constructors are called.
3. The Signature must resolve to a constructor.
4. The preinitialization(Signature) pointcut provides compile-time checking that a constructor is being referenced.
5. Due to a compiler limitation in the AspectJ compiler, the preinitialization(Signature) pointcut cannot be used when associated with around( ) advice.

Example 7-4 shows the preinitialization(Signature) pointcut capturing join points before the initialization of an object using the MyClass constructor with an int and a String as parameters.

Example 7-4. Using the preinitialization(Signature) pointcut to capture join points before the execution of a specific constructor

```
public aspect PreInitializationRecipe
{
    /*
        Specifies calling advice just before an object initializes
        using a constructor that meets the following signature rules:
```

```
    Class Name: MyClass
    Method Name: new (This is a keyword indicating the constructor call)
    Method Parameters: an int followed by a String
*/
pointcut myClassIntStringObjectPreInitializationPointcut() :
        preinitialization(MyClass.new (int, String));

// Advice declaration
before(
    int number,
    String name) : myClassIntStringObjectPreInitializationPointcut()
    && args(number, name)
{
    System.out.println(
        "-------------- Aspect Advice Logic ---------------");
    System.out.println(
        "In the advice picked by "
            + "anyMyClassObjectInitializationPointcut()");
    System.out.println(
        "The current type of object under construction is: ");
    System.out.println(thisJoinPoint.getThis());
    System.out.println(
        "The values passed in were: " + number + ", " + name);
    System.out.println(
        "Signature: "
            + thisJoinPoint.getStaticPart().getSignature());
    System.out.println(
        "Source Line: "
            + thisJoinPoint.getStaticPart().getSourceLocation());
    System.out.println(
        "-----------------------------------------------");
    }
}
```

Figure 7-4 shows how the preinitialization(Signature) pointcut is applied to pick
join points before an object is initialized.

See Also

Recipe 4.1 shows some of the wildcard variations that can be used in a Signature;
The adviceexecution() pointcut is covered in Recipe 6.1; Chapter 13 describes the
different types of advice available in AspectJ.

7.5   Capturing When a Class Is Initialized

Problem

You want to capture when a class is initialized.

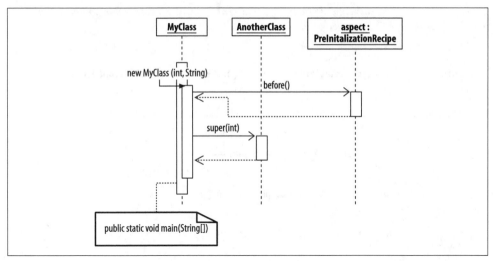

Figure 7-4. How the preinitialization(Signature) pointcut is applied

Solution

Use the staticinitialization(TypePattern) pointcut. The syntax of the staticinitialization(TypePattern) pointcut is:

```
pointcut <pointcut name>(<any values to be picked up>) :
            staticinitialization(<class>);
```

Discussion

The staticinitialization(TypePattern) pointcut has two key characteristics:

1. There are limitations on the environment available to advice picked by the staticinitialization(TypePattern) pointcut. There is no parent object triggering the static initialization; therefore, there is no this reference. There is also no instance object involved, and, therefore, there is no target reference.

2. The TypePattern can include wildcard characters to select a range of different classes.

Example 7-5 shows the staticinitialization(TypePattern) pointcut capturing join points in the static initialization of the MyClass class.

Example 7-5. Using the staticinitialization(TypePattern) pointcut to capture join points on the static initialization of a specific class

```
public aspect StaticInitializationRecipe
{
    /*
        Specifies calling advice when a class is initialized
        that meets the following type pattern rules:
```

Example 7-5. Using the staticinitialization(TypePattern) pointcut to capture join points on the static initialization of a specific class (continued)

```
      Class Name: MyClass
*/
pointcut myClassStaticInitializationPointcut() : staticinitialization(MyClass);

// Advice declaration
before() : myClassStaticInitializationPointcut()
{
   System.out.println(
      "-------------- Aspect Advice Logic ---------------");
   System.out.println(
      "In the advice picked by "
         + "myClassStaticInitializationPointcut()");
   System.out.println(
      "Join Point Kind: "
         + thisJoinPoint.getStaticPart().getKind());
   System.out.println(
      "Signature: "
         + thisJoinPoint.getStaticPart().getSignature());
   System.out.println(
      "Source Line: "
         + thisJoinPoint.getStaticPart().getSourceLocation());
   System.out.println(
      "------------------------------------------------");
}
}
```

Figure 7-5 shows how the staticinitialization(TypePattern) pointcut is applied.

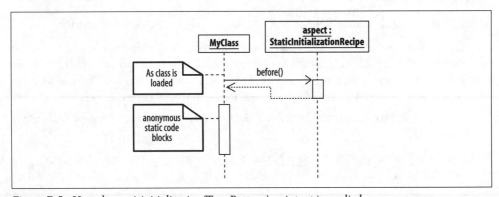

Figure 7-5. How the staticinitialization(TypePattern) pointcut is applied

See Also

Recipe 5.1 shows some of the wildcard variations that can be used in a TypePattern; Chapter 13 describes the different types of advice available in AspectJ including the associated different forms of environment that they expose.

CHAPTER 8

Capturing Join Points on Attributes

8.0   Introduction

One slightly controversial feature of the AspectJ developer's toolkit is the ability to monitor any accesses or modifications that may occur on a class's attribute. AspectJ provides this capability in the form of the get(Signature) and set(Signature) point-cuts that are the focus of this chapter.

Anyone who has practiced traditional object-oriented techniques will be a little worried when they hear this as it effectively breaks encapsulation, especially if the attributes being monitored are declared protected or private. It is good advice to think carefully before you decide your aspect needs to have direct access to a class's internals to avoid unnecessary tight coupling between your aspects and your classes.

However, sometimes a cross-cutting concern requires this level of intimacy with a class's to apply the aspect effectively. Used judiciously the get(Signature) and set(Signature) pointcuts showcased in this chapter can provide a powerful means of advising your classes, but they must be used carefully to ensure that you are not making your classes and your aspects needlessly brittle.

8.1   Capturing When an Object's Attribute Is Accessed

Problem

You want to capture when an object's attribute is accessed.

Solution

Use the get(Signature) pointcut. The syntax of the get(Signature) pointcut is:

```
pointcut <pointcut name>(<any values to be picked up>) :
            get(<optional modifier> <type> <class>.<field>);
```

Discussion

The get(Signature) has four key characteristics:

1. The get(Signature) pointcut triggers advice where the attribute is directly accessed, not just on a call to an accessor method.

2. The get(Signature) pointcut cannot capture access to static attributes although it is perfectly legal within the syntax of AspectJ to define a pointcut in this way.

3. The Signature must resolve to an attribute of a particular class.

4. The Signature can include wildcard characters to select a range of join points on different attributes.

Example 8-1 shows the get(Signature) pointcut being used to capture join points that are encountered whenever the String MyClass.name attribute is accessed.

Example 8-1. Using the get(Signature) pointcut to capture access to attributes

```
public aspect GetRecipe
{

    /*
    Specifies calling advice whenever an attribute
    matching the following rules is accessed:

    Type: String
    Class Name: MyClass
    Attribute Name: name
    */
    pointcut getNamePointcut( ) : get(String MyClass.name);

    // Advice declaration
    before( ) : getNamePointcut( )
    {
        System.out.println(
            "-------------- Aspect Advice Logic ---------------");
        System.out.println(
            "In the advice picked by " + "getNamePointcut( )");
        System.out.println(
            "Signature: "
                + thisJoinPoint.getStaticPart().getSignature( ));
        System.out.println(
            "Source Line: "
                + thisJoinPoint.getStaticPart().getSourceLocation( ));
        System.out.println(
            "-------------------------------------------------");
    }
}
```

Figure 8-1 shows how the get(Signature) pointcut is applied to a simple class.

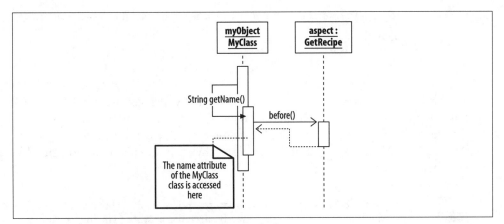

Figure 8-1. How the get(Signature) pointcut is applied

You might expect that where a class has a constant attribute defined, using the static and final keywords, you could capture when that constant is accessed using the get(Signature) pointcut. The getConstantPointcut( ) pointcut in Example 8-2 attempts to capture when the MyClass.CONSTANT attribute is accessed for just this purpose.

Example 8-2. Using the get(Signature) pointcut to capture when a constant is accessed

```
public aspect GetConstant
{
   /*
    Specifies calling advice whenever an attribute
    matching the following rules is accessed.

    Type: String
    Class Name: MyClass
    Attribute Name: CONSTANT
   */
   pointcut getConstantPointcut( ) : get(public static final String MyClass.CONSTANT);

   // Advice declaration
   before() : getConstantPointcut( )
   {
      System.out.println(
        "-------------- Aspect Advice Logic --------------");
      System.out.println(
        "In the advice picked by " + "getConstantPointcut( )");
      System.out.println(
        "Signature: "
          + thisJoinPoint.getStaticPart().getSignature( ));
      System.out.println(
        "Source Line: "
          + thisJoinPoint.getStaticPart().getSourceLocation( ));
```

Example 8-2. Using the get(Signature) pointcut to capture when a constant is accessed (continued)

```
    System.out.println(
        "------------------------------------------------");
  }
}
```

In fact, this form of constant access is *not* caught by the getConstantPointcut( ) pointcut even though this is acceptable AspectJ syntax. Though this is a valid get(Signature) pointcut declaration, unlike regular variable attributes, the Java compiler "inlines" static final attributes; therefore, they do not exist in a form suitable for access with a pointcut.

Take care when using the get(Signature) pointcut as it breaks the encapsulation of attributes that may be declared private. This breaking of encapsulation could lead to brittle software. Because you are specifying pointcuts based on variable names, you must remember that this can add detrimental tighter coupling to your design.

See Also

Recipe 4.1 shows some of the wildcard variations that can be used in a Signature; Chapter 13 describes the different types of advice available in AspectJ; the within(TypePattern) pointcut is described in Recipe 9.1; the NOT(!) operator is described in Recipe 12.4.

8.2   Capturing the Value of the Field Being Accessed

Problem

You want to capture the value of the field being accessed so that it can be used in your corresponding advice.

Solution

Use the after( ) returning(<ReturnValue>) form of advice with an identifier in the returning( ) part of the declaration to contain the value that has been accessed.

Discussion

Example 8-3 shows how the value of the MyClass.name attribute can be passed to the after( ) returning(<ReturnValue>) advice as triggered when the MyClass.name is accessed.

Example 8-3. Accessing the value of a field as it is returned when it is accessed

```
public aspect CaptureAccessedFieldValue
{
    pointcut getNamePointcut() : get(String MyClass.name);

    // Advice declaration
    after() returning(String value) : getNamePointcut()
    {
        System.out.println(
            "-------------- Aspect Advice Logic ---------------");
        System.out.println(
            "In the advice picked by " + "getNamePointcut()");
        System.out.println(
            "Signature: "
                + thisJoinPoint.getStaticPart().getSignature());
        System.out.println(
            "Source Line: "
                + thisJoinPoint.getStaticPart().getSourceLocation());

        System.out.println("Value being accessed is " + value);

        System.out.println(
            "-------------------------------------------------");
    }
}
```

See Also

Recipe 4.1 shows some of the wildcard variations that can be used in a Signature; The get(Signature) pointcut's syntax is examined in Recipe 8.1; the after() returning form of advice is shown in Recipe 13.6.

8.3   Capturing When an Object's Field Is Modified

Problem

You want to capture when an object's field is modified.

Solution

Use the set(Signature) pointcut. The syntax of the set(Signature) pointcut is:

```
pointcut <pointcut name>(<any values to be picked up>) :
        set(<optional modifier> <type> <class>.<field>);
```

Discussion

The set(Signature) pointcut has four key characteristics:

1. The set(Signature) pointcut triggers when a field is modified.

2. The set(Signature) pointcut *cannot* capture modification of static fields although it is perfectly legal within the syntax of AspectJ to define a pointcut in this way.

3. The Signature must resolve to an attribute of a particular class.

4. The Signature can include wildcard characters to select a range of join points on different attributes.

Example 8-4 shows the set(Signature) pointcut capturing join points encountered whenever the String MyClass.name attribute is modified.

Example 8-4. Using the set(Signature) pointcut to capture join points when an attribute is modified

```
public aspect SetRecipe
{
    /*
        Specifies calling advice whenever an attribute
        matching the following rules is modified:

        Type: String
        Class Name: MyClass
        Attribute Name: name
    */
    pointcut setNamePointcut( ) : set(String MyClass.name);

    // Advice declaration
    before() : setNamePointcut( ) && !within(SetRecipe +)
    {
        System.out.println(
            "------------------- Aspect Advice Logic --------------------");
        System.out.println(
            "In the advice picked by " + "setNamePointcut( )");
        System.out.println(
            "Signature: "
                + thisJoinPoint.getStaticPart().getSignature( ));
        System.out.println(
            "Source Line: "
                + thisJoinPoint.getStaticPart().getSourceLocation( ));
        System.out.println(
            "------------------------------------------------------------");
    }
}
```

Figure 8-2 shows how the set(Signature) pointcut is applied to a simple class.

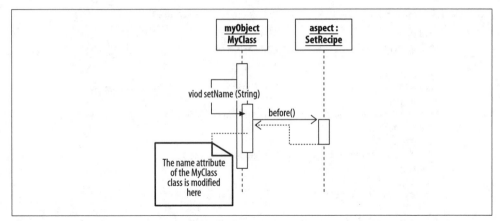

Figure 8-2. How the set(Signature) pointcut is applied

See Also

Recipe 4.1 shows some of the wildcard variations that can be used in a `Signature`; Chapter 13 describes the different types of advice available in AspectJ; the `within(TypePattern)` pointcut is described in Recipe 9.1; the NOT(!) operator is described in Recipe 12.4.

8.4 Capturing the Value of a Field When It Is Modified

Problem

You want to capture the value of the field after it has been modified so it can be used in your corresponding advice.

Solution

Combine the `args([Types | Identifiers])` pointcut with the `set(Signature)` pointcut to expose the new value of the field being set as an identifier on your pointcut that can be passed to the corresponding advice.

Discussion

Example 8-5 shows how the new value, that the `MyClass.name` attribute is being set to, can be passed to the `before( )` advice.

Example 8-5. Accessing the new value of the field being set

```
public aspect CaptureModifiedFieldValue
{
    pointcut setNamePointcut(String newValue) : set(String MyClass.name)
                        && args(newValue);
```

Example 8-5. Accessing the new value of the field being set (continued)

```
// Advice declaration
before(String newValue) : setNamePointcut(newValue)
{
    System.out.println(
        "------------------- Aspect Advice Logic --------------------");
    System.out.println(
        "In the advice picked by " + "setNamePointcut( )");
    System.out.println(
        "Signature: "
            + thisJoinPoint.getStaticPart().getSignature( ));
    System.out.println(
        "Source Line: "
            + thisJoinPoint.getStaticPart().getSourceLocation( ));

    System.out.println("Field Value set to: " + newValue);

    System.out.println(
        "------------------------------------------------------------");
}
}
```

See Also

Recipe 4.1 shows some of the wildcard variations that can be used in a Signature; The set(Signature) pointcut's syntax is examined in Recipe 8.4; the args([Types | Identifiers]) pointcut declaration is explained in Recipe 11.3; combining pointcut logic using a logical AND (&&) is shown in Recipe 12.2; Chapter 13 describes the different types of advice available in AspectJ.

CHAPTER 9

Capturing Join Points Within Programmatic Scope

9.0 Introduction

A common approach in the design of pointcut definitions is to limit the range of join points captured based on the programmatic scope of interest. This gives you some immediate control over what join points are going to be involved in further pointcut definitions.

This chapter describes the set of pointcuts that allow to you explicitly limit the join points captured based upon their programmatic scope. These pointcuts enable you to specify a method right through to package scope.

The pointcuts in this chapter are fairly simple to master, and they are some of the most commonly used elements of AspectJ. For example, a popular use of the `within(TypePattern)` pointcut (discussed in Recipe 5.1) is to use it in the `!within(%THIS_ASPECT%)` form. This AspectJ idiom limits the scope to every join point outside of the current aspect, providing protection against the advice triggering a recursive call to the same advice block and resulting in an infinite loop. The concepts in this chapter are basic to AspectJ programming and form the backbone of many of the operations detailed later in the book.

9.1 Capturing All Join Points Within a Particular Class

Problem

You want to capture all the join points within a particular class.

Solution

Use the within(TypePattern) pointcut, using the TypePattern to specify the particular class type pattern. The syntax of the within(TypePattern) pointcut is:

```
pointcut <pointcut name>(<any values to be picked up>) : within(<class>);
```

Discussion

The within(TypePattern) pointcut has three key characteristics:

1. The within(TypePattern) pointcut captures all join points within the scope of the specified class.
2. The within(TypePattern) pointcut is rarely used in isolation. Rather, it is usually combined with other pointcuts to narrow the join points that will trigger the attached advice.
3. The TypePattern can include wildcard characters to select a range of join points on different classes.

Example 9-1 shows the within(TypePattern) pointcut being used to capture all the join points within the MyClass class.

Example 9-1. Using the within(TypePattern) pointcut to capture join points within a specific class

```
public aspect WithinClassRecipe
{

    /*
        Specifies calling advice on any join point encountered within
        the defined scope:

        Scope: MyClass
    */
    pointcut withinMyClass() : within(MyClass);

    // Advice declaration
    before() : withinMyClass() && !within(WithinClassRecipe +)
    {
        System.out.println(
            "-------------- Aspect Advice Logic --------------");
        System.out.println(
            "In the advice picked by " + "withinMyClass()");
        System.out.println(
            "Join Point Kind: " + thisJoinPoint.getKind());
        System.out.println(
            "Signature: "
                + thisJoinPoint.getStaticPart().getSignature());
        System.out.println(
            "Source Line: "
                + thisJoinPoint.getStaticPart().getSourceLocation());
```

Example 9-1. Using the within(TypePattern) pointcut to capture join points within a specific class (continued)

```
    System.out.println(
        "--------------------------------------------------");
    }
}
```

Figure 9-1 shows how the within(TypePattern) pointcut is applied to a single class.

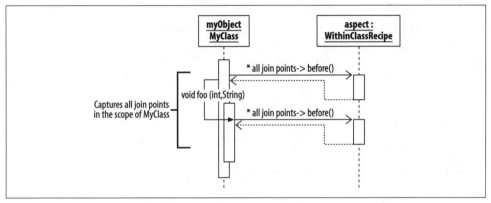

Figure 9-1. How the within(TypePattern) pointcut is applied

See Also

Recipe 5.1 shows some of the wildcard variations that can be used in a TypePattern; see the recipes in Chapter 12 for examples of the mechanisms by which pointcuts can be combined; the within(TypePattern) pointcut is often negated to remove an aspect from the scope of the weaving using the unary NOT (!) operator as described in Recipe 12.4; Chapter 13 contains recipes that describe the different types of advice available in AspectJ.

9.2   Capturing All Join Points Within a Particular Package

Problem

You want to capture all the join points within classes that are, in turn, within a particular package scope.

Solution

Use the within(TypePattern) pointcut using the TypePattern to specify a package.

Discussion

The within(TypePattern) pointcut provides a useful means of specifying an interest in the join points that occur in every class within a package by using wildcards. Entire packages of join points can be included or excluded from the rest of the point-cut logic using the appropriate wildcards in the TypePattern.

Example 9-2 shows the within(TypePattern) pointcut being used to capture all the join points within the packageA package.

Example 9-2. Using the within(TypePattern) pointcut to capture join points within a specific package

```
public aspect WithinPackageRecipe
{
    /*
        Specifies calling advice on any join point is encountered within
        the defined scope:

        Scope: packageA
    */
    pointcut withinPackageA() : within(packageA.*);

    // Advice declaration
    before() : withinPackageA() && !within(WithinPackageRecipe +)
    {
        System.out.println("-------------- Aspect Advice Logic ---------------");
        System.out.println("In the advice picked by " + "withinPackageA()");
        System.out.println("Join Point Kind: " + thisJoinPoint.getKind());
        System.out.println("Signature: " +
            thisJoinPoint.getStaticPart().getSignature());
        System.out.println(
            "Source Line: " + thisJoinPoint.getStaticPart().getSourceLocation());
        System.out.println("--------------------------------------------------");
    }
}
```

The within(TypePattern) pointcut's key characteristics are listed in Recipe 6.1.

See Also

Recipe 5.1 shows some of the wildcard variations that can be used in a TypePattern; Recipe 9.1 shows the more traditional use of the within(TypePattern) pointcut defi-nition for capturing the join points within a specific class; the mechanisms by which pointcuts can be combined are described in the recipes in Chapter 12; the within(TypePattern) pointcut is often negated to remove an aspect from the scope of the weaving using the unary NOT (!) operator as described in Recipe 12.4.

9.3 Capturing All Join Points Within a Particular Method

Problem

You want to capture all the join points within the scope of a particular method or methods.

Solution

Use the `withincode(Signature)` pointcut. The syntax of the `withincode(Signature)` pointcut is:

```
pointcut <pointcut name>(<any values to be picked up>) :
        withincode(<modifier> <class>.<method>(<parameter types>));
```

Discussion

There are three key characteristics of the `withincode(Signature)` pointcut:

1. The `withincode(Signature)` pointcut specifies all join points within the local scope of a particular method.

2. The `withincode(Signature)` pointcut is rarely used in isolation. Rather, it is usually combined with other pointcuts to narrow the join points that will trigger the attached advice.

3. The `Signature` can include wildcard characters to select a range of join points on different methods across different classes.

Example 9-3 shows the `withincode(Signature)` pointcut capturing all join points within the scope of the `* MyClass.foo(int,String)` method.

Example 9-3. Using the withincode(Signature) pointcut to capture all join points within a method's scope

```
public aspect WithinMethodRecipe
{
  /*
      Specifies calling advice whenever a method
      matching the following rules gets called:

      Class Name: MyClass
      Method Name: foo
      Method Return Type: * (any return type)
      Method Parameters: an int followed by a String
  */
  pointcut withinFooIntStringAnyReturnPointcut() :
      withincode(* MyClass.foo(int, String));

  // Advice declaration
  before() : withinFooIntStringAnyReturnPointcut()
```

Example 9-3. Using the withincode(Signature) pointcut to capture all join points within a method's scope (continued)

```
      && !within(WithinMethodRecipe +)
{
    System.out.println(
        "-------------- Aspect Advice Logic --------------");
    System.out.println(
        "In the advice picked by withinFooIntStringAnyReturnPointcut");
    System.out.println(
        "Join Point Kind: "
            + thisJoinPoint.getStaticPart().getKind( ));
    System.out.println(
        "Signature: "
            + thisJoinPoint.getStaticPart().getSignature( ));
    System.out.println(
        "Source Line: "
            + thisJoinPoint.getStaticPart().getSourceLocation( ));
    System.out.println(
        "------------------------------------------------");
    }
}
```

Figure 9-2 shows how the withincode(Signature) pointcut is applied.

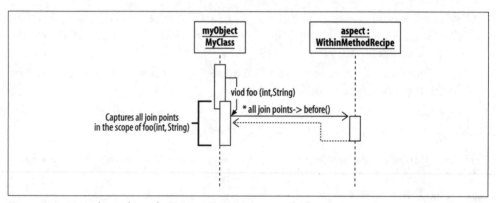

Figure 9-2. How the withincode(Signature) pointcut is applied

See Also

Recipe 4.1 shows some of the wildcard variations that can be used in a Signature; the withincode(Signature) pointcut can be negated to remove a specific method from the scope of the weaving using the NOT (!) operator as described in Recipe 12.4; Chapter 13 describes the different types of advice available in AspectJ.

CHAPTER 10

Capturing Join Points Based on Control Flow

10.0 Introduction

The pointcuts described in this chapter support capturing all join points within the scope or context of another initial join point. Every join point has a discrete location in the control flow of a program, and this provides the context for join points that are captured by the pointcut declarations described here.

This may seem confusing at first. If you imagine that a join point is a specific point in your code providing a marker at which a scope can be defined, then these pointcut definitions pick that scope. To understand these pointcuts, you must delve into this chapter's recipes and try things out. It is particularly worth examining the figures that accompany the recipes as these serve to illustrate what is actually going on when the pointcut's logic is applied.

These pointcuts can be the hardest to grasp for newcomers to AspectJ, but it is worth persevering because they provide some unique and powerful mechanisms for capturing join points that are often useful once you have added them to your repertoire.

10.1 Capturing All Join Points Within a Program's Control Flow Initiated by an Initial Join Point

Problem

You want to capture all join points encountered within the program control flow after and including an initiating join point selected by a separate pointcut.

Solution

Use the `cflow(Pointcut)` pointcut. The syntax of the `cflow(Pointcut)` pointcut is:

```
pointcut <pointcut name>(<any values to be picked up>) : cflow(<pointcut>)
```

Discussion

The `cflow(Pointcut)` pointcut has three key characteristics:

1. The `cflow(Pointcut)` pointcut picks all join points encountered within the context of an initial specific join point and picked by another pointcut.
2. The join points caught include the initial join point.
3. Scope is the important discriminator in the `cflow(pointcut)` pointcut. This pointcut will capture all join points within the control flow of the join point captured by the pointcut parameter.

Example 10-1 shows how the `cflow(Pointcut)` is used to capture all join points in the program control flow after and including an initial join point as captured by the `callInitialPointcut()` pointcut.

Example 10-1. Using the cflow(Pointcut) pointcut to capture all join points after and including a specific pointcut

```
public aspect CFlowRecipe
{
    /*
    Specifies calling advice whenever a method
    matching the following rules gets called:

    Class Name: MyClass
    Method Name: foo
    Method Return Type: void
    Method Parameters: an int followed by a String
    */
    pointcut callInitialPointcut() : call(
        void MyClass.foo(int, String));

    /*
      Specifies calling advice whenever a join point is encountered
      including and after the initial join point that triggers the pointcut
      that is specified in the parameter:

      Pointcut Name: callInitialPointcut
    */
    pointcut cflowPointcut() : cflow(callInitialPointcut());

    // Advice declaration
    before() : cflowPointcut() && !within(CFlowRecipe +)
    {
        System.out.println(
```

```
                "------------------- Aspect Advice Logic --------------------");
        System.out.println(
            "In the advice attached to the cflowPointcut point cut");
        System.out.println(
            "Join Point Kind: "
                + thisJoinPoint.getStaticPart().getKind());
        System.out.println(
            "Signature: "
                + thisJoinPoint.getStaticPart().getSignature());
        System.out.println(
            "Source Line: "
                + thisJoinPoint.getStaticPart().getSourceLocation());
        System.out.println(
                "------------------------------------------------------------");
    }
}
```

Figure 10-1 gives a more practical example of how the cflow(Pointcut) pointcut can
be applied.

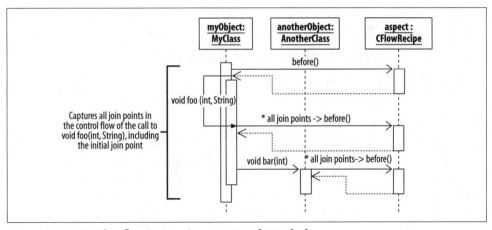

Figure 10-1. How the cflow(Pointcut) pointcut can be applied

It is worth going into a little more detail about what the cflow(Pointcut) does. This
particular pointcut introduces the concept of a join point context. This is to say that
every join point has a scope within which it is considered to be part of the control
flow of the executing program.

It is within this control flow that any encountered join point will trigger the
cflow(Pointcut) pointcut and invoke any associated advice. The cflow(Pointcut)
pointcut comes into effect and triggers its associated advice when the specified pointcut parameter is triggered by an initial join point. The advice associated with the
cflow(Pointcut) will then be invoked for every join point encountered in the control

flow within the context of the initial join point. Finally, the set of join points caught include the initial join point itself, which is the major difference between this pointcut and the `cflowbelow(Pointcut)`.

In the current implementation of the `cflow(Pointcut)` is implemented in such a way as to incur significant overhead when it is used. Where possible, and when pointcut reuse is not impacted, consider using the `withincode(Signature)` pointcut in preference over the `cflow(Pointcut)`.

See Also

The paper "Measuring the Dynamic Behaviour of AspectJ Programs" by Ganesh Sittampalam et al, available at *http://www.sable.mcgill.ca/publications/papers/ #oopsla2004*, discusses some of the problems with performance that an AspectJ implementation may have over a handcoded solution; the `withincode(Signature)` pointcut is described in Recipe 9.3; the `cflowbelow(Pointcut)` pointcut is examined in Recipe 10.2; more information on a join point's context and environment is available in Chapter 13; the recipes in Chapter 12 describe techniques for combining pointcut definitions.

10.2 Capturing All Join Points Within a Program's Control Flow, Excluding the Initial Join Point

Problem

You want to capture all join points encountered within the program control flow after the initiating join point selected by a separate pointcut.

Solution

Use the `cflowbelow(Pointcut)` pointcut. The syntax of the `cflowbelow(Pointcut)` pointcut is:

```
pointcut <pointcut name>(<any values to be picked up>) : cflowbelow(<pointcut>);
```

Discussion

Example 10-2 shows the `cflowbelow(Pointcut)` pointcut being used to capture all of the join points that occur after an initial join point captured by the `callInitialPointcut( )` pointcut.

Example 10-2. Using the cflowbelow(Pointcut) pointcut to capture join points after an initially captured join point

```
public aspect CFlowBelowRecipe
{
    /*
    Specifies calling advice whenever a method
    matching the following rules gets called:

    Class Name: MyClass
    Method Name: foo
    Method Return Type: void
    Method Parameters: an int followed by a String
    */
    pointcut callInitialPointcut( ) : call(
        void MyClass.foo(int, String));

    /*
      Specifies calling advice whenever a join point is encountered
      after but excluding the initial join point that triggers the pointcut
      that is specified in the parameter:

      Pointcut Name: callInitialPointcut
    */
    pointcut cflowPointcut( ) : cflowbelow(callInitialPointcut( ));

    // Advice declaration
    before( ) : cflowPointcut( ) && !within(CFlowBelowRecipe +)
    {
        System.out.println(
           "------------------ Aspect Advice Logic -------------------");
        System.out.println(
           "In the advice attached to the cflowbelowPointcut point cut");
        System.out.println(
           "Join Point Kind: " + thisJoinPoint.getKind( ));
        System.out.println(
           "Signature: "
              + thisJoinPoint.getStaticPart().getSignature( ));
        System.out.println(
           "Source Line: "
              + thisJoinPoint.getStaticPart().getSourceLocation( ));
        System.out.println(
           "-----------------------------------------------------------");
    }
}
```

Figure 10-2 shows how the cflowbelow(Pointcut) pointcut can be applied.

This recipe differs only slightly from Recipe 10.1; the difference is in the number of join points that are actually captured. Whereas the cflow(Pointcut) pointcut triggers advice on all join points encountered within an initial join point's context *including* the initial join point, the cflowbelow(Pointcut) pointcut *excludes* that initial join point.

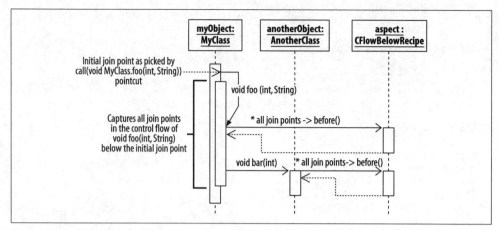

Figure 10-2. How the cflowbelow(Pointcut) pointcut can be applied

See Also

Recipe 10.1 describes the cflow(Pointcut) pointcut; Chapter 12 describes techniques for combining pointcut definitions; more information on a join point's context and environment is available in Chapter 13.

CHAPTER 11

Capturing Join Points Based on Object Type

11.0 Introduction

The pointcuts covered in this chapter enable you to examine the type of the this reference, the optional target reference or arguments at a particular join point.

The this([Type | Identifier]) examines the type of the object that is referenced by this at the captured join point. The *target* of a join point, specified by the target([Type | Identifier]) pointcut, differs depending on the join point type but is commonly the object upon which a method is being called, or an attribute that is being accessed in some way where the join point is encountered. The *args* of a join point, specified by the args([Types | Identifiers]) pointcut, are the arguments, if any, available at the captured join point.

The types of the this, target, and args references can be examined in one of two ways: using static Type specifications, or by using an Identifier that references an actual runtime object.

A Type specification provides a static compile-time evaluation of the object type at the join point and takes the form of a fully qualified class name (for example, com.oreilly.Foo is acceptable, but Foo or *Foo.class* is not).

An Identifier provides a means by which the actual types of runtime objects at the captured join point can be evaluated rather than just static types. An Identifier is dynamically assigned to the appropriate object at runtime.

11.1 Capturing When the this Reference Is a Specific Type

Problem

You want to capture all join points where the this reference at a join point is of a specific type.

Solution

Use the this([Type | Identifier]) pointcut. The syntax of the this([Type | Identifier]) pointcut is:

```
pointcut <pointcut name>(<any values to be picked up>) :
        this(<type> or <identifier> or *);
```

Discussion

The this([Type | Identifier]) pointcut examines the this reference at the captured join point to decide whether to invoke the associated advice and has five key characteristics:

1. The this([Type | Identifier]) pointcut captures all join points when the executing object is of the specified type.

2. A Type definition parameter must resolve to a valid class. This is not the same as a TypePattern, where wildcards may be employed.

3. An Identifier is used to examine the type of the runtime object referenced to by this and to expose that object to the advice if required.

4. Using a * wildcard allows you to state a valid object must be pointed to by the this reference at the join point, but you are not interested in what type it is.

5. Join points that occur on exception handling do not have a value for using the handler(TypePattern) pointcut, when they use the handler(TypePattern) within any static block of code including static class initialization specified using the staticinitialization(TypePattern) pointcut, and interestingly the object pre-initialization using the preinitialization(Signature) pointcut, *do not* have a value for the this reference to expose using the this([Type | Identifier]) pointcut.

Example 11-1 shows two examples of the this([Type | Identifier]) pointcut being used to:

- Capture join points where the this reference is pointing to an object of type MyClass using an Identifier

- Capture when the this reference's type is AnotherClass using a Type specification

Example 11-1. Using the this(Type | Identifier) pointcut to capture join points based on the type of the this reference

```
public aspect ThisRecipe
{
    /*
        Specifies calling advice whenever the executing
        object is of a type that matches the following rules:

        Identifier/s: MyClass object
    */
    pointcut thisIdentifierMyClassPointcut(MyClass object) : this(object);
```

```
    /*
        Specifies calling advice whenever the executing
        object is of a type that matches the following rules:

        Type Pattern: AnotherClass
    */
    pointcut thisTypePatternAnotherClassPointcut() : this(AnotherClass);

    // Advice declaration
    before(MyClass object) : thisIdentifierMyClassPointcut(object)
        && !within(ThisRecipe +)
    {
        System.out.println(
            "------------------ Aspect Advice Logic --------------------");
        System.out.println(
            "In the advice picked by thisIdentifierMyClassPointcut");
        System.out.println("Join Point Kind: " + thisJoinPoint.getKind());
        System.out.println(
            "this reference as passed by Identifier " + object);
        System.out.println(
            "Object referenced by this: " + thisJoinPoint.getThis());
        System.out.println(
            "Signature: " + thisJoinPoint.getStaticPart().getSignature());
        System.out.println(
            "Source Line: " + thisJoinPoint.getStaticPart().getSourceLocation());
        System.out.println(
            "---------------------------------------------------------");
    }


    // Advice declaration
    before() : thisTypePatternAnotherClassPointcut() && !within(ThisRecipe +)
    {
        System.out.println(
            "------------------ Aspect Advice Logic --------------------");
        System.out.println(
            "In the advice picked by thisTypePatternAnotherClassPointcut");
        System.out.println("Join Point Kind: " + thisJoinPoint.getKind());
        System.out.println(
            "Type of executing object: "
                + thisJoinPoint.getThis().getClass().getName());
        System.out.println(
            "Object referenced by this: " + thisJoinPoint.getThis());
        System.out.println(
            "Signature: " + thisJoinPoint.getStaticPart().getSignature());
        System.out.println(
            "Source Line: " + thisJoinPoint.getStaticPart().getSourceLocation());
        System.out.println(
            "---------------------------------------------------------");
    }
}
```

Figure 11-1 shows how the this([Type | Identifier]) pointcut is applied.

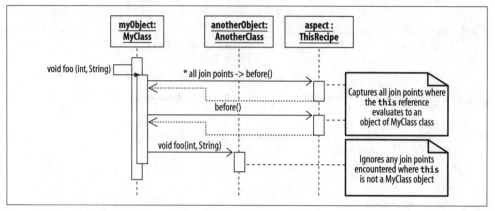

Figure 11-1. How the this([Type | Identifier]) pointcut is applied

See Also

The calling context that is available to advice is covered in Chapter 13; the handler(TypePattern) pointcut is described in Recipe 5.1; the preinitialization(Signature) pointcut is described in Recipe 7.4; the staticinitialization(TypePattern) pointcut is described in Recipe 7.5; the within(TypePattern) pointcut is described in Recipe 9.1; the NOT(!) operator is described in Recipe 12.4.

11.2 Capturing When a Join Point's Target Object Is a Specific Type

Problem

You want to capture all join points encountered when a join point's target object, if any, is of a specific type.

Solution

Use the target([Type | Identifier]) pointcut. The syntax of the target([Type or Identifier]) pointcut is:

```
pointcut <pointcut name>(<any values to be picked up>) :
        target(<type> or <identifier> or *);
```

Discussion

The target([Type | Identifier]) pointcut has five key characteristics:

1. The target([Type | Identifier]) pointcut picks all join points when the target object is of the specified type.

2. A Type definition parameter must resolve to a valid class to pick up on the relevant join points. This is different from a TypePattern where wildcards may be employed.

3. An Identifier is used to examine the type of the runtime object referenced as the target at the captured join point and to expose that object to the advice if required.

4. Using a * wildcard allows you to state there must be a target for the join point, but you are not interested in what type it is.

5. Join points that occur on exception handling using the handler(TypePattern) pointcut, static class initialization using the staticinitialization(TypePattern) and interestingly the object preinitialization using the preinitialization(Signature) pointcut *do not* have any target context to expose using the target([Type | Identifier]) pointcut.

Example 11-2 shows two examples of the target([Type | Identifier]) pointcut being used to:

- Capture join points when the target is a MyClass object indicated by Identifier
- Capture join points where the type of the target of a method call is AnotherClass specified by Type

Example 11-2. Using the target([Type | Identifier]) pointcut to capture join points based on the type of a methods target

```
public aspect TargetRecipe
{
   /*
       Specifies calling advice whenever the target of a methods
       is of a type that matches the following rules:

       Identifier/s: MyClass object
   */
   pointcut targetIdentifierMyClassPointcut(MyClass object) : target(object);

   /*
       Specifies calling advice whenever the target of a methods
       is of a type that matches the following rules:

       Type Pattern: AnotherClass
   */
   pointcut targetTypePatternAnotherClassPointcut() : target(AnotherClass);
```

Example 11-2. Using the target([Type | Identifier]) pointcut to capture join points based on the type of a methods target (continued)

```
// Advice declaration
before(MyClass object) : targetIdentifierMyClassPointcut(object)
    && !within(TargetRecipe +)
{
    System.out.println(
        "------------------ Aspect Advice Logic --------------------");
    System.out.println(
        "In the advice picked by targetIdentifierMyClassPointcut");
    System.out.println("Join Point Kind: " + thisJoinPoint.getKind());
    System.out.println("Object referenced by Target passed by Identifier: " + object);
    System.out.println(
        "Signature: " + thisJoinPoint.getStaticPart().getSignature());
    System.out.println(
        "Source Line: " + thisJoinPoint.getStaticPart().getSourceLocation());
    System.out.println(
        "----------------------------------------------------------");
}

// Advice declaration
before() : targetTypePatternAnotherClassPointcut() && !within(TargetRecipe +)
{
    System.out.println(
        "------------------ Aspect Advice Logic --------------------");
    System.out.println(
        "In the advice picked by targetTypePatternAnotherClassPointcut");
    System.out.println("Join Point Kind: " + thisJoinPoint.getKind());
    System.out.println(
        "Object referenced by Target: " + thisJoinPoint.getTarget());
    System.out.println(
        "Signature: " + thisJoinPoint.getStaticPart().getSignature());
    System.out.println(
        "Source Line: " + thisJoinPoint.getStaticPart().getSourceLocation());
    System.out.println(
        "----------------------------------------------------------");
}
}
```

Figure 11-2 shows how the target([Type | Identifier]) pointcut is applied.

See Also

The calling context that is available to advice is covered in Chapter 13; the handler(TypePattern) pointcut is described in Recipe 5.1; the preinitialization(Signature) pointcut is described in Recipe 7.4; the staticinitialization(TypePattern) pointcut is described in Recipe 7.5; the within(TypePattern) pointcut is described in Recipe 9.1; the NOT(!) operator is described in Recipe 12.4.

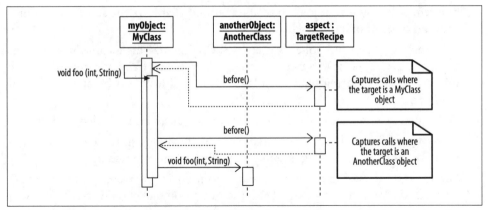

Figure 11-2. How the target(Type | Identifier) pointcut is applied

11.3 Capturing When the Arguments to a Join Point Are a Certain Number, Type, and Ordering

Problem

You want to capture all join points encountered when a join point's arguments, if any, are of a specific type, number, and ordering.

Solution

Use the args([Types | Identifiers]) pointcut. The syntax for this pointcut is:

```
pointcut <pointcut name>(<any values to be picked up>) :
        args(<types> or <identifiers> | .. | *, <repeat>);
```

Discussion

The args([Types | Identifiers]) pointcut has seven key characteristics:

1. Any combination of Types and Identifiers can be used to narrow to the right join points and expose the right context to the advice.

2. An Identifier is used to examine the type of the runtime objects that are the arguments at the captured join point and to expose those objects to the advice if required.

3. Using .. allows you some flexibility in the number of arguments that a particular join point must have to match against your args([Types | Identifiers]) declaration.

4. *Without* the .., the args([Types | Identifiers]) pointcut picks all join points that exactly match the types of the arguments specified. This is to say that the

pointcut will only match join points on methods that have the same order, number, and types of parameters at runtime.

With the `..`, a "best fit" policy is used by the pointcut. This means the statement `args(MyClass,..,float)` would result in any join points being matched that have two arguments, starting with a `MyClass` object and followed by any number of arguments that include a float amongst them.

5. Only one `..` can be used in a single `args([Types | Identifiers])` declaration.

6. Using a `*` wildcard allows you to express some flexibility in the type of an argument, but the number of arguments to a join point must match up.

   For example, if a single `*` is specified within an `args([Types | Identifiers])` pointcut declaration—e.g., `args(*)`—then this pointcut would match any join point that had one argument of any type and ignore any join points that had no arguments. Similarly, the statement `args(*,*)` would match any join point that contained two arguments of any type.

7. Join points that occur on a field access, caught by either the `get(TypePattern)` and `set(TypePattern)` pointcuts, or static class initialization, caught by the `staticinitialization(TypePattern)` pointcut, *do not* have any arguments to expose using the `args([Types | Identifiers])` pointcut.

8. If `Object` is used as the type for an identifier to be picked up by the `args([Types | Identifiers])` pointcut, then this will successfully match against primitive types as well as specific instances of `Object`. The primitive type is automatically "boxed" into its corresponding object type, `Float` in the case of a float primitive for example, before being passed to the advice. This behavior provides a means by which you can get primitive argument values into your advice.

Example 11-3 shows two examples of the `args([Types | Identifiers])` pointcut being used to:

- Capture all join points where the arguments to the methods are an object of the `MyClass` class as indicated by `Identifier`

- Capture join points where the type of the argument is that of the `AnotherClass` class as specified by `Type`

Example 11-3. Using the args([Types | Identifiers]) pointcut to capture join points based on the types of a methods arguments

```
public aspect ArgsRecipe
{
    /*
        Specifies calling advice whenever the type of a methods argument
        is of a type that matches the following rules:

        Identifier/s: MyClass object
    */
    pointcut argIdentifierMyClassPointcut(MyClass object) : args(object);
```

Example 11-3. Using the args([Types | Identifiers]) pointcut to capture join points based on the types of a methods arguments (continued)

```
/*
    Specifies calling advice whenever the type of a methods argument
    is of a type that matches the following rules:

    Type Pattern: AnotherClass
*/
pointcut argTypePatternAnotherClassPointcut( ) : args(AnotherClass);

// Advice declaration
before(MyClass object) : argIdentifierMyClassPointcut(object)
    && !within(ArgsRecipe +)
{
    System.out.println(
        "------------------ Aspect Advice Logic --------------------");
    System.out.println(
        "In the advice picked by argIdentifierMyClassPointcut");
    System.out.println("Join Point Kind: " + thisJoinPoint.getKind( ));
    System.out.println(
        "Signature: " + thisJoinPoint.getStaticPart().getSignature( ));
    System.out.println(
        "Source Line: " + thisJoinPoint.getStaticPart().getSourceLocation( ));
    System.out.println(
        "Arguments picked up using Identifiers: " + object);
    System.out.println(
        "----------------------------------------------------------");
}

// Advice declaration
before() : argTypePatternAnotherClassPointcut( ) && !within(ArgsRecipe +)
{
    System.out.println(
        "------------------ Aspect Advice Logic --------------------");
    System.out.println(
        "In the advice picked by argTypePatternAnotherClassPointcut");
    System.out.println("Join Point Kind: " + thisJoinPoint.getKind( ));
    System.out.println(
        "Signature: " + thisJoinPoint.getStaticPart().getSignature( ));
    System.out.println(
        "Source Line: " + thisJoinPoint.getStaticPart().getSourceLocation( ));
    System.out.println(
        "----------------------------------------------------------");
}
}
```

Figure 11-3 shows how the args([Types | Identifiers]) pointcut is applied.

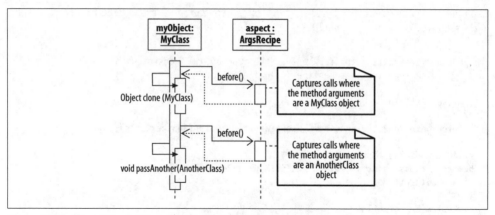

Figure 11-3. How the args(Types | Identifiers) pointcut is applied

 Problems can occur with method overloading if you overload by creating a new method with fewer parameters than the original method. The args([Types | Identifiers]) pointcut examines the number, types, and order of the arguments at a join point, and so an overloaded method that provides *fewer* parameters may not trigger advice that *was* triggered by the original method.

See Also

Recipes 11.1 and 11.2 describe the this([Type | Identifier]) and target([Type | Identifier]) pointcuts respectively; the get(TypePattern) and set(TypePattern) pointcuts are described in Recipes 8.1 and 8.3 respectively; the calling context that is available to advice is covered in Chapter 13; the within(TypePattern) pointcut is described in Recipe 9.1; the NOT(!) operator is described in Recipe 12.4.

CHAPTER 12

Capturing Join Points Based on a Boolean or Combined Expression

12.0 Introduction

This chapter examines how pointcuts can be combined and evaluated as Boolean expressions. Pointcut logic is evaluated to determine whether a particular join point is caught. The Boolean nature of pointcut logic allows for pointcut declarations to be combined using traditional Boolean expressions such as logical AND, logical OR, and logical NOT.

Conditional logic can also be expressed in pointcut declarations using an `if` statement. An `if` statement is used to compare expressions that contain values other than Booleans. The `if` statement evaluates the values passed to it at runtime to come to a `true` or `false` result.

Anonymous pointcuts are the building blocks of more complexly named pointcut declarations. Anonymous pointcuts can be declared as part of compound-named pointcuts or as part of an advice declaration. *Named pointcuts* are then, in turn, the building blocks of pointcut logic reuse. *Pointcut reuse* allows efficient management of the complex logic that can be defined using the available pointcut within AspectJ. This chapter closes by examining how to declare anonymous pointcuts and combine those pointcuts into reusable named pointcuts.

12.1 Capturing When a Runtime Condition Evaluates to True on a Join Point

Problem

You want to trigger advice based on a true result when comparing some runtime values that can be evaluated at a captured join point.

Solution

Use the if(Expression) statement to assess a Boolean expression that contains the runtime variables to be compared. The syntax of the if(Expression) statement is:

```
pointcut <pointcut name>(<any values to be picked up>) :
        if(<Boolean expression>);
```

Discussion

The if(Expression) statement has two key characteristics:

1. The if(Expression) pointcut evaluates variables provided at runtime to come to a true or false result as to whether a join point should trigger the corresponding advice.

2. The Expression can be made up of various logical elements, including exposed join point context, static variables, and other pointcut declarations.

Example 12-1 shows the if(Expression) statement in use. The after advice will only be executed if the runtime values of the variables that make up the expression result in true.

Example 12-1. The if(Expression) statement being used to assess target application variables

```
public aspect IfRecipe
{
    // Define some variables for comparison
    private static final long realisticSalary = 30000l;

    /*
     * Specifies calling advice if this is referencing an object of class MyClass
     * and the object has a realistic salary:
     */
    pointcut ifJoinPointThisHasRealisticSalaryPointcut() : if (
        thisJoinPoint.getThis() instanceof MyClass
            && ((MyClass) thisJoinPoint.getThis()).getSalary()
                < realisticSalary
            && ((MyClass) thisJoinPoint.getThis()).getSalary() > 0)
        && !withincode(* MyClass.get*());

    // Advice declaration
    //This advice will be executed before the pointcut that picks it
    after() : ifJoinPointThisHasRealisticSalaryPointcut()
        && !within(IfRecipe +)
    {
        System.out.println(
            "------------------ Aspect Advice Logic -------------------");
        System.out.println(
            "In the advice picked by ifJoinPointThisHasRealisticSalaryPointcut");
        System.out.println(
            "Join Point Kind: " + thisJoinPoint.getKind());
```

```
    System.out.println(
        "Executing object: " + thisJoinPoint.getThis());
    System.out.println(
        "MyClass instance: "
        + ((MyClass) thisJoinPoint.getThis()).getName()
        + " : "
        + ((MyClass) thisJoinPoint.getThis()).getSalary());
    System.out.println(
        "Signature: " + thisJoinPoint.getSignature());
    System.out.println(
        "Source Line: " + thisJoinPoint.getSourceLocation());
    System.out.println(
        "------------------------------------------------------------");
    }
}
```

The if(Expression) statement allows you to define conditional logic as to whether a piece of advice should be applied to a particular join point. This conditional logic is executed at runtime and must work on valid types at the point when the join points are reached.

The conditional logic contained in the ifJoinPointThisHasRealisticSalaryPointcut() pointcut in Example 12-1 specifies that the corresponding after advice should be triggered when the following occur:

- The executing object is of type MyClass.
- The salary attribute of the object is less than the realisticSalary constant.
- The salary attribute of the object is greater than 0.
- The current join point is not within the getSalary() method. By using the wildcard, the join point must not be within any method in the MyClass class that begins with get.

Each of the conditions is logically combined using the AND (&&) operator. The first three conditions are fairly easily understood as part of the pointcut's Boolean logic, but the final one is a little more interesting. The !withincode(* MyClass.get*()) condition has to be included to prevent the call to getSalary() from within the advice in turn triggering a recursive call to the advice and resulting in an infinite loop.

See Also

The AND (&&) operator and the OR (||) operator are described in Recipes 12.2 and 12.3, respectively; the NOT(!) operator is described in Recipe 12.4; Chapter 13 describes the different forms of advice that AspectJ supports.

12.2 Combining Pointcuts Using a Logical AND (&&)

Problem

You want to combine some pointcut declarations, so advice is executed on a join point as long as all conditions within the pointcut declarations evaluate to true.

Solution

Use the && operator. The syntax of the && operator is:

```
pointcut <pointcut name>(<any values to be picked up>) :
          <pointcut declaration> && <pointcut declaration>
```

Discussion

Example 12-2 shows an example of the && operator combining the logic of two pointcuts into a single pointcut declaration.

Example 12-2. Using the && operator to combine two pointcuts

```
public aspect LogicalAndRecipe
{
  /*
    Specifies calling advice whenever a method
    matching the following rules gets called:

    Class Name: MyClass
    Method Name: Any Method
    Method Return Type: Any Return Type
    Method Parameters: Any Parameters
  */
  pointcut callAnyMethodOnMyClass() : call(* MyClass.* (..));

  /*
    Specifies calling advice whenever a method
    matching the following rules gets called:

    Class Name: MyClass
    Method Name: bar
    Method Return Type: void
    Method Parameters: None
  */
  pointcut callBarPointcut() : call(void MyClass.bar());

  /*
    Specifies calling advice whenever a join points is
    encountered that would be picked by both pointcuts
    specified:

    Pointcut name: callAnyMethodOnMyClass
    Pointcut name: callBarPointcut
```

Example 12-2. Using the && operator to combine two pointcuts (continued)

```
  Method Return Type: void
  Method Parameters: None
*/
pointcut callIntersectionAnyAndBar() : callAnyMethodOnMyClass()
                        && callBarPointcut();

// Advice declaration
before() : callAnyMethodOnMyClass() && !within(LogicalAndRecipe +)
{
   System.out.println(
      "------------------- Aspect Advice Logic --------------------");
   System.out.println(
      "In the advice picked by callAnyMethodOnMyClass");
   System.out.println(
      "Signature: " + thisJoinPoint.getSignature());
   System.out.println(
      "Source Line: " + thisJoinPoint.getSourceLocation());
   System.out.println(
      "-----------------------------------------------------------");
}

// Advice declaration
before() : callBarPointcut() && !within(LogicalAndRecipe +)
{
   System.out.println(
      "------------------- Aspect Advice Logic --------------------");
   System.out.println("In the advice picked by callBarPointcut");
   System.out.println(
      "Signature: " + thisJoinPoint.getSignature());
   System.out.println(
      "Source Line: " + thisJoinPoint.getSourceLocation());
   System.out.println(
      "-----------------------------------------------------------");
}

// Advice declaration
before() : callIntersectionAnyAndBar()
   && !within(LogicalAndRecipe +)
{
   System.out.println(
      "------------------- Aspect Advice Logic --------------------");
   System.out.println(
      "In the advice picked by callIntersectionAnyAndBar");
   System.out.println(
      "Signature: " + thisJoinPoint.getSignature());
   System.out.println(
      "Source Line: " + thisJoinPoint.getSourceLocation());
   System.out.println(
      "-----------------------------------------------------------");
}
}
```

Most developers are familiar with the behavior of the && operator. However, for the newcomers, a mathematical explanation is that when two sets of things are combined using a logical AND, they combine to give the intersection of the two sets. Putting these mathematical terms into an AspectJ context, when two or more simple pointcuts are combined with the && operator into a compound pointcut, the join points that would be picked by both the individual pointcuts will trigger the compound pointcut's associated advice. More simply, if any one join point has been picked by either of the simple pointcuts, then it will not be picked by the overall compound pointcut.

The order of the pointcuts being combined using the && operator also has an effect on how the compound pointcut is interpreted. The runtime analysis of the && operators is executed from left to right. This means that as a candidate join point is examined, the first pointcut that indicates it would not include the join point is where the comparison stops. This is true for the && operator in Java and is especially useful when one of the comparisons in the combination must be protected by a previous condition, as shown in Example 12-3 (replicated from Recipe 9.1).

Example 12-3. Using the && operator ordering protecting later comparisons

```
pointcut ifJoinPointThisHasUnRealisticSalaryPointcut( ) : if (
        thisJoinPoint.getThis( ) instanceof MyClass
        && ((MyClass) thisJoinPoint.getThis()).getSalary( ) >= realisticSalary)
        && !withincode(long MyClass.getSalary( ));
```

In this example, the first condition states that the this reference must be an instance of MyClass to continue with the evaluation of the rest of the statement. This protects the call in the next part of the statement, which casts the this reference to MyClass. If the first condition fails, then the second will never be reached; because of this behavior, the && operator is sometimes called a short-circuit operator.

See Also

Recipe 12.1 describes the if(Expression) pointcut; the within(TypePattern) pointcut is described in Recipe 9.1; the NOT(!) operator is described in Recipe 12.4; Chapter 13 describes the different types of advice available in AspectJ.

12.3   Combining Pointcuts Using a Logical OR (||)

Problem

You want to combine some pointcut declarations, so advice is executed on a join point as long as one of the conditions within the pointcut declarations evaluates to true.

Solution

Use the || operator. The syntax of the || operator is:

```
pointcut <pointcut name>(<any values to be picked up>) :
            <pointcut declaration> || <pointcut declaration>
```

Discussion

Example 12-4 shows the || operator combining callFooIntStringPointcut() and callBarPointcut() into a single compound pointcut called callIntersectionFooOrBar().

Example 12-4. Using the || operator to combine two pointcut declarations

```
public aspect LogicalOrRecipe
{
    /*
    Specifies calling advice whenever a method
    matching the following rules gets called:

    Class Name: MyClass
    Method Name: foo
    Method Return Type: void
    Method Parameters: int and a String
    */
    pointcut callFooIntStringPointcut() : call(
        void MyClass.foo(int, String));

    /*
    Specifies calling advice whenever a method
    matching the following rules gets called:

    Class Name: MyClass
    Method Name: bar
    Method Return Type: void
    Method Parameters: None
    */
    pointcut callBarPointcut() : call(void MyClass.bar());

    /*
    Specifies calling advice whenever a join points is
    encountered that would be picked by both pointcuts
    specified:

    Pointcut name: callFooIntStringPointcut
    Pointcut name: callBarPointcut
    Method Return Type: void
    Method Parameters: None
    */
    pointcut callIntersectionFooOrBar() : callFooIntStringPointcut()
                            || callBarPointcut();

    // Advice declaration
    before() : callFooIntStringPointcut()
```

```
         && !within(LogicalOrRecipe +)
    {
        System.out.println(
            "------------------ Aspect Advice Logic --------------------");
        System.out.println(
            "In the advice picked by callFooIntStringPointcut");
        System.out.println(
            "Signature: " + thisJoinPoint.getSignature( ));
        System.out.println(
            "Source Line: " + thisJoinPoint.getSourceLocation( ));
        System.out.println(
            "----------------------------------------------------------");
    }

    // Advice declaration
    before() : callBarPointcut( ) && !within(LogicalOrRecipe +)
    {
        System.out.println(
            "------------------ Aspect Advice Logic --------------------");
        System.out.println("In the advice picked by callBarPointcut");
        System.out.println(
            "Signature: " + thisJoinPoint.getSignature( ));
        System.out.println(
            "Source Line: " + thisJoinPoint.getSourceLocation( ));
        System.out.println(
            "----------------------------------------------------------");
    }

    // Advice declaration
    before() : callIntersectionFooOrBar( )
        && !within(LogicalOrRecipe +)
    {
        System.out.println(
            "------------------ Aspect Advice Logic --------------------");
        System.out.println(
            "In the advice picked by callIntersectionFooOrBar");
        System.out.println(
            "Signature: " + thisJoinPoint.getSignature( ));
        System.out.println(
            "Source Line: " + thisJoinPoint.getSourceLocation( ));
        System.out.println(
            "----------------------------------------------------------");
    }
}
```

In addition to combining pointcuts using a logical AND, as shown in Recipe 12.2, pointcuts and other logical expressions can be combined using a logical OR. Those familiar with the nature of logical operations will know that the result of a logical OR comparison is seen as positive if *any* of the constituent parts meet the comparison condition. In the language of AspectJ, if a join point initiates the advice on any of the constituent pointcuts combined using a logical OR into a compound pointcut, then the join point will trigger that advice.

The || operator in AspectJ also exhibits short-circuiting behavior, similar to the && operator. However, the short-circuiting rule is the opposite of the && operator. With the || operator, the moment a condition is evaluated as positive, the compound statement can be evaluated as positive and completed.

See Also

Recipe 12.2 covers the AND (&&) operator and its short-circuiting evaluations features; the within(TypePattern) pointcut is described in Recipe 9.1; the NOT(!) operator is described in Recipe 12.4; Chapter 13 describes the different types of advice available in AspectJ.

12.4   Capturing All Join Points NOT Specified by a Pointcut Declaration

Problem

You want to capture all the join points *not* caught by a particular pointcut.

Solution

Use the unary ! *operator* to specify that the join points normally captured by a specific pointcut declaration are to be ignored. The syntax of the ! operator is:

```
pointcut <pointcut name>(<any values to be picked up>) :
          !<pointcut declaration>
```

Discussion

Example 12-5 shows an example of the ! operator being used to capture all join points not captured by the call(void MyClass.foo(int,String) pointcut.

Example 12-5. Using the ! operator to capture join points not caught by a call(Signature) pointcut

```
public aspect LogicalNotRecipe
{
    /*
      Specifies calling advice whenever a method
      does NOT match the following rules
      gets called:

      Class Name: MyClass
      Method Name: foo
      Method Return Type: void
      Method Parameters: an int followed by a String
```

```
    */
    pointcut notCallPointCutFooIntString( ) : !call(void MyClass.foo(int, String));

    // Advice declaration
    before( ) : notCallPointCutFooIntString( )
        && !within(LogicalNotRecipe +)
    {
        System.out.println(
            "------------------- Aspect Advice Logic --------------------");
        System.out.println(
            "In the advice picked by notCallPointCutFooIntStringAnyReturn( )");
        System.out.println(
            "Signature: " + thisJoinPoint.getSignature( ));
        System.out.println(
            "Source Line: " + thisJoinPoint.getSourceLocation( ));
        System.out.println(
            "-----------------------------------------------------------");
    }
}
```

See Also

Techniques for combining pointcut declarations are covered in Recipes 12.2 and 12.3; the within(TypePattern) pointcut is described in Recipe 9.1; Chapter 13 describes the different types of advice available in AspectJ.

12.5   Declaring Anonymous Pointcuts

Problem

You want to declare a simple pointcut anonymously within a named pointcut declaration, or attached directly to an advice.

Solution

Anonymous pointcuts are the building blocks of pointcut declarations. They have been used throughout all the pointcut-based chapters, but this recipe gives anonymous pointcuts more detailed attention.

Example 12-6 shows an example of anonymous pointcuts being used as the foundation for more complexly named pointcuts, as well as directly on an advice declaration.

Example 12-6. Using anonymous pointcuts

```
public aspect AnonymousPointcutRecipe
{
    /*
    A pointcut declaration that is built up from one
    anonymous pointcut:
```

Example 12-6. Using anonymous pointcuts (continued)

```
  Anonymous Pointcuts: call(void MyClass.foo(int,String)
*/
pointcut singleAnonymousPointcut( ) : call(void MyClass.foo(int, String));

/*
  A pointcut declaration that is built up from two
  anonymous pointcuts:

  Anonymous Pointcuts: call(void MyClass.foo(int,String)
                       call(void MyClass.foo(int,String)
                       !within(AnonymousPointcutRecipe +)

*/
pointcut multipleAnonymousPointcut( ) : (
   call(void MyClass.bar( ))
   || call(void MyClass.foo(int, String))
   && !within(AnonymosPointcutRecipe +));

/*
  A pointcut declaration attached to the advice it will invoke,
  built up from anonymous pointcuts:

  Anonymous Pointcuts: within(LogicalOrRecipe +)
*/
before( ) : singleAnonymousPointcut( )
   && !within(AnonymousPointcutRecipe +)
{
   System.out.println(
     "------------------ Aspect Advice Logic -------------------");
   System.out.println(
     "In the advice picked by singleAnonymousPointcut and");
   System.out.println("!within(AnonymousPointcutRecipe +");
   System.out.println(
     "Signature: " + thisJoinPoint.getSignature( ));
   System.out.println(
     "Source Line: " + thisJoinPoint.getSourceLocation( ));
   System.out.println(
     "---------------------------------------------------------");
}

/*
  A pointcut declaration attached to the advice it will invoke,
  built up from anonymous pointcuts:

  Anonymous Pointcuts: None
*/
before( ) : multipleAnonymousPointcut( )
{
   System.out.println(
     "------------------ Aspect Advice Logic -------------------");
   System.out.println(
     "In the advice picked by multipleAnonymousPointcut( )");
```

Example 12-6. Using anonymous pointcuts (continued)

```
    System.out.println(
        "Signature: " + thisJoinPoint.getSignature());
    System.out.println(
        "Source Line: " + thisJoinPoint.getSourceLocation());
    System.out.println(
        "------------------------------------------------------------");
    }
}
```

Discussion

This recipe differs from the other pointcut-based recipes in this book because it deals with one of two particular mechanisms for declaring pointcuts rather than examining a specific pointcut type. Pointcuts can be declared anonymously within named pointcut declarations or by being directly attached to the advice they will invoke.

See Also

Recipes 12.2 and 12.3 cover techniques for combining pointcut declarations; the within(TypePattern) pointcut is described in Recipe 9.1; the NOT(!) operator is described in Recipe 12.4; Chapter 13 describes the different types of advice available in AspectJ.

12.6   Reusing Pointcuts

Problem

You want to reuse a pointcut expression.

Solution

Declare a pointcut that can be referenced by name in the places where it is to be reused.

Discussion

Example 12-7 shows an example where the foundationNamedPointcut() named pointcut is reused when declaring the reuseNamedPointcut().

Example 12-7. Reuse of named pointcuts

```
public aspect PointcutReuseRecipe
{
    /*
      A pointcut declaration that is to be used and reused:

      Anonymous Pointcuts: call(void MyClass.foo(int,String)
```

Example 12-7. Reuse of named pointcuts (continued)

```
*/
pointcut foundationNamedPointcut( ) : call(
   void MyClass.foo(int, String));

/*
 A pointcut declaration that is built up from two
 pointcuts:

 Anonymous Pointcuts: !within(AnonymousPointcutRecipe +)
 Named Pointcuts: foundationNamedPointcut( )

*/
pointcut reuseNamedPointcut( ) : foundationNamedPointcut( )
   && !within(PointcutReuseRecipe +);

/*
 A pointcut declaration attached to the advice it will invoke,
 built up from simple named and anonymous pointcuts:

 Anonymous Pointcuts: !within(LogicalOrRecipe +)
 Named Pointcuts: foundationNamedPointcut( );
*/
before( ) : foundationNamedPointcut( )
   && !within(PointcutReuseRecipe +)
{
   System.out.println(
      "------------------ Aspect Advice Logic -------------------");
   System.out.println(
      "In the advice picked by foundationNamedPointcut( ) and");
   System.out.println("!within(AnonymousPointcutRecipe( ) +");
   System.out.println(
      "Signature: " + thisJoinPoint.getSignature( ));
   System.out.println(
      "Source Line: " + thisJoinPoint.getSourceLocation( ));
   System.out.println(
      "----------------------------------------------------------");
}

/*
 A pointcut declaration attached to the advice it will invoke,
 built up from complex pointcuts built reusing other pointcut
 declarations:

 Named Pointcuts: reuseNamedPointcut
*/
before( ) : reuseNamedPointcut( )
{
   System.out.println(
      "------------------ Aspect Advice Logic -------------------");
   System.out.println(
      "In the advice picked by reuseNamedPointcut( )");
   System.out.println(
```

Example 12-7. Reuse of named pointcuts (continued)

```
        "Signature: " + thisJoinPoint.getSignature( ));
    System.out.println(
        "Source Line: " + thisJoinPoint.getSourceLocation( ));
    System.out.println(
        "------------------------------------------------------------");
    }
}
```

A named pointcut is similar to a method. It has a signature and can be referenced throughout the rest of the pointcut declarations within a particular aspect or even in other aspects according to the named pointcut's access modifier. This becomes increasingly important when we consider inheritance between aspects where point-cuts can be declared abstract and the actual pointcut logic can be implemented by the inheriting aspects.

When declaring pointcuts for reuse it is important that you consider *where* your pointcut delcarations are going to be reused. You use access modifiers in relation to your pointcut declarations in order to control where your pointcut declarations are visible within your application.

In AspectJ, pointcut declarations have the same access modifiers as regular Java methods: public, the pointcut delcaration is visible throughout your entire applica-tions aspects; default (no modifier specified), the pointcut declaration is visible to all other aspects in the same package; protected, the pointcut delcaration is visible only to subaspects; private, the pointcut delcaration is only visible in the aspect within it is declared.

See Also

Inheritance between aspects and the implications on pointcut declarations is dis-cussed in Chapter 15; techniques for combining pointcut declarations are covered in Recipes 12.2 and 12.3; the within(TypePattern) pointcut is described in Recipe 9.1; the NOT(!) operator is described in Recipe 12.6; Chapter 13 describes the different types of advice available in AspectJ.

Defining Advice

13.0 Introduction

This chapter examines the different ways that advice can be specified in AspectJ. Pointcuts define *which* join points you are interested in and *advice* defines *what* to do when those join points are encountered.

An advice block contains straightforward Java code. Advice looks much like a Java method, except that it cannot be called directly from your application. It is the AspectJ runtime system that executes the advice according to the pointcut logic associated with that advice.

This chapter begins by examining how advice can interact with your application's classes, including the mechanisms by which to access the triggering join point context. The different types of advice are then discussed before finally covering advice precedence and how the order in which advice is invoked can be controlled where more than one piece of advice is applied to the same join point.

13.1 Accessing Class Members

Problem

You want to access attributes and methods of a particular object from within your advice.

Solution

Pass the appropriate object to the advice as a parameter on your pointcut declaration.

Discussion

Example 13-1 shows how to access public and private members of a class whose object is available as the call join point is encountered.

Example 13-1. Passing an object to advice for access to its methods and attributes

```
public privileged aspect MemberAccessRecipe
{
    /*
    Specifies calling advice whenever a method
    matching the following rules gets executed:

    Class Name: MyClass
    Method Name: foo
    Method Return Type: void
    Method Parameters: an int followed by a String
    */
    pointcut executionOfFooPointCut( ) : execution(
        void MyClass.foo(int, String));

    // Advice declaration
    after(MyClass myClass) : executionOfFooPointCut( ) && this(myClass)
    {
        System.out.println(
            "------------------- Aspect Advice Logic --------------------");
        System.out.println(
            "Accessing the set(float) member of the MyClass object");
        System.out.println(
            "Privileged access not required for this method call as it is public");
        myClass.setF(2.0f);
        System.out.println(
            "Using the privileged aspect access to the private f member variable");
        System.out.print("The current value of f is: ");
        System.out.println(myClass.f);
        System.out.println(
            "Signature: " + thisJoinPoint.getSignature( ));
        System.out.println(
            "Source Line: " + thisJoinPoint.getSourceLocation( ));
        System.out.println(
            "-----------------------------------------------------------");
    }
}
```

An object of the MyClass class is made available to the advice by using the
this(Identifier) pointcut definition. The this(Identifier) pointcut definition
effectively exposes the advice to the object that is pointed at by the this reference at
the triggering join point. The setF(float) method is called from within the advice
and shows access to the MyClass object's public methods. To gain access to the private MyClass.f attribute, the aspect has to have some additional changes made to its
structure. The aspect is attempting to break encapsulation by accessing the private
member directly, and, therefore, the aspect must be declared as privileged because it
is committing a potentially intrusive act.

AspectJ provides the privileged keyword to be used where an aspect requires full
and unrestricted access to the classes it is applied to, including those member variables and methods that are not declared on the class's public interface. The

privileged status of an aspect should serve as a warning that care must be taken in any changes to that aspect, or the classes to which it is applied, as these changes can potentially cause other problems throughout the application.

See Also

The call(Signature) pointcut is described in Recipe 4.1; the within(TypePattern) pointcut is described in Recipe 9.1; the this(TypePattern or Identifier) pointcut is described in Recipe 11.1; the Appendix contains a quick reference for the JoinPoint class and its subclasses.

13.2   Accessing the Join Point Context

Problem

You want to access the join point context from within your advice.

Solution

Use the thisJoinPoint and thisJoinPointStaticPart variable.

Discussion

Classes in Java have a this variable to allow their objects to reference and work with themselves. Aspects are converted by the AspectJ compiler into classes; therefore, the aspects have a this reference.

However, an additional join point context can be exposed to advice from the join points that trigger it. AspectJ provides the thisJoinPoint variable to expose this join point context. In addition to thisJoinPoint, the thisJoinPointStaticPart variable is useful if the context that is being accessed can be assessed statically.

Example 13-2 shows some of the information that is available from the generic thisJoinPoint variable.

Example 13-2. Using the thisJoinPoint variable

```
public aspect ThisJoinPointRecipe
{
    /*
    Specifies calling advice whenever a method
    matching the following rules gets called:

    Class Name: MyClass
    Method Name: foo
    Method Return Type: void
    Method Parameters: an int followed by a String
    */
    pointcut callPointCut( ) : call(void MyClass.foo(int, String));
```

Example 13-2. Using the thisJoinPoint variable (continued)

```
// Advice declaration
before() : callPointCut( ) && !within(ThisJoinPointRecipe +)
{

    System.out.println(
        "------------------ Aspect Advice Logic -------------------");
    System.out.println(
        "Exercising the static parts of AspectJ 1.1.1 thisJoinPoint");
    System.out.println(
        "Source Line: "
            + thisJoinPointStaticPart.getSourceLocation( ));
    System.out.println(
        "Join Point Kind: "
            + thisJoinPointStaticPart.getKind( ));
    System.out.println(
        "Simple toString: "
            + thisJoinPointStaticPart.toString( ));
    System.out.println(
        "Simple toShortString: "
            + thisJoinPointStaticPart.toShortString( ));
    System.out.println(
        "Simple toLongString: "
            + thisJoinPointStaticPart.toLongString( ));
    System.out.println(
        "Exercising the join point generic signature of AspectJ 1.1.1 thisJoinPoint");
    System.out.println(
        "Signature: "
            + thisJoinPointStaticPart.getSignature( ));
    System.out.println(
        "Signature name: "
            + thisJoinPointStaticPart.getSignature().getName( ));
    System.out.println(
        "Signature declaring type: "
            + thisJoinPointStaticPart.getSignature().getDeclaringType( ));
    System.out.println(
        "-------------------------------------------------------------");
}

// Advice declaration
before() : callPointCut( ) && !within(ThisJoinPointRecipe +)
{

    System.out.println(
        "------------------ Aspect Advice Logic -------------------");
    System.out.println(
        "Exercising the dynamic parts of AspectJ 1.1.1 thisJoinPoint");
    System.out.println(
        "Get the this reference: " + thisJoinPoint.getThis( ));
    System.out.println(
        "Getting the Target: " + thisJoinPoint.getTarget( ));
    System.out.println("Join Point Arguments: ");
    Object[] args = thisJoinPoint.getArgs( );
```

Example 13-2. Using the thisJoinPoint variable (continued)

```
    for (int count = 0; count < args.length; count++)
    {
        System.out.println(args[count]);
    }
    System.out.println(
        "-----------------------------------------------------------");
    }
}
```

The code in Example 13-2 produces the following output:

```
------------------ Aspect Advice Logic --------------------
Exercising the static parts of AspectJ 1.1.1 thisJoinPoint
Source Line: MyClass.java:14
Join Point Kind: method-call
Simple toString: call(void MyClass.foo(int, String))
Simple toShortString: call(MyClass.foo(..))
Simple toLongString: call(public void MyClass.foo(int, java.lang.String))
Exercising the join point generic signature of AspectJ 1.1.1 thisJoinPoint
Signature: void MyClass.foo(int, String)
Signature name: foo
Signature declaring type: class MyClass
-----------------------------------------------------------
------------------ Aspect Advice Logic --------------------
Exercising the dynamic parts of AspectJ 1.1.1 thisJoinPoint
Get the this reference: null
Getting the Target: MyClass@d19bc8
Join Point Arguments:
1
Russ Miles
-----------------------------------------------------------
```

The thisJoinPoint variable contains static and dynamic context information about the triggering join point. *Static join point context* information contains anything that can be decided at compile and weave time, as explained in Chapter 1. *Dynamic join point context* information can only be populated at runtime because it is dependent on the actual runtime state of the join point context.

To keep things as efficient as possible, the static join point information can be accessed by using the thisJoinPoint.getStaticPart() method or, as shown in Example 13-2, by accessing the thisJoinPointStaticPart variable. If a particular advice only uses the getStaticPart() method or thisJoinPointStaticPart, then the AspectJ compiler can perform compilation optimizations to reduce the overhead associated with accessing the join point context.

> The thisJoinPoint variable is an object of the JoinPoint class declared within the AspectJ runtime libraries. Different subclasses of the generic JoinPoint class can be instantiated as thisJoinPoint variables depending on the type of the triggering join point. A quick reference for the JoinPoint class and its subclasses is provided in the Appendix.

See Also

The call(Signature) pointcut is described in Recipe 4.1; the within(TypePattern) pointcut is described in Recipe 9.1; the Appendix contains a quick reference for the JoinPoint class and its subclasses.

13.3   Executing Advice Before a Join Point

Problem

You want advice to execute before the join points that trigger it.

Solution

Use the before( ) type of advice.

Discussion

Example 13-3 shows how to execute advice before a call to the void MyClass.foo(int,String) method.

Example 13-3. Executing advice before a method call

```
public aspect BeforeAdviceRecipe
{
    /*
    Specifies calling advice whenever a method
    matching the following rules gets called:

    Class Name: MyClass
    Method Name: foo
    Method Return Type: void
    Method Parameters: an int followed by a String
    */
    pointcut callPointCut() : call(void MyClass.foo(int, String));

    // Advice declaration
    before() : callPointCut() && !within(BeforeAdviceRecipe +)
    {
        System.out.println(
            "------------------- Aspect Advice Logic --------------------");
        System.out.println(
            "Source Location: "
                + thisJoinPoint.getStaticPart().getSourceLocation());
        System.out.println(
            "------------------------------------------------------------");
    }
}
```

See Also

The call(Signature) pointcut is described in Recipe 4.1; the within(TypePattern) pointcut is described in Recipe 9.1; the thisJoinPoint variable is examined in Recipe 13.2.

13.4   Executing Advice Around a Join Point

Problem

You want advice to execute around the join points that trigger it.

Solution

Use the around( ) type of advice.

Discussion

Example 13-4 shows how to execute advice around the void MyClass.foo(int, String) method.

Example 13-4. Executing advice around a method call

```
public aspect AroundAdviceRecipe
{
    /*
      Specifies calling advice whenever a method
      matching the following rules gets called:

      Class Name: MyClass
      Method Name: bar
      Method Return Type: int
      Method Parameters:
      */
    pointcut callFooPointCut() : call(int MyClass.foo( ));

    /*
      Specifies calling advice whenever a method
      matching the following rules gets called:

      Class Name: MyClass
      Method Name: bar2
      Method Return Type: int
      Method Parameters: int
      */
    pointcut callBarPointCut(int value) : call(int MyClass.bar(int))
        && args(value);

    /*
      Specifies calling advice whenever a method
      matching the following rules gets called:
```

Example 13-4. Executing advice around a method call (continued)

```
   Class Name: MyClass
   Method Name: baz
   Method Return Type: int
   Method Parameters:
   */
  pointcut callBazPointCut() : call(int MyClass.baz());

   // Advice declaration
   // This advice will be executed before the pointcut that picks it
  int around() : callFooPointCut() && !within(AroundAdviceRecipe +)
  {
      System.out.println(
          "------------------ Aspect Advice Logic --------------------");
      System.out.println(
          "Signature: " + thisJoinPoint.getSignature());
      System.out.println(
          "Source Location: "
             + thisJoinPoint.getStaticPart().getSourceLocation());
      System.out.println(
          "----------------------------------------------------------");
      return proceed();
  }


   // Advice declaration
   // This advice will be executed before the pointcut that picks it
  int around(int value) : callBarPointCut(value)
      && !within(AroundAdviceRecipe +)
  {
      System.out.println(
          "------------------ Aspect Advice Logic --------------------");
      System.out.println(
          "Signature: " + thisJoinPoint.getSignature());
      System.out.println(
          "Source Location: "
             + thisJoinPoint.getStaticPart().getSourceLocation());
      System.out.println(
          "----------------------------------------------------------");
      return proceed(value);
  }

   // Advice declaration
   // This advice will be executed before the pointcut that picks it
  int around() : callBazPointCut() && !within(AroundAdviceRecipe +)
  {
      System.out.println(
          "------------------ Aspect Advice Logic --------------------");
      System.out.println(
          "Signature: " + thisJoinPoint.getSignature());
      System.out.println(
          "Source Location: "
             + thisJoinPoint.getStaticPart().getSourceLocation());
```

Example 13-4. Executing advice around a method call (continued)

```
    System.out.println(
      "-------------------------------------------------------------");
    return 200;
  }
}
```

The around( ) advice is a powerful construct that indicates to AspectJ the advice should be run instead of the join point that has triggered it. This allows overriding the original logic present in the application. This recipe shows the around( ) advice being applied passively and actively according to whether the proceed( ) call is made from within the around( ) advice block. according to whether the proceed( ) call is made from within the around( ) advice block. Figure 13-1 shows the behavior from Example 13-4 where passive and active around( ) advice are being applied.

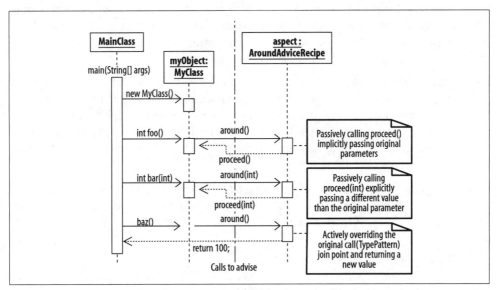

Figure 13-1. Using around( ) advice passively and actively on a call(TypePattern) pointcut

The proceed( ) call indicates the around( ) advice should continue with executing the original join point logic, passing any values that were originally available. In the first piece of advice in Example 13-4, there were no parameters to pass; in the second, there was an int available on the call join point, and for this reason the parameter must be passed on to the proceed( ) call. The parameter could have a completely different value than the original but not a different type or class; otherwise, this will cause a compilation error.

Contrasting with the more passive form of the around( ) advice type shown in the first two pieces of advice in Example 13-4, around( ) advice can be used to override the join point that has triggered it. The MyClass.baz( ) method is overridden by the third around( ) advice because of the `proceed( )` call. To complete the overriding of the original join point, the around( ) advice returns a value different from what was originally intended.

The same overriding approach can be used to override constructors. This mechanism is useful when the actual object being instantiated needs to be controlled by the aspect. The return object from a constructor is the newly instantiated object and as such can be decided by the advice. The advice could return a different class of object than the one expected by the target application as long as it is an appropriate class.

The around( ) advice *must* have a return value specified, but this can be `void` if no value is needed. A return value can be obtained from the original logic in terms of the return from the `proceed( )` call or a totally new object of a class appropriate for the join points captured.

If the advice is applied to join points with different return types, then the advice may declare that its return value will be of the `Object` class. In the case where one of those return types is a primitive type, such as a `float` or an `int`, the AspectJ will automatically "unbox" the primitive return value at runtime.

For example, when an around( ) advice block that returns an `Object` advises a method call join point on a method that returns a `float` primitive type, the advice must "box" the return value as an instance of the Float class so it can be returned as an `Object` according to the advice declaration. Where the join point returns, the return value is automatically and transparently unboxed back to the primitive `float` according to the method's original signature.

Performance is a consideration when using around( ) advice. There is a performance penalty when using around( ) advice in AspectJ, which means that a combination of the `before()` and `after()` returning form of advice wherever possible.

See Also

The paper "Measuring the Dynamic Behaviour of AspectJ Programs" by Ganesh Sittampalam et al, available at *http://www.sable.mcgill.ca/publications/papers/#oopsla2004*, discusses some of the problems with performance that an AspectJ implementation may have over a hand-coded solution; The `after( )` returning form of advice is discussed in Recipe 13.6; the `call(Signature)` pointcut is described in Recipe 4.1; the `within(TypePattern)` pointcut is described in Recipe 9.1; the `thisJoinPoint` variable and the context it encapsulates is examined in Recipe 13.2; discusses some common pointcut idioms, one of which being the ability to ignore exception handling and object initialization join points, as these do not support around( ) advice.

13.5 Executing Advice Unconditionally After a Join Point

Problem

You want advice to execute after a specific join point regardless of how the join point returned.

Solution

Use the after( ) type of advice.

Discussion

Example 13-5 shows how to execute advice after the void MyClass.foo(int,String) method regardless of how the method returns.

Example 13-5. Executing advice after a method call

```
public aspect AfterAdviceRecipe
{
   /*
   Specifies calling advice whenever a method
   matching the following rules gets called:

   Class Name: MyClass
   Method Name: foo
   Method Return Type: void
   Method Parameters: an int followed by a String
   */
   pointcut callPointCut( ) : call(void MyClass.foo(int, String));

   // Advice declaration
   after( ) : callPointCut( ) && !within(AfterAdviceRecipe +)
   {

      System.out.println(
         "------------------ Aspect Advice Logic -------------------");
      System.out.println(
         "Source Location: "
            + thisJoinPoint.getStaticPart().getSourceLocation( ));
      System.out.println(
         "--------------------------------------------------------");
   }
}
```

See Also

The call(Signature) pointcut is described in Recipe 4.1; the within(TypePattern) pointcut is described in Recipe 9.1; the thisJoinPoint variable and the context it encapsulates is examined in Recipe 13.2; discusses some common pointcut idioms, one of which being the ability to ignore exception handling join points as these do not support after( ) advice.

13.6   Executing Advice Only After a Normal Return from a Join Point

Problem

You want advice to execute after a specific join point only if that join point returned normally.

Solution

Use the after( ) returning or after( ) returning(<ReturnType> <Identifier>) types of advice.

Discussion

Example 13-6 shows how to specify that the advice should only be executed after the call to void MyClass.foo(int) if the call to the method returns normally.

Example 13-6. Executing advice after a method call if that call returns normally

```
public aspect AfterReturningAdviceRecipe
{
    /*
    Specifies calling advice whenever a method
    matching the following rules gets called:

    Class Name: MyClass
    Method Name: foo
    Method Return Type: void
    Method Parameters: an int followed by a String
    */
    pointcut callPointCut( ) : call(void MyClass.foo(int));

    // Advice declaration
    after( ) returning : callPointCut( ) && !within(AfterReturningAdviceRecipe +)
    {
        System.out.println(
           "------------------ Aspect Advice Logic --------------------");
        System.out.println(
           "Source Location: "
              + thisJoinPoint.getStaticPart().getSourceLocation( ));
        System.out.println(
           "-----------------------------------------------------------");
    }
}
```

The after( ) returning advice in Example 13-6 does not access a returning value from the join point because the void MyClass.foo(int) method does not return any value. If the join point did return a value, then AspectJ provides the after( ) returning(ReturnType Identifier) variation that lets you assign the returning value to an identifier() and access the value in the corresponding advice block, as shown in Example 13-7.

Example 13-7. Accessing a method's return value if the method returned normally

```
public aspect AfterReturningValueAdviceRecipe
{
    /*
    Specifies calling advice whenever a method
    matching the following rules gets called:

    Class Name: MyClass
    Method Name: foo
    Method Return Type: int
    Method Parameters: an int followed by a String
    */
    pointcut callPointCut( ) : call(int MyClass.foo(int));

    // Advice declaration
    after( ) returning(Object value) : callPointCut( )
        && !within(AfterReturningAdviceRecipe +)
    {
        System.out.println(
            "------------------- Aspect Advice Logic --------------------");
        System.out.println(
            "Source Location: "
                + thisJoinPoint.getStaticPart().getSourceLocation( ));
        System.out.println(
            "Value being returned: "
                + value);
        System.out.println(
            "-----------------------------------------------------------");
    }
}
```

An interesting side effect of using the after( ) returning(<Type> <Identifier>) advice to access a primitive type, as shown in Example 13-7, is that the primitive int value must be boxed in an instance of the Integer class to be passed to the advice. When the return type expected by the advice is of type Object, and if the return value is a primitive type, AspectJ will automatically and transparently box the primitive value into its corresponding Java class. This automatic and transparent boxing behavior, where a value of type Object is expected and primitives are to be passed to or from the advice, is also used by the around( ) form of advice.

The after( ) returning forms of advice provide a finer filter of the join points that trigger the advice than the normal after( ) type of advice (covered in Recipe 13.5).

The code within the after( ) returning advice block will be executed if the encountered join point returns without raising an exception offering a mechanism by which to avoid capturing join points on methods that have experienced problems.

See Also

The call(Signature) pointcut is described in Recipe 4.1; the within(TypePattern) pointcut is described in Recipe 9.1; the thisJoinPoint variable and the context it encapsulates is examined in Recipe 13.2; the around( ) advice is described in Recipe 13.4; the after( ) advice is shown in Recipe 13.5.

13.7   Executing Advice Only After an Exception Has Been Raised in a Join Point

Problem

You want advice to execute after a specific join point only if that join point raised an exception.

Solution

Use the after( ) throwing or after( ) throwing(<ExceptionType> <Identifier>) types of advice

Discussion

Example 13-8 shows how to specify that advice should be executed if the call to the void MyClass.foo(int) method returns with an exception.

Example 13-8. Executing advice after a method call if that call raises an exception

```
public aspect AfterThrowingAdviceRecipe
{
   /*
   Specifies calling advice whenever a method
   matching the following rules gets called:

   Class Name: MyClass
   Method Name: foo
   Method Return Type: void
   Method Parameters: an int followed by a String
   */
   pointcut callPointCut() : call(void MyClass.foo(int));

   // Advice declaration
   after() throwing : callPointCut()
      && !within(AfterThrowingAdviceRecipe +)
   {
      System.out.println(
```

Example 13-8. Executing advice after a method call if that call raises an exception (continued)

```
        "------------------- Aspect Advice Logic -------------------");
    System.out.println(
      "Source Location: "
        + thisJoinPoint.getStaticPart().getSourceLocation());
    System.out.println(
      "------------------------------------------------------------");
  }
}
```

The after() throwing advice type completes the picture for applying advice to be executed after a join point returns. In this case, the advice should be executed when an exception has occurred. This gives the developer the capability to handle exceptional circumstances after a join point has been executed.

See Also

The call(Signature) pointcut is described in Recipe 4.1; the handler(TypePattern) pointcut is shown in more detail in Recipe 5.1; the within(TypePattern) pointcut is described in Recipe 9.1; the thisJoinPoint variable and the context it encapsulates is examined in Recipe 13.2; the after() and after() returning advice types are described in Recipes 13.5 and 13.6 respectively.

13.8   Controlling Advice Precedence

Problem

You want to control the precedence of multiple advice blocks as they are applied to the same join point.

Solution

If the same types of advice located in different aspects are applied to the same join point, you can use the declare precedence statement. The syntax of the declare precedence statement is:

```
declare precedence : TypePattern, TypePattern, ..;
```

If the same types of advice are located in the same aspect, then the location of the advice declaration is used to denote its precedence as it is applied to the shared join point.

Discussion

Example 13-9 shows using the declare precedence statement to specify that AspectA is of a higher precedence than AspectB.

Example 13-9. Using the declare precedence statement to control aspect precedence

```
public aspect AspectA
{
    // Declare precedence rules
    declare precedence : AspectA, AspectB;

    /*
    Specifies calling advice whenever a method
    matching the following rules gets called:

    Class Name: MyClass
    Method Name: foo
    Method Return Type: * (any return type)
    Method Parameters: an int followed by a String
    */
    pointcut callPointCut() : call(void MyClass.foo(int, String));

    // Advice declaration
    before() : callPointCut() && !within(AspectA +)
    {

        System.out.println(
            "------------------ Aspect Advice Logic --------------------");
        System.out.println("In the advice of AspectA");
        System.out.println("Target: " + thisJoinPoint.getTarget());
        System.out.println("This: " + thisJoinPoint.getThis());
        System.out.println("Aspect Instance: " + AspectA.aspectOf());
        System.out.println(
            "----------------------------------------------------------");
    }
}
```

Aspects can work in relative isolation in some applications, but as your aspect-oriented architecture becomes more complex, having two aspects advising the same join point is reasonable. In these cases, you must control the precedence of the aspects when applying their advice to any shared join points.

TypePatterns are used in the declare precedence statements to specify the different aspects and their explicit orderings. The TypePatterns can be specified using wildcards to indicate the precedence for sets of particular aspects or to entire packages of aspects if required.

The same problem occurs when two blocks of the same type of advice in the same aspect are applied to the same join point. In this case, it does not make sense to use the declare precedence statement because the advice is all in the same aspect. To handle this, AspectJ applies an implicit order of precedence based upon the type and location of the advice within the aspect declaration.

In the case where the same types of advice within the same aspect are advising the same join point the implicit rules of precedence are:

- The implicit precedence rules for the before( ) and around( ) types of advice are applied in the order they are declared in the aspect. If two blocks of before( ) advice in the same aspect are applied to the same join point, then the first block that is declared will have the highest precedence and the last will have the lowest.

- The implicit precedence for the after( ), after( ) returning, and around( ) throwing types of advice are applied in the reverse order to the before and around( ) types of advice. This means that if two or more blocks of the after( ) types of advice in the same aspect are applied to the same join point, then the block that is declared last will have the highest precedence and the first will have the lowest.

Whether advice is declared in the same or separate aspects, advice precedence means different things depending on the advice type. Figure 13-2 shows the different precedence orderings in relation to a join point and their implications for the different forms of advice.

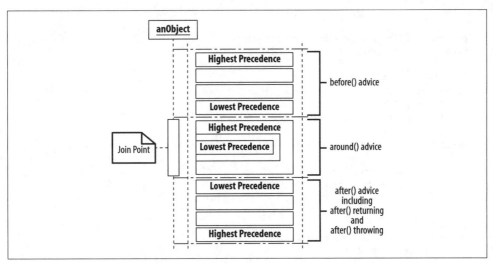

Figure 13-2. Advice order of precedence in relation to a join point

See Also

The call(Signature) pointcut is covered in Recipe 4.1; the within(TypePattern) pointcut is described in Recipe 9.1; the NOT(!) operator is described in Recipe 12.4; the before( ) type of advice is described in Recipe 13.3; the around( ) type of advice is covered in Recipe 13.4; the after( ) type of advice and its variations are described in Recipes 13.5, 13.6, and 13.7, respectively.

13.9   Advising Aspects

Problem

You want to apply advice to other aspects.

Solution

Use the pointcuts available within AspectJ to specify the aspects to be advised.

Discussion

AspectJ includes aspects within the scope of advisable things, so the various point-cuts available in AspectJ can be used to specify advising other aspects in addition to the classes within the application. Example 13-10 shows how to declare advice to be applied to advice within another aspect.

Example 13-10. Applying advice to other advice

```
public aspect AdviseAspectRecipe
{
    /*
    Specifies calling advice whenever a method
    matching the following rules gets called:

    Class Name: MyClass
    Method Name: foo
    Method Return Type: void
    Method Parameters: an int followed by a String
    */
    pointcut callPointCut() : call(void MyClass.foo(int, String));

    // Advice declaration
    before() : callPointCut() && within(AdvisedAspect +)
    {

        System.out.println(
            "------------------ Aspect Advice Logic --------------------");
        System.out.println(
            "In the advice attached to the call point cut");
        System.out.println(
            "Signature: "
                + thisJoinPoint.getStaticPart().getSignature());
        System.out.println(
            "Source Line: "
                + thisJoinPoint.getStaticPart().getSourceLocation());
        System.out.println(
            "----------------------------------------------------------");

    }
}
```

See Also

The call(Signature) pointcut is described in Recipe 4.1; the within(TypePattern) pointcut is described in Recipe 9.1; the thisJoinPoint variable and the context it encapsulates is examined in Recipe 13.2.

CHAPTER 14
Defining Aspect Instantiation

14.0 Introduction

In Chapter 9, the recipes on advice hinted at an interesting characteristic of how AspectJ implements aspects. When AspectJ was being designed, the decision was made to reuse as much as possible from the existing Java language. This decision meant that even though the nature and intent of aspect orientation was at the forefront of the work on AspectJ, this goal was tempered by an attempt to keep within the constraints of Java so specialized runtime environments would not be needed.

To achieve this goal the designers decided to implement aspects as classes within the post-processed aspect-oriented application. This clever approach meant that 100% of the world's virtual machines could run AspectJ programs unaltered. This approach is interesting for another reason: since aspects are transformed into regular classes during the weaving process (see Chapter 1 for details), then they must have their own regular object lifecycle. Further, since aspects have their own lifecycle, they must have an associated instantiation policy by which the compiler can decide when a new aspect object is to be created. In this chapter, you see how to declare and control the specific instantiation policies that govern when an aspect object is created within the flow of your application.

14.1 Defining Singleton Aspects

Problem

You want to declare that an aspect is to be instantiated as a singleton.

Solution

Use the `issingleton()` explicit aspect instantiation policy declaration or rely on the default implicit aspect instantiation policy.

Discussion

AspectJ assigns a singleton behavior to aspects by default. Every aspect you have seen so far has been a singleton because the instantiation policy has not been explicitly declared.

The singleton aspect instantiation policy can be made explicit by adding the issingleton( ) statement to the aspect declaration, as shown in Example 14-1.

Example 14-1. Declaring a singleton aspect explicitly

```
public aspect Singleton issingleton( )
{
   /*
   Specifies calling advice whenever a method
   matching the following rules gets called:

   Class Name: MyClass
   Method Name: foo
   Method Return Type: void
   Method Parameters: an int followed by a String
   */
   pointcut callPointCut( ) : call(void MyClass.foo(int, String));

   // Advice declaration
   before() : callPointCut( ) && !within(Singleton +)
   {

      System.out.println(
         "------------------- Aspect Advice Logic -------------------");
      System.out.println(
         "In the advice attached to the call point cut");
      System.out.println(
         "Target: " + thisJoinPoint.getTarget( ));
      System.out.println(
         "This: " + thisJoinPoint.getThis( ));
      System.out.println("Aspect Instance: " + Singleton.aspectOf( ));
      System.out.println(
         "-----------------------------------------------------------");

   }
}
```

At the core of the singleton pattern is the goal of declaring a class that constrains itself to one object instance for the lifetime of an application. Figure 14-1 shows how each different object is advised by the same aspect instance in an application.

Singletons are a great way for applying a common component throughout an application. Declaring your aspects as singletons allows you to share the instantiated aspect across all the areas that the aspect is applied in your application. The memory space taken by that aspect instantiation is shared across all objects and threads and can provide a useful means of sharing data when used carefully.

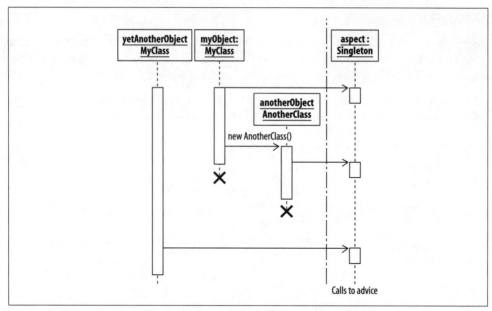

Figure 14-1. Calls from all objects are received by the same singleton aspect

The primary disadvantage of using traditional object-oriented singletons is that every class that uses the singleton is closely coupled to the singleton's public interface. If the singleton's public interface changes, then all of the classes that use the singleton must change. This produces a complicated ripple effect of changes throughout your application.

The aspect-oriented singleton aspect does not suffer from this disadvantage. By modularizing the rules for how the singleton is applied with the behavior that the singleton provides in one place, then only the aspect needs to be amended if its behavior changes.

See Also

The singleton pattern is discussed in more detail in Recipe 17.1; the call(Signature) pointcut is covered in Recipe 4.1; the within(TypePattern) pointcut is described in Recipe 9.1; the NOT(!) operator is described in Recipe 12.4; inheritance between aspects is described in more detail in Chapter 15.

14.2 Defining an Aspect per Instance

Problem

You want to declare that an aspect is to be instantiated on a per-object-instance basis.

Solution

Use the perthis(Pointcut) or pertarget(Pointcut) aspect instantiation policy declarations.

Discussion

AspectJ provides the perthis(Pointcut) and pertarget(Pointcut) aspect instantiation policies to declare an aspect should be instantiated for every new object instance according to the classes selected with the Pointcut definition.

The difference between the perthis(Pointcut) and the pertarget(Pointcut) declarations has to do with what object is examined when an advised join point is reached. The perthis(Pointcut) declaration specifies that a new aspect will be instantiated for every new object referenced by this at the advice triggering join point. The pertarget(Pointcut) instantiation policy specifies that a new aspect will be instantiated for every new object that is the target of an advice triggering join point. Despite these subtle differences, both declarations explicitly associate a single aspect instance to a single object instance.

Example 14-2 shows how a perthis(Pointcut) declaration can be assigned to a particular aspect, and Figure 14-2 shows how the aspect instantiation policy is realized within the flow of an application.

Example 14-2. Using the perthis(Pointcut) declaration to instantiate an aspect for every executing object

```
public aspect PerThis perthis(callPointCut( ))
{
  /*
  Specifies calling advice whenever a method
  matching the following rules is executed:

  Class Name: MyClass
  Method Name: foo
  Method Return Type: void
  Method Parameters: an int followed by a String
  */
  pointcut callPointCut( ) : call(
    void MyClass.foo(int, String));
```

Example 14-2. Using the perthis(Pointcut) declaration to instantiate an aspect for every executing object (continued)

```
    // Advice declaration
    before() : callPointCut( ) && !within(PerThis +)
    {

        System.out.println(
            "------------------ Aspect Advice Logic -------------------");
        System.out.println(
            "In the advice attached to the call point cut");
        System.out.println("Target: " + thisJoinPoint.getTarget( ));
        System.out.println("This: " + thisJoinPoint.getThis( ));
        System.out.println(
            "Aspect Instance: "
                + PerThis.aspectOf(thisJoinPoint.getThis( )));
        System.out.println(
            "---------------------------------------------------------");

    }
}
```

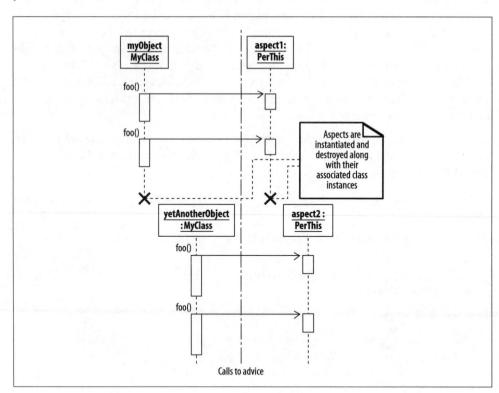

Figure 14-2. Creating one aspect instance per object advised

The `Pointcut` parameter on the `perthis(Pointcut)` and `pertarget(Pointcut)` aspect instantiation policy declarations raises some interesting questions when you consider that multiple classes can be advised by a single aspect. Example 14-3 shows how an aspect can be declared to advise multiple classes where the `perthis(Pointcut)` aspect instantiation policy is only relevant on objects of the `MyClass` class as specified by the `executeMyClassFoo( )` pointcut.

Example 14-3. Attempting to advise multiple classes but specifying an aspect instantiation policy that is only interested in one class

```
public aspect AdviseMultipleClasses perthis(executeMyClassFoo( ))
{
    public pointcut executeMyClassFoo() : execution(void MyClass.foo( ));

    public pointcut executeAnotherClassFoo() : execution(void AnotherClass.foo( ));

    before() : executeMyClassFoo( )
    {
        System.out.println("Advising foo");
        System.out.println("Aspect is: " + this);
    }

    before() : executeAnotherClassFoo( )
    {
        System.out.println("Advising foo");
        System.out.println("Aspect is: " + this);
    }
}
```

Declaring that the `AdviseMultipleClasses` aspect is only to be instantiated for every new object as specified by the `executeMyClassFoo( )` pointcut implicitly excludes other classes of object. Even though the `executeAnotherClassFoo( )` pointcut is declared and has corresponding advice, it will not result in any aspects being applied to classes other than those that it shares with `executeMyClassFoo( )`.

In Example 14-3, no common classes are shared between the two pointcuts, so the `executeMyClassFoo( )` pointcut and associated advice is ignored because this pointcut is taking part in the definition of the `perthis(Pointcut)` instantiation policy, as shown in Figure 14-3.

An aspect cannot have two instantiation policies for two different types of object. To ensure that an aspect's instantiation policy is relevant for all objects of the classes that it advises, a useful idiom is to declare a pointcut that combines all other pointcut declarations in the aspect purely for the use of the aspect's instantiation policy, as shown in Example 14-4.

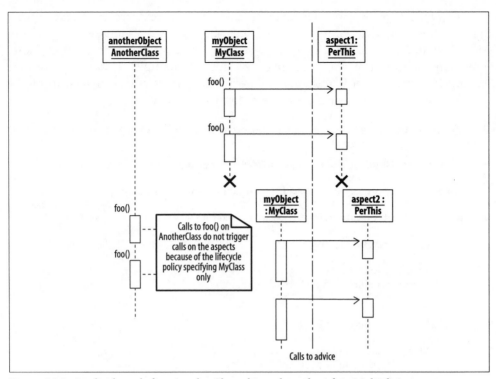

Figure 14-3. Implicitly excluding AnotherClass objects from the AdviseMultipleAspects aspect according to the aspect instantiation policy

Example 14-4. Capturing all classes that are advised by an aspect for inclusion into the aspect instantiation policy definition

```
public aspect AdviseMultipleClasses perthis(applyLifecyclePolicy( ))
{
    public pointcut executeMyClassFoo() : execution(void MyClass.foo( ));

    public pointcut executeAnotherClassFoo() : execution(void AnotherClass.foo( ));

    public pointcut applyLifecyclePolicy() : executeMyClassFoo( ) ||
                            executeAnotherClassFoo( );

    before() : executeMyClassFoo( )
    {
        System.out.println("Advising foo");
        System.out.println("Aspect is: " + this);
    }

    before() : executeAnotherClassFoo( )
    {
        System.out.println("Advising foo");
        System.out.println("Aspect is: " + this);
    }
}
```

See Also

The execution(Signature) pointcut is covered in Recipe 4.4; the within(TypePattern) pointcut is described in Recipe 7.1; the OR(||) operator is described in Recipe 12.3; the NOT(!) operator is described in Recipe 12.4; the Singleton aspect instantiation policy is described in Recipe 14.1.

14.3   Defining an Aspect per Control Flow

Problem

You want to declare that an aspect is to be instantiated on a per-control-flow basis.

Solution

Use the percflow(Pointcut) aspect instantiation declaration.

Discussion

The percflow(Pointcut) statement indicates to the AspectJ compiler that it should create a new instance of the aspect for every new control flow that is entered within the set of join points indicated by the Pointcut parameter.

Example 14-5 shows the percflow(Pointcut) instantiation declaration being used to specify a new instance of the PerControlFlow aspect for every new program control flow where the join points specified by the callPointCut() are encountered.

Example 14-5. Using the percflow(Pointcut) to create a new instance of an aspect for every new program control flow entered

```
public aspect PerControlFlow percflow(callPointCut())
{
    /*
    Specifies calling advice whenever a method
    matching the following rules gets called:

    Class Name: MyClass
    Method Name: foo
    Method Return Type: * (any return type)
    Method Parameters: an int followed by a String
    */
    pointcut callPointCut() :
        call(void MyClass.foo(int, String));

    // Advice declaration
    before() : callPointCut() && !within(PerControlFlow +)
    {

        System.out.println(
            "------------------- Aspect Advice Logic -------------------");
```

Example 14-5. Using the percflow(Pointcut) to create a new instance of an aspect for every new program control flow entered (continued)

```
    System.out.println(
        "In the advice attached to the call point cut");
    System.out.println("Target: " + thisJoinPoint.getTarget());
    System.out.println("This: " + thisJoinPoint.getThis());
    System.out.println(
        "Aspect Instance: " + PerControlFlow.aspectOf());
    System.out.println(
        "-------------------------------------------------------");
    }
}
```

Figure 14-4 shows how this relationship works in the case of the percflow(Pointcut) declaration.

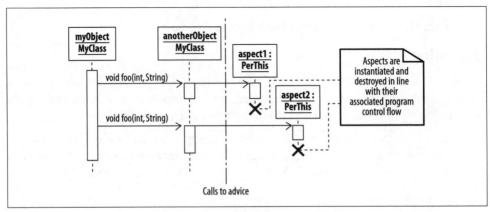

Figure 14-4. Creating a new aspect instance per program control flow

The percflow(Pointcut) statement represents the finest granularity of aspect instanti-ation policy and creates the largest number of distinct aspect instances for a particu-lar piece of code. With this type of aspect instantiation declaration, the memory requirements of your aspects becomes more important.

See Also

The call(Signature) pointcut is covered in Recipe 4.1; the within(TypePattern) pointcut is described in Recipe 7.1; the NOT(!) operator is described in Recipe 12.4.

Defining Aspect Relationships

15.0 Introduction

Aspects in AspectJ are objects in their own right and they benefit from the traditional object-oriented (OO) mechanisms that make object orientation such a great approach for software development.

When using the OO concepts of association and composition, then the rules for aspects are fairly simple: an aspect can contain or use other classes without using any unique syntax. If you ignore some irregular method signatures, a class can use an aspect as if it were just another class.

This chapter deals with the details of inheritance between aspects and classes and some of the special things to consider when defining these relationships.

15.1 Inheriting Pointcut Definitions

Problem

You want to create pointcut declarations in an aspect that can then be reused using inheritance.

Solution

Create an abstract aspect. Define within the abstract aspect the reusable pointcut logic using the appropriate public, protected, or default access modifiers. Finally, inherit that abstract aspect into your subaspects to reuse the declared pointcuts.

Discussion

Pointcuts are subject to a similar set of rules as normal methods when using inheritance. If a pointcut is declared public, protected, or default, then its logic can be inherited and reused within other aspects.

Example 15-1 shows an abstract aspect that provides a base for inheriting its defined pointcuts.

Example 15-1. Using an abstract aspect to define reusable pointcut logic

```
public abstract aspect BasePointcutDefinitionsAspect
{
    public pointcut callPointcut() : call(void MyClass.foo(int, String));
}
```

 In Example 15-1, no obvious need exists for the BasePointcutDefini-tionsAspect to be abstract. The aspect is declared as abstract because the AspectJ language states that only abstract aspects can be extended by subaspects.

Example 15-2 shows the ReusePointcutsRecipe aspect inheriting the callPointcut() declaration from the aspect in Example 15-1.

Example 15-2. Reusing pointcut logic from the abstract base aspect

```
public aspect ReusePointcutsRecipe extends BasePointcutDefinitionsAspect
{

    // Advice declaration
    before() : callPointcut() && !within(ReusePointcutsRecipe +)
    {

        System.out.println(
           "------------------- Aspect Advice Logic --------------------");
        System.out.println(
           "In the advice attached to the call point cut");
        System.out.println(
           "Signature: "
              + thisJoinPoint.getStaticPart().getSignature());
        System.out.println(
           "Source Line: "
              + thisJoinPoint.getStaticPart().getSourceLocation());

        System.out.println(
           "----------------------------------------------------------");
    }
}
```

Figure 15-1 shows the static structure of the inheritance relationship defined in Examples 15-1 and 15-2.

The ability to define abstract aspects that encapsulate just pointcut logic opens up the possibilities for pointcut libraries. This powerful concept is useful in large-scale enterprise environments. Specific pointcuts for patterns of weaving throughout the

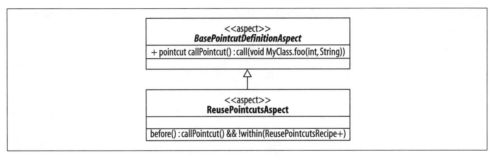

Figure 15-1. Inheritance between aspects

application can be defined and reused without having to repeat the generic pointcut logic over and over again.

See Also

Recipe 4.1 shows the definition of the call(Signature) pointcut; the within(TypePattern) pointcut is described in Recipe 9.1; the NOT(!) operator is described in Recipe 12.4.

15.2   Implementing Abstract Pointcuts

Problem

You want to declare and reference a pointcut but leave the definition of the pointcut logic to be implemented by specialized subaspects.

Solution

Use the abstract keyword when declaring the pointcut and the surrounding aspect, and do not supply any pointcut logic.

Discussion

Example 15-3 shows an abstract pointcut being declared and used throughout an aspect.

Example 15-3. Declaring abstract pointcuts for implementation by derived aspects

```
public abstract aspect BaseAbstractAspect
{
    /*
    Specifies an abstract pointcut placeholder
    for derived aspects to specify
    */
    public abstract pointcut abstractBasePointcut();
```

Example 15-3. Declaring abstract pointcuts for implementation by derived aspects (continued)

```
    /*
      Specifies calling advice whenever a jhin point
      picked by the abstractBasePointcut (specified
      by specialized aspects) is encountered, and not within
      this aspect or any inheriting aspects.
    */
    pointcut runAdvicePointcut() : abstractBasePointcut()
       && !within(BaseAbstractAspect +);
}
```

Example 15-4 shows how the abstract pointcut declared in Example 15-3 can be fully defined in the subaspect.

Example 15-4. Implementing the full pointcut logic of the inherited abstract base pointcut

```
public aspect AbstractImplementationAspect extends BaseAbstractAspect
{
    /*
    Specifies calling advice whenever a method
    matching the following rules gets called:

    Class Name: MyClass
    Method Name: foo
    Method Return Type: void
    Method Parameters: an int followed by a String
    */
    public pointcut abstractBasePointcut() : call(void MyClass.foo(int, String));

    // Advice declaration
    before() : runAdvicePointcut()
    {

        System.out.println(
           "------------------ Aspect Advice Logic --------------------");
        System.out.println(
           "In the advice attached to the call point cut");
        System.out.println(
           "Signature: "
             + thisJoinPoint.getStaticPart().getSignature());
        System.out.println(
           "Source Line: "
             + thisJoinPoint.getStaticPart().getSourceLocation());
        System.out.println(
           "---------------------------------------------------------");
    }
}
```

Figure 15-2 shows the inheritance relationship between the aspects in Examples 15-3 and 15-4.

An abstract pointcut declaration is useful when you want to postpone the definition of specific pointcut logic while still declaring more generic and potentially reusable

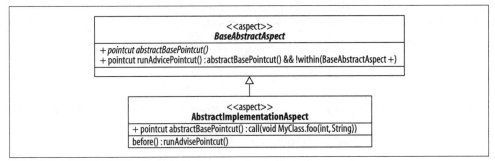

Figure 15-2. Implementing abstract pointcuts

pointcuts. Using this approach, generic abstract aspects can be created that can be extended specifically for a particular application. This can lead to libraries of reusable aspects.

See Also

Recipe 4.1 shows the definition of the call(Signature) pointcut; the within(TypePattern) pointcut is described in Recipe 9.1; the NOT(!) operator is described in Recipe 12.4; Chapters 17 through 19 use the techniques shown in this example to define reusable aspects when implementing object-oriented design patterns.

15.3   Inheriting Classes into Aspects

Problem

You want to refactor an existing class as an aspect by inheriting the existing class's behavior.

Solution

Use the extends keyword to declare that the aspect extends the class.

Discussion

Example 15-5 shows a pseudo-logging class that represents an existing logging mechanism. The aim is to refactor all existing calls to the logging class from the application and modularize the logging into an aspect that can more flexibly be woven into the application.

Example 15-5. A pseudo-traditional logging class representing an existing logging class within the application prior to being refactored for aspects

```
public class OOLogging
{
    public void logEntry(String entry)
```

Example 15-5. A pseudo-traditional logging class representing an existing logging class within the application prior to being refactored for aspects (continued)

```
    {
        System.out.println("Entry logged: " + entry);
    }
}
```

Once the existing calls to the class have been refactored out of the application, an aspect can be created to reapply logging to the application, reusing the original logging class through inheritance, as shown in Example 15-6.

Example 15-6. Using inheritance of a traditional class to reuse behavior being refactored into an aspect

```
public aspect AOLogging extends OOLogging
{
    /*
    Specifies calling advice whenever a method
    matching the following rules gets called:

    Class Name: MyClass
    Method Name: foo
    Method Return Type: void
    Method Parameters: an int followed by a String
    */
    pointcut callPointcut( ) : call(void MyClass.foo(int, String));

    // Advice declaration
    before() : callPointcut( )
        && !within(AOLogging +)
        && !within(OOLogging)
    {
        this.logEntry(thisJoinPoint.toShortString( ));
    }
}
```

 Refactoring is the term used for making changes to an existing design to improve it in some way. Refactoring doesn't necessarily incorporate any new features into the solution; rather, it re-engineers the software to provide a design that can be more easily maintained and more elegant, or it incorporates other design improvements. *Refactoring: Improving the Design of Existing Code* by Martin Fowler (Addison-Wesley) is the definitive work to date on refactoring.

Figure 15-3 shows the static structure after declaring the aspect shown in Example 15-6.

Although aspects can reuse class behavior using inheritance, this can sometimes be a brittle approach. A more elegant solution would be to perform reuse by aggregation incorporating the logging class as an attribute of the logging aspect. The logging

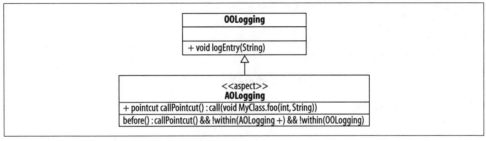

Figure 15-3. Applying reuse using inheritance between aspects and classes

aspect could then be woven against the target application and effectively delegate the logging behavior to the internal instance of the logging class.

See Also

Recipe 4.1 shows the definition of the call(Signature) pointcut; the within(TypePattern) pointcut is described in Recipe 9.1; the NOT(!) operator is described in Recipe 12.4; refactoring can often be achieved using inner aspects, which are discussed in Recipe 15.4.

15.4 Declaring Aspects Inside Classes

Problem

You want to declare an internal class-wide cross-cutting concern.

Solution

Use an inner aspect declaration.

Discussion

Example 15-7 shows how to define an inner aspect that is applied to its containing class. The call(TypePattern) pointcut is used to capture join points on all calls to the MyClass class.

Example 15-7. Declaring an inner aspect

```
public class MyClass
{

    /*
        Specifies calling advice whenever a method
        matching the following rules gets called:

        Class Name: MyClass
        Method Name: *
        Method Return Type: * (any return type)
```

Example 15-7. Declaring an inner aspect (continued)

```
    Method Parameters: .. (any parameters0
    */
private static aspect CallMethods
{
    pointcut callPointCut() : call(* MyClass.* (..));

    // Advice declaration
    before() : callPointCut() && !within(CallMethods +)
    {

        System.out.println(
            "--------------- Aspect Advice Logic ----------------");
        System.out.println(
            "In the advice attached to the call point cut");
        System.out.println(
            "Signature: "
                + thisJoinPoint.getStaticPart().getSignature());
        System.out.println(
            "Source Line: "
                + thisJoinPoint.getStaticPart().getSourceLocation());
        System.out.println(
            "----------------------------------------------------");
    }
}

public void foo(int number, String name)
{
    System.out.println("Inside foo (int, String)");
}

public void bar(String name)
{
    System.out.println("Inside bar (String)");
    this.privateMethod();
}

private void privateMethod()
{
    System.out.println("In privateMethod ()");
}

public static void main(String[] args)
{
    // Create an instance of MyClass
    MyClass myObject = new MyClass();
    // Make the call to foo
    myObject.foo(1, "Russ");
    // Make the call to bar
    myObject.bar("Kim");
}
}
```

Cross-cutting behavior is often thought of as system-wide in scope, but the classes may exhibit cross-cutting concerns internally. Any behavior, common across a group of methods in a class, is a candidate for being a cross-cutting concern especially if it is not core to the classes purpose within the business logic.

Inner aspects have three key characteristics:

1. Inner aspects must be explicitly declared static as their instantiation is controlled by an aspect instantiation policy and not by the construction of the surrounding class.

2. Inner aspects may have all of the regular access modifiers applied to them to allow encapsulation protection and static inheritance reuse where appropriate.

3. An inner aspect is not restricted to being woven against the surrounding class. By declaring an inner aspect, you are implying that the aspect is strongly related to the surrounding class but the aspect is not constrained in that way.

Inner aspects are useful when refactoring your existing code. The first step is to identify behavior that is cross-cutting in nature, i.e., that it affects more than one area of your class and may not naturally sit with the fundamental business purpose of the class.

One or more inner aspects can then be declared that modularize this cross-cutting behavior. Some commonality may exist between the inner aspects in your application, so the next stage could be to refactor the inner aspects into more traditional system scoped aspects.

See Also

Recipe 4.1 shows the definition of the call(Signature) pointcut; the within(TypePattern) pointcut is described in Recipe 9.1; the NOT(!) operator is described in Recipe 12.4; the before( ) form of advice is explained in Recipe 13.3; aspect instantiation policies are covered in Chapter 14; more refactoring concerns and approaches are shown in Recipe 15.3; a series of articles from Ramnivas Laddad, at *http://www.theserverside.com/ articles/article.tss?l=AspectOrientedRefactoringPart1/1* provides more information on aspect-oriented refactoring.

CHAPTER 16

Enhancing Classes and the Compiler

16.0 Introduction

This chapter shows how aspects in AspectJ can be used statically to introduce behavior and interfaces to existing classes using *static cross-cutting* techniques. Using these techniques, classes can be extended to implement interfaces, extend from new parent classes, introduce new methods and attributes, soften exceptions that are raised, and inherit from multiple base classes.

Static cross-cutting is powerful and must be used with care. Problems that were deliberately avoided by language constraints, such as multiple inheritance complications, are possible and must be considered before they are used. There are two schools of thought on this. Some people argue the developer should decide if they want to use the more complex techniques and, therefore, accept the potential problems. Others, such as the designers of Java, attempt to constrain these decisions as much as possible using the language.

Ultimately, the individual's opinions or the organization's style determines whether static cross-cutting techniques are acceptable. However, it is useful to know that these techniques exist within the aspect developers toolbox.

16.1 Extending an Existing Class

Problem

You want to extend an existing class.

Solution

Declare the new methods and attributes to be added to the existing class within the aspect.

Discussion

Example 16-1 shows how an attribute and a method can be introduced to the
MyClass class.

Example 16-1. Adding an attribute and a method to an existing class

```
public aspect ExtendClassRecipe
{

    private int MyClass.newVariable = 20;

    public int MyClass.bar(String name)
    {
        System.out.println("In bar(String name), name:" + name);
        return this.newVariable;
    }
}
```

Figure 16-1 shows the class structure of the MyClass class before and after the aspect
in Example 16-1 is applied.

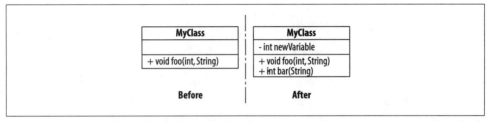

Figure 16-1. The MyClass class before and after the aspect introduces a new attribute and method

See Also

Recipe 16.2 shows how to specify a new inheritance relationship between classes;
Recipe 16.3 shows how to apply new interfaces to an existing class using aspects.

16.2 Declaring Inheritance Between Classes

Problem

You want to introduce a new inheritance relationship between two classes.

Solution

Use the declare parents statement to specify a particular class that extends from
another class.

Discussion

Example 16-2 shows how a new inheritance relationship can be specified for the MyClass class.

Example 16-2. Adding a new inheritance relationship between classes

```
public aspect IntroduceInheritanceRecipe
{

    declare  parents : MyClass extends AnotherClass;
}
```

Figure 16-2 shows the class structure of the MyClass class before and after the aspect in Example 16-2 is applied.

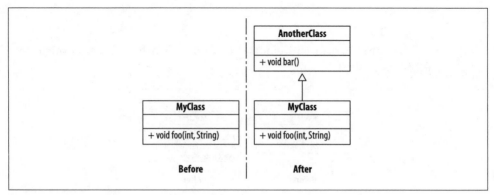

Figure 16-2. The MyClass class before and after the aspect introduces a new inheritance relationship

See Also

Recipe 16.3 shows how to apply new interfaces to an existing class using aspects.

16.3 Implementing Interfaces Using Aspects

Problem

You want to add an interface to a class.

Solution

Use the declare parents statement to specify a particular class that implements a specific interface or interfaces.

Discussion

Example 16-3 shows how the declare parents statement in AspectJ can apply an interface to a class that may have had no knowledge of the interface prior to the aspect being applied.

Example 16-3. Using aspects to declare a new interface on an existing class

```
public aspect ImplementInterfaceRecipe
{
    declare parents : MyClass implements MyInterface;
}
```

Figure 16-3 shows how the static class architecture is affected by the application of the aspect in Example 16-3.

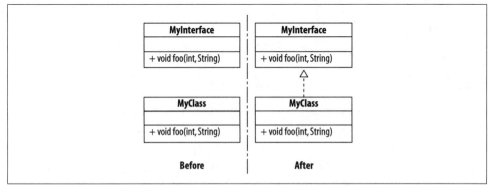

Figure 16-3. The static class structure before and after the aspect introduces a new interface

Having the capability to apply an interface to an existing class allows objects of that class to be referenced by the interface type, as shown in Example 16-4.

Example 16-4. Referring to an object according to an aspect declared interface

```
// Create an instance of MyClass
MyInterface myObject = new MyClass();

// ...

// Work with the interface reference
myObject.foo(1, "Russ");
```

By applying a new interface to a class, the class can be used in ways in which it was not originally designed. This is particularly useful when a new role is assigned to a class.

The class must implement any methods the interface declares. In traditional object orientation, the Adapter design pattern would be a good solution. However, AspectJ does offer an alternative implementation of the Adapter pattern. Using the mechanisms shown in Recipe 12.1, an aspect can add implementations of the interfaces methods to the class without the need for a separate Adapter.

See Also

Recipe 16.1 shows how to extend an existing class with a new method; Chapters 17 through 19 give various examples of how roles can be assigned to classes using aspects when implementing OO design patterns; Recipe 18.3 discusses an aspect-oriented approach to implementing the Adapter design pattern; Recipe 23.2 shows how a generic design pattern for aspect-oriented role declaration.

16.4   Declaring a Default Interface Implementation

Problem

You want to provide a default implementation for an interface.

Solution

Declare the default implementations for the interface's methods within the aspect.

Discussion

Example 16-5 shows how a default implementation is provided for the MyInterface interface by implementing the void bar(String) method.

Example 16-5. Using aspects to provide a default implementation of an interface method

```
public aspect DefaultInterfaceImplementationRecipe
{
    declare parents : MyClass implements MyInterface;

    // Declare the default implementation of the bar method
    public void MyInterface.bar(String name)
    {
        System.out.println("bar(String) called on " + this);
    }
}
```

Figure 16-4 shows how the static class structure is affected by the application of the aspect in Example 16-5.

Figure 16-4 gives a misleading picture of the outcome of applying Example 16-5. You won't see a DefaultImplementation class when the aspects are woven and compiled. However, for the sake of visualizing the architecture, the result is similar to how this figure presents it except that the void bar(int,String) is transparently added to the MyClass class.

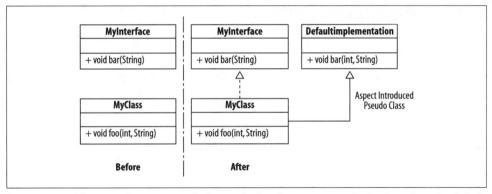

Figure 16-4. The static class structure before and after the aspect is applied to introduce the default interface implementation

What you end up with is something like multiple inheritance. Interfaces in Java provide a means by which a class can have an explicitly declared public interface, or role, to which it can be used. This allows multiple interfaces to be implemented by a single class because no method implementations to worry exist. Traditionally, a Java class can explicitly inherit from only one other class, which prohibits multiple inheritance. This is not the case with aspects in AspectJ.

A Java interface can have an implementation of its methods declared by an aspect and still be declared an interface allowing a form of multiple inheritance. A good candidate situation where it is useful to provide default implementations of an interface is when traditional OO design patterns are applied. A design pattern can be an invasive element of an applications design. This result may not always be a good thing when the business logic of the classes becomes blurred with the pattern logic being applied. You should probably apply the patterns wherever possible as aspects, incorporating default implementations of the appropriate roles where needed, and keep the business logic within the classes clear and manageable.

Many of the traditional design patterns use abstract classes as their base for the different roles they use. In Java, only one base class is allowed and this means that the architecture can be complicated by the conflicting desire for having a clear expression of the business relationships between classes and the desire to apply good practice design patterns. AspectJ, by providing the means of specifying a default implementation for an interface, has removed the need to have an abstract class as the base for many design patterns.

See Also

Recipe 16.1 explains how classes can be extended by aspects introducing new methods and attributes; OO design patterns and the benefits that those patterns can gain by using an aspect-oriented approach are examined in Chapters 17 through 19.

16.5 Softening Exceptions

Problem

You want to specify a set of exceptions that should be softened—i.e., converted to uncaught exceptions—when raised on the join points selected by a specific pointcut.

Solution

Use the declare soft statement.

Discussion

Example 16-6 shows softening the ExceptionA exception that is raised on the void foo( ) method so the users of that method do not have to worry about handling that exception.

Example 16-6. Softening exceptions on a method call

```
public aspect SoftenExceptionRecipe
{
    pointcut callPointCut() : call(void MyClass.foo());

    declare soft : ExceptionA : callPointCut();
}
```

Java supports two types of exception; checked and unchecked (runtime) exceptions. Checked exceptions extend from java.lang.Exception and get their name because of the following reason: if they are declared as being raised by a particular method, then calling methods *must* handle those exceptions explicitly otherwise the compiler will complain. Runtime exceptions extended from java.lang.RuntimeException or java.lang.Error, can be raised at any point during an applications lifetime, but do not need to be explicitly caught.

Softening exceptions involves wrapping a checked exception raised on a particular join point in an instance of the org.aspectj.lang.SoftException runtime exception class. Prior to applying softening of the ExceptionA exception, it would have to be caught or re-thrown, as shown in Example 16-7.

Example 16-7. The exception handling required if the exception is not softened

```
...

try
{
    myObject.foo();
}
catch (ExceptionA ea)
{
```

Example 16-7. The exception handling required if the exception is not softened (continued)

```
    ea.printStackTrace( );
}
```

...

By converting the checked exception to a runtime exception, the class can be used without the need for exception handling, as shown in Example 16-8.

Example 16-8. When the exception is softened, then no exception handling is necessary

...

```
myObject.foo( );
```

...

Declaring exceptions should be softened in this manner so the surrounding methods do not have to worry about catching those exceptions. Though the exception has been softened, it can still be raised and is more likely not to be caught until it reaches the surrounding system producing an output similar to that shown in Example 16-9.

Example 16-9. Output from a softened exception being thrown and not caught in this recipe's example application

```
Exception in thread "main" org.aspectj.lang.SoftException
    at MyClass.main(MyClass.java:14)
Caused by: ExceptionA
    at MyClass.foo(MyClass.java:7)
    ... 1 more
```

See Also

The AspectJ language API, including the `SoftException` class, is covered in more detail in the Appendix; using the `handler(TypePattern)` pointcut to capture join points when types of exceptions are caught is covered in Recipe 5.1.

16.6   Extending Compilation

Problem

You want to extend the capabilities of the compiler to enforce application specific rules.

Solution

Use the `declare error` or `declare warning` statement to specify conditions that should raise a compiler error or warning respectively.

Discussion

AspectJ supports advising most of the Java system but perhaps the most interesting and odd construct is the Java compiler. Example 16-10 shows how to declare a new error and warning that will be raised by the compiler if the specified condition is found within the application being compiled.

Example 16-10. Using aspects to declare new warnings and errors that can be raised by the compiler

```
public aspect CompilationAdviceRecipe
{
    declare error : call(void ProtectedAccessClass.setValue(int))
        && !this(MyClass)
        : "Must only set the ProtectedAccessClass.value from a MyClass object";

    declare warning : call(int ProtectedAccessClass.getValue())
        && !this(MyClass)
        : "Should only be reading ProtectedAccessClass.value from a MyClass object";
}
```

The capability to enforce new rules regarding what Java constructs are allowed and how they should be used is useful when you are potentially creating an application that may have changing needs depending on its target environment and as to what functionality it is allowed to expose. This allows you to define system policy warnings and to guide developers in their implementations.

 The error and warning messages must be simple, declared string literals. You cannot reference any other part of the software architecture, even static pieces of the structure, from within these messages.

See Also

Recipe 17.5 shows how this form of warning is used to indicate to developers that they are breaking the rules of Builder design pattern; for real-world examples of using declare error and declare warning to enforce design constraints and general developer guidance, take a look at the aTrack bug-tracking project available at *https://atrack.java.net*.

CHAPTER 17

Implementing Creational Object-Oriented Design Patterns

17.0 Introduction

With the release of the seminal book *Design Patterns: Elements of Reusable Object-Oriented Software* by Erich Gamma, Richard Helm, Ralph Johnson, and John Vlissides (Addison-Wesley), the now infamous Gang of Four (GoF) design patterns became formally recognized as a useful practice in object-oriented (OO) software development.

The GoF book was split into three categories of design pattern: Creational, Structural, and Behavioral. The original GoF design patterns were designed to be implemented using the mechanisms available in most OO languages. Aspect orientation, when implemented using AspectJ, adds new mechanisms with which these patterns can be applied:

- The code that deals with the mechanics of a design pattern can be modularized out of the rest of the business logic so as to be less intrusive.

- In Java, inheritance relationships between classes must be used with care since Java allows only one inheritance relationship between two classes. Aspects can provide mechanisms by which the more generic pattern-oriented relationships can be applied seperately from any core business relationships between classes. Therefore, aspects can remove the need for an abstract base class leaving the classes with as much freedom as possible to define the right relationships for their business logic without the design pattern getting in the way.

- A by-product of the above two advantages is that code is clearer and easier to understand because of the removal of pattern-focused relationships and logic from the business logic classes thanks to the modularization of the patterns into aspects.

All three categories of design pattern from the GoF book can benefit from an aspect-oriented implementation and this chapter focuses on the Creational patterns.

The pattern implementations described in the next three chapters are based on Jan Hannemann and Gregor Kiczales's work for the 17th Annual ACM conference on Object-Oriented ProProgramming, Systems, Languages, and Applications (OOPSLE). Go to *http://www.cs. ubc.ca/~jan/AODPs/* to check out the original research.

17.1   Implementing the Singleton Pattern

Problem

You want to apply the singleton pattern using AspectJ.

Solution

The *Singleton* pattern allows the definition of a class as having one runtime instance within an application. A singleton is normally met by providing no default constructor for a particular class, often overridden as a protected constructor, so an object of the class cannot be directly instantiated by the application. Access to the singleton object is usually implemented by creating a static method that returns the single instance of the class.

Example 17-1 shows an abstract aspect that uses the Director aspect-oriented design pattern (see Chapter 23) to provide a generic foundation for applying the singleton pattern.

Example 17-1. Using an aspect to define the Singleton Pattern

```
public abstract aspect SingletonPattern issingleton()
{
    private Hashtable singletons = new Hashtable();

    public interface Singleton
    {
    }

    public interface NonSingleton
    {
    }

    // Pointcut to define specify an interest in all creations
    // of all Classes that extend Singleton
    pointcut selectSingletons() : call((Singleton +).new (..));

    // Pointcut to ensure that any classes in the Singleton inheritance tree
    // that are marked as Non Singletons are not included in the Singleton
    // logic.
    pointcut excludeNonSingletons() : !call((NonSingleton +).new (..));
```

Example 17-1. Using an aspect to define the Singleton Pattern (continued)

```
Object around() : selectSingletons() && excludeNonSingletons()
{
    Class singleton = thisJoinPoint.getSignature().getDeclaringType();

    synchronized(singletons)
    {
        if (singletons.get(singleton) == null)
        {
            singletons.put(singleton, proceed());
        }
    }

    return (Object) singletons.get(singleton);
}
}
```

Discussion

The `SingletonPattern` abstract aspect defines two roles: `Singleton` and `NonSingleton`. The roles are implemented as interfaces so that the abstract aspect can work with the singletons without worrying about implementation details.

Figure 17-1 shows the structure of the `SingletonPattern` abstract aspect with the interfaces and behavior that it defines to support the singleton design pattern.

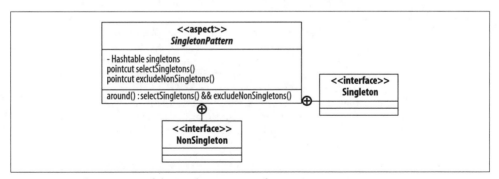

Figure 17-1. The structure of the SingletonPattern abstract aspect

The `Singleton` interface is applied by subaspects of the abstract `SingletonPattern` aspect to any classes within the target application that are to be treated as singletons. Similarly, the `NonSingleton` interface is applied to classes that may pick up singleton behavior from their parent class by inheritance. If you decide the child class is not to be a singleton, then the `NonSingleton` interface can be employed so that the singleton characteristic of the parent is overridden.

Two pointcuts are declared to capture when classes that have the `Singleton` interface are instantiated. The `selectSingletons()` pointcut definition picks the calls to the constructors on classes that extend the `Singleton` interface. To support the need to turn off the singleton behavior for subclasses of singletons, the excludeNonSingletons( ) point-cut is declared. This pointcut can be overridden by the specific aspects when you need to stop a subclass from being affected by a superclass's singleton behavior.

The around( ) advice captures calls to constructors on classes that have had the Singleton interface applied. The around( ) advice overrides the constructor to check that the type of the object being instantiated has not been created.

A lookup of the object's class being created is performed on the singletons hash table using the class information supplied by the thisJoinPoint variable. If the type of class is not present within the hash table, then its class is added and an object of that class is constructed by calling proceed( ), which executes the original construc-tors logic. The proceed( ) call returns the constructed object and this is added with the class object to the hash table.

If the type of the class is present within the hash table, then no new objects need to be created. The singleton object is retrieved from the hash map according to its class and returned from the around( ) of advice as the result of the constructor call.

By default, an aspect in AspectJ is a singleton. The SingletonPattern aspect uses the explicit issingleton( ) instantiation policy to highlight this aspect's important behavioral characteric.

> The implementation of the singleton pattern in this recipe is thread-safe because the hash table is locked during the execution of the around( ) advice using a synchronize block for simplicity. This incurs a performance penalty when the singleton is accessed for the first time and created, but it means that the pattern can then be applied within a multithreaded application. A more efficient mechanism could be to use an instance of the ThreadLocal class as a variable inside the aspect to ensure that the locked check is only performed once for a single thread, as discussed in the article by Brian Goetz, available at *http://www.javaworld.com/javaworld/jw-11-2001/jw-1116-dcl.html.*

Example 17-2 shows how the abstract SingletonPattern aspect can be applied for a specific application.

Example 17-2. Applying the abstract SingletonPattern aspect to target application classes

```
public aspect PrinterSingleton extends SingletonPattern
{
    declare parents: Printer implements Singleton;

    declare parents: SpecializedPrinter implements NonSingleton;
}
```

Figure 17-2 shows how the `PrinterSingleton` aspect affects an applications classes.

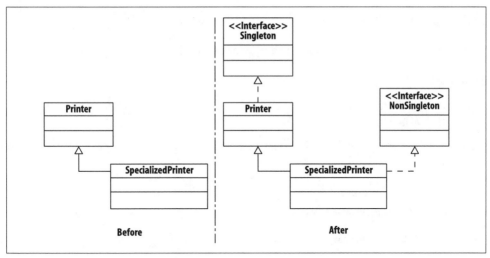

Figure 17-2. How the static application structure is affected by the PrinterSingleton aspect

Figure 17-3 shows how the new singleton behavior of the `Printer` class behaves in an example application.

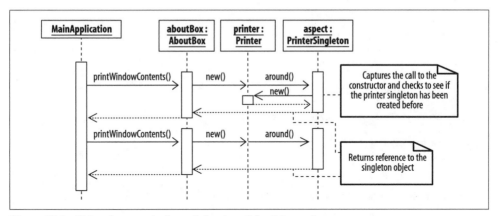

Figure 17-3. Using the new singleton behavior of the Printer class

See Also

Recipe 13.4 provides more detail on the proceed( ) call and its usage within around( ) advice; Recipe 7.1 describes the call(Signature) pointcut when capturing calls to a classes constructor; more information on aspect instantiation policies is available in Chapter 14; the Director aspect-oriented design pattern is explained in Recipe 23.3.

17.2   Implementing the Prototype Pattern

Problem

You want to apply the prototype pattern using AspectJ.

Solution

The *prototype* pattern supports the creation of duplicate objects based on an original object, the prototype.

Example 17-3 uses the Director aspect-oriented design pattern (see Chapter 23) to define the generic behavior needed to apply this pattern.

Example 17-3. Using an aspect to define the prototype pattern

```
public abstract aspect PrototypePattern
{
   protected interface Prototype
   {
   }

   public Object Prototype.clone( ) throws CloneNotSupportedException
   {
      return super.clone( );
   }

   public Object cloneObject(Prototype object)
   {
      try
      {
         return object.clone( );
      }
      catch (CloneNotSupportedException ex)
      {
         return createCloneFor(object);
      }
   }

   protected Object createCloneFor(Prototype object)
   {
      return null;
   }
}
```

Discussion

The abstract `PrototypePattern` aspect defines the `Prototype` interface that can be applied to any class within the target application that is to be a prototype. Those classes are extended with a `clone( )` method to support prototype duplication.

Figure 17-4 shows the structure of the PrototypePattern abstract aspect with the interfaces and behavior that it defines to support the prototype design pattern.

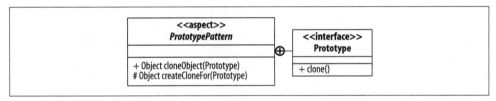

Figure 17-4. The structure of the PrototypePattern abstract aspect

A clone( ) method is the Java mechanism for implementing a deep copy of the object. Some base classes may not support being cloned; the PrototypePattern aspect provides the createCloneFor(Prototype) method, so it can be overridden by sub-aspects to perform specific cloning operations that the generic aspect will not know.

Example 17-4 shows how the abstract PrototypePattern aspect can be applied for a specific application.

Example 17-4. Applying the abstract PrototypePattern aspect to a target application

```
public aspect GraphicPrototypes extends PrototypePattern
{
    declare parents : Graphic implements Prototype;

    declare parents : MusicalNote implements Prototype;

    declare parents : Staff implements Prototype;

    protected Object createCloneFor(Prototype object)
    {
        if (object instanceof MusicalNote)
        {
            return new MusicalNote(
                ((MusicalNote) object).getX( ),
                ((MusicalNote) object).getY( ));
        }
        else if (object instanceof Staff)
        {
            return new Staff(((Staff) object).getX(), ((Staff) object).getY( ));
        }
        else
        {
            return null;
        }
    }
}
```

Figure 17-5 shows an example of the effects that the GraphicsPrototype aspect has on an application's class.

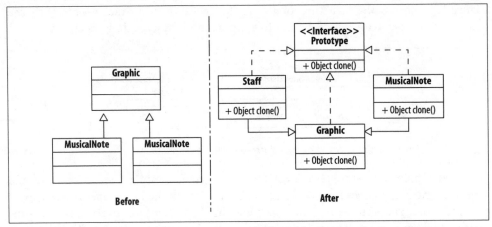

Figure 17-5. How the static application structure is affected by the GraphicsPrototype aspect

Figure 17-6 shows how the new prototype pattern behavior interacts in an example application.

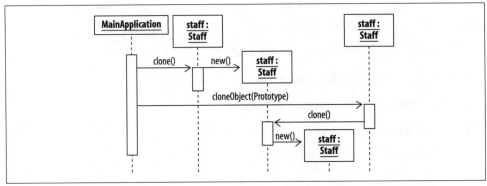

Figure 17-6. Using the new prototype behavior of the Staff class

See Also

Using the declare keyword to affect a class hierarchies static structure is explained in more detail in Recipe 16.2; the Director aspect-oriented design pattern is explained in Recipe 23.3.

17.3   Implementing the Abstract Factory Pattern

Problem

You want to apply the abstract factory pattern using AspectJ.

Solution

The *abstract factory* pattern supports groups of related classes being instantiated while shielding the clients of the factory from the exact implementations.

To implement the abstract factory pattern using AspectJ, create an aspect that can remove the abstract factory pattern's reliance on an abstract base class using static cross-cutting techniques to provide default implementations of the factory methods.

Discussion

Creating a generic factory using abstract aspects makes no sense because the factory contains methods specific to the objects that can be created. The only advantage an AspectJ implementation offers to this design pattern is the ability to remove the reliance on an abstract base class for the abstract factory and replace it with a simple interface. This means that the specialized factories can inherit from other more appropriate classes rather than having use their one allowed inheritance relationship to support the design pattern.

Example 17-5 shows how the abstract factory pattern could be applied to the factory needs of a simple application by providing default implementations of the methods declared in a Java interface.

Example 17-5. Applying the abstract factory pattern using aspects

```
public interface ComputerFactory
{
    public Computer createPentiumProcessorComputer( );

    public Computer createComputerWithHardDisk(HardDisk hardDisk);
}

public aspect DefaultComputerFactoryImplementation
{

    public Computer ComputerFactory.createPentiumProcessorComputer( )
    {
        Processor processor = new Processor("Pentium 4 : 9089085043");
        Motherboard motherboard = new Motherboard("019283", processor);
        HardDisk hardDisk = new HardDisk("738947");
        FloppyDisk floppyDisk = new FloppyDisk("93746");
        Computer computer = new Computer("12345", motherboard, hardDisk, floppyDisk);
        return computer;
    }

    public Computer ComputerFactory.createComputerWithHardDisk(HardDisk hardDisk)
    {
        Processor processor = new Processor("Pentium Standard : 123478");
        Motherboard motherboard = new Motherboard("434244", processor);
        FloppyDisk floppyDisk = new FloppyDisk("432434");
```

```
        Computer computer = new Computer("56789", motherboard, hardDisk, floppyDisk);
        return computer;
    }
}
```

See Also

Chapter 16 contains recipes that show how static cross-cutting techniques can be used to extend classes and provide default implementations of interface elements.

17.4   Implementing the Factory Method Pattern

Problem

You want to apply the factory method pattern using AspectJ.

Solution

The *factory method* pattern is similar to the abstract factory pattern in that it provides mechanisms by which the exact implementation of an object is decoupled from the clients of the factory. However, the factory method provides a single method for instantiating different implementations of a single interface.

The abstract class that contains the abstract factory method is implemented by specialized classes that explicitly override the factory method to provide mechanisms for instantiating different implementations of the desired object.

To implement the factory method pattern using AspectJ, use the same mechanisms as the abstract factory pattern to create an aspect that can remove the factory method pattern's reliance on an abstract base class using static cross-cutting techniques, providing a default implementation of the factory method or methods.

Discussion

A specialized aspect is shown in Example 17-6 that provides a default implementation for the factory method.

Example 17-6. Applying the factory method pattern using aspects

```
public interface ComputerCreator
{
    public Computer createComputer(String serial);
}

public aspect DefaultComputerCreatorImplementation
{
    public void ComputerCreator.createComputerAndPrintInventory(String serial)
    {
```

```
    System.out.println("Inventory of computerparts:");
    System.out.println(this.createComputer(serial).toString( ));
  }
}
```

Traditionally, the ComputerCreator interface in this solution would be an abstract class. However, static cross-cutting techniques can provide more freedom when applying the factory method design pattern by removing the need for the abstract base class.

See Also

Chapter 16 contains recipes that show static cross-cutting techniques for extending classes and providing default implementations of interface elements; Recipe 20.3 shows how to decouple the decision as to which implementation classes of an interface are instantiated solely using aspects.

17.5   Implementing the Builder Pattern

Problem

You want to apply the builder pattern using AspectJ.

Solution

The *builder* pattern captures the complex steps that may be needed in the creation of a particular object. The steps are implemented as methods on the builder class; after each of the required steps has been completed, then the builder can be called to create the resulting built object.

To implement the builder pattern using AspectJ, create an aspect that adds to the top-level builder class a field to store the build result and a method to access that result using static cross-cutting techniques. This enables the builder to be an interface and not an abstract class.

Discussion

The builder pattern can be implemented using aspects, as shown in Example 17-7.

Example 17-7. Applying the builder pattern using aspects

```
public interface TextPhraseBuilder
{
    public void buildHeader(String title);

    public void buildBody(String content);
```

Example 17-7. Applying the builder pattern using aspects (continued)

```
    public void buildFooter(String closingContent);

    public String getResult( );
}

public aspect TextPhraseBuilderDefaultImplementation
{
    public StringBuffer TextPhraseBuilder.result = new StringBuffer( );

    public String TextPhraseBuilder.getResult( )
    {
        return result.toString( );
    }

    /**
     * Declares a compiler error that gets reported if other classes
     * (except Builders or this aspect) try to access the result variable.
     */
    declare error : (
        set(public StringBuffer TextPhraseBuilder +.result)
          || get(public StringBuffer TextPhraseBuilder +.result))
          && !(within(TextPhraseBuilder +)
          || within(TextPhraseBuilderDefaultImplementation)) :
          "variable result is aspect protected. use getResult( ) to access it";
}
```

The TextPhraseDefaultImplementationBuilder aspect provides a default implementation of the getResult( ) method. This frees the specialized builders from exhausting their single inheritance relationship with an abstract base class. The getResult( ) method provides access to the result field that is also added to the interface and its implementing classes to provide a place to store the result of the builder.

Ideally, the result field would be declared protected since it is only used internally by the TextPhraseBuilder and its subclasses. The AspectJ compiler will not allow protected fields to be introduced on an interface, public is the only option.

This leads to a second problem. How can the pattern's use be constrained so direct access of the public result field is flagged to the developers as the wrong mechanism by which to obtain the fields value? The solution is provided by another powerful feature of AspectJ, the ability to define new compile time checking and error notifications.

Until aspect orientation, the compiler had been a fairly rigid piece of software, not to be tampered with by the developers. However, a few circumstances occur when interaction with the compiler can influence its validation of the code could be useful and this feature is available with AspectJ.

The TextPhraseBuilderDefaultImplementation aspect defines an error to be triggered by the compiler should your code attempt to access the newly added result attribute directly. This will provide a final check that the rules of the pattern are being followed. Although the problem being protected against is a disadvantage of the aspect-oriented implementation of the design pattern, the problem is reduced by incorporating this compile time check.

See Also

Chapter 16 provides specific recipes showing static cross-cutting techniques for extending classes, providing default implementations, and extending the compilers capabilities.

CHAPTER 18

Implementing Structural Object-Oriented Design Patterns

18.0   Introduction

Continuing on from the creational design patterns in the previous chapter, you are going to harness the advantages in implementing structural design patterns using AspectJ.

Although the benefits of applying aspects vary depending on the specific pattern, structural object-oriented (OO) design patterns gain more from aspects than their creational cousins. This is mostly due to the cross-cutting and generic nature of structural design patterns which tends to lend itself nicely to aspect-oriented implementations.

Unfortunately, aspect orientation does not provide any real benefits when designing or implementing the façade pattern. The goal of the façade is to provide a simpler interface to a larger collection of objects of complex components. This goal can be achieved in a system where the source code is known using standard classes and method calls, requiring none of the additional mechanisms of AspectJ.

18.1   Implementing the Composite Pattern

Problem

You want to apply the composite pattern using AspectJ.

Solution

The *composite* pattern provides the capability to group objects together in a collection and interact with the group as a whole in a similar manner as you would interact with an individual member of the group.

Example 18-1 uses the Director aspect-oriented design pattern (see Chapter 23) to provide a generic implementation of the composite pattern using AspectJ.

Example 18-1. Using an aspect to define the composite pattern

```
public abstract aspect CompositePattern
{
    public interface Component
    {
    }

    protected interface Composite extends Component
    {
    }

    protected interface Leaf extends Component
    {
    }

    private WeakHashMap perComponentChildren = new WeakHashMap( );

    private Vector getChildren(Component s)
    {
        Vector children = (Vector) perComponentChildren.get(s);
        if (children == null)
        {
            children = new Vector( );
            perComponentChildren.put(s, children);
        }
        return children;
    }

    public void addChild(Composite composite, Component component)
    {
        getChildren(composite).add(component);
    }

    public void removeChild(Composite composite, Component component)
    {
        getChildren(composite).remove(component);
    }

    public Enumeration getAllChildren(Component c) {
        return getChildren(c).elements( );
    }

    public interface Visitor {

        public void doOperation(Component c);
    }

    public void recurseOperation(Component c, Visitor v) {
        for (Enumeration enum = getAllChildren(c); enum.hasMoreElements( );) {
            Component child = (Component) enum.nextElement( );
            v.doOperation(child);
        }
    }
```

Example 18-1. Using an aspect to define the composite pattern (continued)

```
public interface FunctionVisitor
{
    public Object doFunction(Component c);
}

public Enumeration recurseFunction(Component c, FunctionVisitor fv)
{
    Vector results = new Vector();
    for (Enumeration enum = getAllChildren(c); enum.hasMoreElements();) {
    Component child = (Component) enum.nextElement();
      results.add(fv.doFunction(child));
    }
    return results.elements();
}
}
```

Discussion

The `CompositePattern` aspect defines the `Composite` and `Leaf` interfaces to be applied to classes within your application playing those roles. The aspect uses the visitor pattern to recursively visit and work with each of the components of a composite.

Figure 18-1 shows the structure of the `CompositePattern` abstract aspect and the interfaces and behavior that it defines to support the composite design pattern.

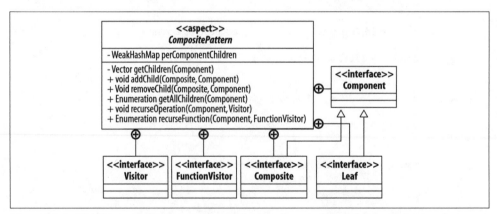

Figure 18-1. The CompositePattern aspect and the interfaces it defines for the design pattern's roles

This `CompositePattern` abstract aspect is extended into specialized subaspects that specify the classes that play the `Composite` and `Leaf` roles. Example 18-2 shows how the abstract `CompositePattern` aspect can be applied for a specific application.

Example 18-2. Applying the CompositePattern aspect to a target application

```
public aspect GraphicsComposite extends CompositePattern
{
```

Example 18-2. Applying the CompositePattern aspect to a target application (continued)

```
declare parents : Window implements Composite;
declare parents : Line implements Leaf;
declare parents : Rectangle implements Leaf;

public void Component.draw(PrintStream s)
{
    s.println("Drawing: " + this);
}

public void Composite.draw(final PrintStream s)
{
    s.println("Composite: " + this);
    GraphicsComposite.aspectOf().recurseOperation(this, new Visitor( )
        {
            public void doOperation(Component c)
            {
                c.draw(s);
            }
        });
}

public void Leaf.draw(PrintStream s)
{
    s.println("Drawing Leaf: " + this);
}
}
```

Figure 18-2 shows an example set of application classes before the GraphicsComposite aspect is applied.

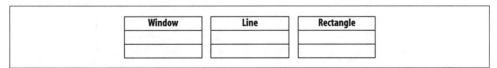

Figure 18-2. The Window, Line, and Rectangle business logic classes

Figure 18-3 shows the effects of applying the GraphicsComposite aspect shown in Example 18-2 to a set of application classes.

Figure 18-4 shows how the new composite behavior of the Window class is interacted with in an example application.

See Also

More information on the extension of existing classes using aspects can be found in Chapter 16; the Director aspect-oriented design pattern is explained in Recipe 23.3.

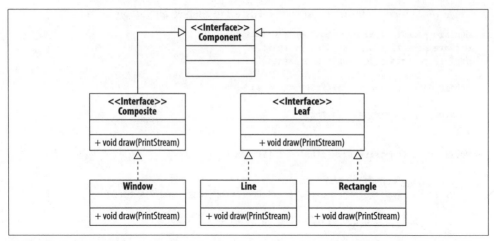

Figure 18-3. *The static structure after the composite pattern has been applied to the Window, Line, and Rectangle classes*

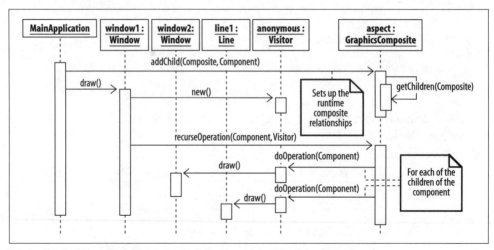

Figure 18-4. *Using the new composite behavior of the Window class*

18.2   Implementing the Flyweight Pattern

Problem

You want to apply the flyweight pattern using AspectJ.

Solution

The *flyweight* pattern provides mechanisms by which fine-grained objects can be incorporated into an OO design without incurring a resource and performance penalty by sharing the objects where appropriate. A heavyweight object encapsulates the actual data to be referred to by potentially many flyweight objects.

The abstract aspect in Example 18-3 uses the Director aspect-oriented design pattern (see Chapter 23) to provide a template by which application specific aspects can apply the flyweight pattern.

Example 18-3. Using an abstract aspect to define the flyweight pattern

```
public abstract aspect FlyweightPattern
{
    private Hashtable flyweightPool = new Hashtable( );

    public interface Flyweight
    {
    };

    protected abstract pointcut flyweightCreation(Object key);

    Object around(Object key) : flyweightCreation(key) &&
        !within(com.oreilly.aspectjcookbook.oopatterns.FlyweightPattern+)
    {
        return this.checkFlyweight(key);
    }

    public synchronized Flyweight checkFlyweight(Object key)
    {
        if (flyweightPool.containsKey(key))
        {
            return (Flyweight) flyweightPool.get(key);
        }
        else
        {
            Flyweight flyweight = createNewFlyweight(key);
            flyweightPool.put(key, flyweight);
            return flyweight;
        }
    }

    protected abstract Flyweight createNewFlyweight(Object key);
}
```

Discussion

Figure 18-5 shows the structure of the FlyweightPattern abstract aspect and the interfaces and behavior that it defines to support the flyweight design pattern.

The abstract FlyweightPattern aspect in Example 18-3 contains a flyweight pool collection. This collection, implemented as a hash table, remembers the heavyweight objects that have already been created so flyweights can be set to the existing heavyweight objects where available.

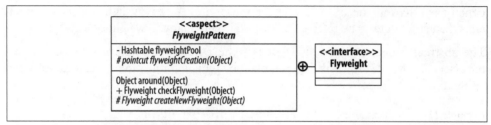

Figure 18-5. The FlyweightPattern aspect and the interfaces it defines for the design pattern's roles

Because the abstract aspect does not know how to create the different concrete flyweight objects, it defines an abstract method createNewFlyweight(...). This abstract method allows subaspects to implement how they will create the specific flyweight objects.

The FlyweightPattern aspect also contains the flyweightCreation(Object) abstract pointcut used to capture when objects, designated as flyweights, are being created. This pointcut enables the FlyweightPattern to override the creation of the flyweight objects using the associated around() advice to apply the design pattern's rules by checking whether an existing heavyweight object can be employed using the checkFlyweight(..) method, creating a new heavyweight object if necessary.

The aspect in Example 18-4 shows how the abstract FlyweightPattern aspect can be applied for a specific application.

Example 18-4. Applying the FlyweightPattern aspect to an application's classes

```
public aspect PrintableCharacterFlyweight extends FlyweightPattern
{
    declare parents : PrintableCharacter implements Flyweight;

    protected pointcut flyweightCreation(Object key) :
        call(public com.oreilly.aspectjcookbook.PrintableCharacter.new(Character))
        && args(key);

    protected Flyweight createNewFlyweight(Object key)
    {
        return new PrintableCharacter((Character) key);
    }
}
```

The PrintableCharacterFlyweight specifies that the PrintableCharacter class is to be managed as a flyweight. The flyweightCreation(..) pointcut is implemented to capture when the PrintableCharacter objects are created. The createNewFlyweight(Object) method is implemented to create new PrintableCharacter objects where necessary.

Figure 18-6 shows the effects before and after the PrintableCharacterFlyweight aspect is applied to an application.

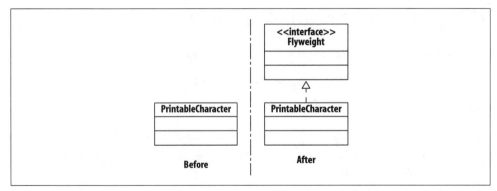

Figure 18-6. The effects of applying the flyweight pattern to the PrintableCharacter class

Figure 18-7 shows how the new flyweight behavior of the PrintableCharacter class behaves in an example application.

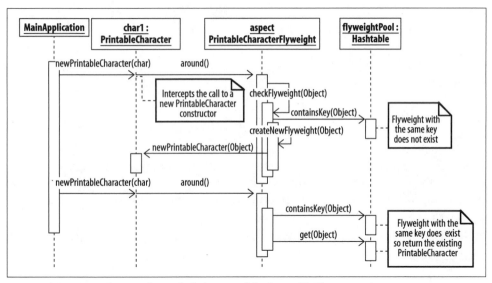

Figure 18-7. Using the new flyweight behavior of the PrintableCharacter class

See Also

For more information on defining abstract aspects and specializing them, please refer to the recipes in Chapter 15; the Director aspect-oriented design pattern is explained in Recipe 23.3.

18.3   Implementing the Adapter Pattern

Problem

You want to apply the adapter pattern using AspectJ.

Solution

The *adapter* pattern provides a means of changing the message sent from one class to the message expected by the real destination class, adapting the messages to glue two classes together.

Example 18-5 shows how to define an application specific adapter pattern aspect.

Example 18-5. Adapting an existing class using aspects

```
public aspect PrinterScreenAdapter
{

  declare parents : Screen implements Printer;

  public void Screen.print(String s)
  {
    outputToScreen(s);
  }
}
```

Discussion

The specific PrinterScreenAdapter aspect extends the behavior of the class that is to adapt to the new capabilities required of it by using AspectJ's capabilities to extend an existing class with new methods and potentially new parent classes, being careful at all times to respect the original capabilities of the class.

Figure 18-8 shows the effects before and after the PrinterScreenAdapter aspect is applied to a Screen class that is adapted to support printing behavior.

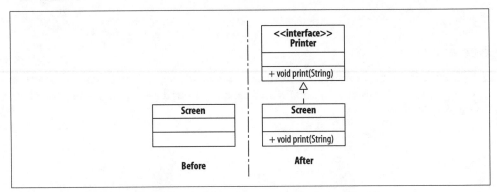

Figure 18-8. The effects of applying the adapter pattern to the Screen class

See Also

The recipes in Chapter 16 provide more information on how to extend existing classes and incorporate interfaces when defining aspects.

18.4 Implementing the Bridge Pattern

Problem

You want to apply the bridge pattern using AspectJ.

Solution

The *bridge* pattern decouples a class from the underlying characteristics of one particular implementation so different implementations can be applied without affecting the class's clients.

Example 18-6 shows how to define an application specific bridge pattern aspect.

Example 18-6. Bridging between an implementation independent window and the means by which it is implemented using a specific windowing system

```
public class Window
{
    public void drawText(String text)
    {

    }

    public void drawRect( )
    {

    }
}

public aspect XWindowBridge perthis(captureAllBridgedCalls( ))
{
    private XWindow imp = new XWindow( );

    public pointcut captureDrawText(String text) :
        execution(public void Window.drawText(String))
        && args(text);

    public pointcut captureDrawRect() : execution(public void Window.drawRect( ));

    public pointcut captureAllBridgedCalls( ) :
        captureDrawText(String)
        || captureDrawRect( );

    void around(String text) : captureDrawText(text)
    {
```

Example 18-6. Bridging between an implementation independent window and the means by which it is implemented using a specific windowing system (continued)

```
        imp.drawText(text);
    }

    void around() : captureDrawRect()
    {
        imp.drawLine( );
        imp.drawLine( );
        imp.drawLine( );
        imp.drawLine( );
    }
}
```

Discussion

Figure 18-9 shows the structure of the XWindowBridge aspect and the behavior that it defines to support the bridge design pattern.

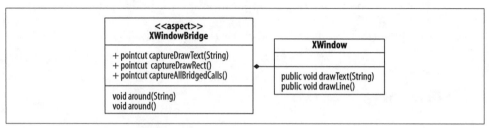

Figure 18-9. The XWindowBridge aspect's structure

The XWindowBridge aspect captures all of the methods on the Window class that need to be channeled to specific calls on the XWindow class. For example, the drawRect( ) method on the Window class results in four calls on the XWindow class, but by using the bridge pattern the Window class does not need to have those calls hard coded into its behavior. In Example 18-6, the Window class does not know exactly how it is going to be implemented on different systems, but that is all taken care of by the XWindowBridge aspect.

By using the perthis(..) aspect instantiation policy, a new aspect is created for every new bridged Window object as specified by the captureAllBridgedCalls( ) pointcut. This means that every Window object has its own copy of the XWindow implementation object. If you wanted to share the XWindow object across multiple Window objects, then all you need is to delete the perthis(..) policy and remove the redundant captureAllBridgedCalls( ) pointcut definition.

If another means were used for drawing windows, then a separate aspect that bridges the calls on the Window class differently could be created and woven into the application instead of the XWindowBridge aspect.

Figure 18-10 shows how the new bridged behavior of the Window class behaves in an example application.

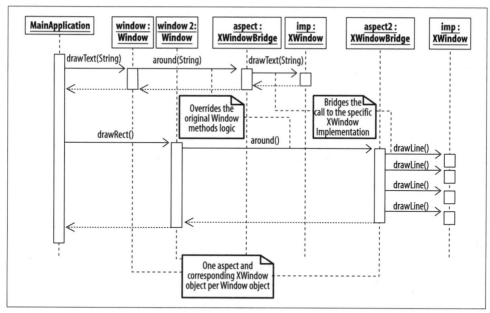

Figure 18-10. Using the bridged behavior of the Window class

See Also

The execution(Signature) pointcut is explained in Recipe 4.4; the args([Types | Identifiers]) is explained in Recipe 11.3; the around( ) form of advice is shown in Recipe 13.4; Recipe 14.2 explains perthis(Pointcut) aspect instantiation policy; specifying the aspects that are built into an application at compile time is covered in Recipe 2.6.

18.5   Implementing the Decorator Pattern

Problem

You want to apply the decorator pattern using AspectJ.

Solution

The *decorator* pattern extends the behavior of a classes methods while maintaining its existing public interface without the class knowing about or caring about the extension.

Example 18-7 shows an abstract aspect that lays the foundation of the decorator pattern that can then be applied using more specific subaspects in a target application.

Example 18-7. Using aspects to define the decorator pattern

```
public abstract aspect DecoratorPattern
{
    public interface DecoratedComponent
    {
    };

    private boolean DecoratedComponent.decorated = false;

    public void DecoratedComponent.setDecorated(boolean decorated)
    {
        this.decorated = decorated;
    }

    public void DecoratedComponent.isDecorated(boolean decorated)
    {
        return this.decorated ;
    }
}
```

Discussion

Figure 18-11 shows the structure of the DecoratorPattern abstract aspect and the interfaces and behavior that it defines to support the decorator design pattern.

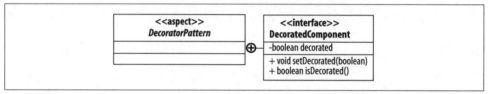

Figure 18-11. The DecoratorPattern aspect and the interfaces and behavior it defines for the design pattern's roles

The DecoratorPattern abstract aspect defines the DecoratedComponent interface to provide a common base interface for all classes that are to be decorated implement. The decorated field is introduced into those classes along with a pair of accessor and modifier methods.

Example 18-8 shows how the abstract DecoratorPattern aspect could be applied for a specific application. The TextDisplayDecorator specifies that the TextDisplay class can be decorated, and that the display(..) method is decorated before and after the method is called if the particular object is decorated.

Example 18-8. Applying the DecoratorPattern to an application's classes

```
public aspect TextDisplayDecorator extends DecoratorPattern
{
    declare parents : TextDisplay implements DecoratedComponent;
```

```
public pointcut selectDecorators(Object object) :
    call(public void TextDisplay.display(String))
    && target(object);

before(Object object) : selectDecorators(object) &&
    if(((DecoratedComponent)object).getDecorated)
{
    System.out.print("<Decoration>");
}

after(Object object) : selectDecorators(object) &&
    if(((DecoratedComponent)object).getDecorated)
{
    System.out.print("</Decoration>");
}
}
```

Figure 18-12 shows the effects when the TextDisplayDecorator aspect, shown in Example 18-8, is applied to the TextDisplay class.

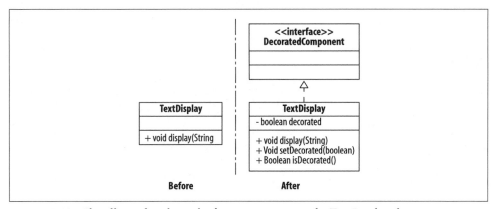

Figure 18-12. The effects of applying the decorator pattern to the TextDisplay class

Figure 18-13 shows how the new decorated behavior of the TextDisplay class behaves in an example application.

See Also

The recipes in Chapter 16 contain more details on the mechanisms by which existing classes can be extended using aspects and the declare keyword; the call(Signature) pointcut is covered in Recipe 4.1; exposing join point context is examined in Recipe 13.2; the args(Type or Identifier) pointcut is described in Recipe 11.3.

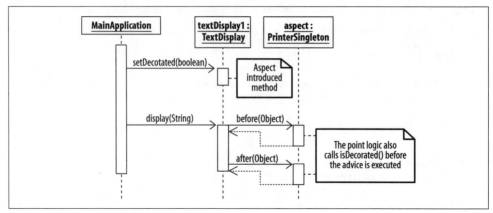

Figure 18-13. Using the decorated behavior of the TextDisplay class

18.6   Implementing the Proxy Pattern

Problem

You want to apply the proxy pattern using AspectJ.

Solution

The *proxy* pattern allows the developer to provide a surrogate object in place of the actual object in case access to the real object needs to be delegated or controlled.

Example 18-9 uses the Director aspect-oriented design pattern (see Chapter 23) to provide an abstract implementation of the proxy pattern.

Example 18-9. Using an abstract aspect to define the proxy pattern

```
public abstract aspect ProxyPattern
{
   protected interface Subject
   {
   }

   protected abstract pointcut requestTriggered();

   private pointcut accessByCaller(Object caller) : requestTriggered() && this(caller);

   private pointcut accessByUnknown() : requestTriggered() && !accessByCaller(Object);

   Object around(Object caller, Subject subject) : accessByCaller(caller)
      && target(subject)
   {
      if (reject(caller, subject, thisJoinPoint))
      {
         return rejectRequest(caller, subject, thisJoinPoint);
```

Example 18-9. Using an abstract aspect to define the proxy pattern (continued)

```
        }
        else if (delegate(caller, subject, thisJoinPoint))
        {
            return delegateRequest(caller, subject, thisJoinPoint);
        }
        return proceed(caller, subject);
    }

    Object around(Subject subject) : accessByUnknown( )
        && target(subject)
    {
        // Without a caller then reject does not really make sense
        // as there is no way of deciding to reject or not
        if (delegate(null, subject, thisJoinPoint))
        {
            return delegateRequest(null, subject, thisJoinPoint);
        }
        return proceed(subject);
    }

    protected abstract boolean reject(
        Object caller,
        Subject subject,
        JoinPoint joinPoint);

    protected abstract boolean delegate(
        Object caller,
        Subject subject,
        JoinPoint joinPoint);

    protected abstract Object rejectRequest(
        Object caller,
        Subject subject,
        JoinPoint joinPoint);

    protected abstract Object delegateRequest(
        Object caller,
        Subject subject,
        JoinPoint joinPoint);
}
```

Discussion

Figure 18-14 shows the structure of the ProxyPattern abstract aspect and the interfaces and behavior that it defines to support the proxy design pattern.

The abstract aspect definition of the proxy pattern in Example 18-9 encapsulates the role of the Subject applied to objects that need proxy logic defined. For each of the two possible situations that a proxy is applied, delegation and protection, there is a defined route by which calls to the subject are examined and delegated or denied depending on the logic contained in the inheriting subaspects.

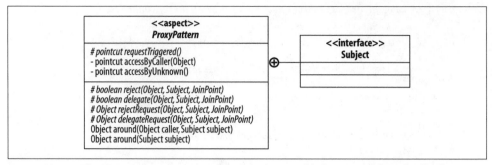

Figure 18-14. The ProxyPattern aspect and the interfaces and behavior it defines for the design pattern's roles

The most important advantage of this aspect implementation of the proxy pattern is that the original classes of the target application do not have to know they are going to be involved in a proxy situation. This is absolutely key since collections of objects in an application can be subjected to security and other proxy sensitive concerns without affecting the design goals of the original classes.

Example 18-10 shows how the abstract `ProxyPattern` aspect could be applied for a specific application. The `DelegationProxy` aspect defines a proxy that intercepts and delegates calls to the subject objects.

Example 18-10. Applying delegation using the ProxyPattern aspect

```
public aspect DelegationProxy extends ProxyPattern
{
    declare parents : RealSubject implements Subject;

    protected pointcut requestTriggered( ) : call(* RealSubject.write(..));

    protected boolean reject(
        Object caller,
        Subject subject,
        JoinPoint joinPoint)
    {
        return false;
    }

    protected boolean delegate(
        Object caller,
        Subject subject,
        JoinPoint joinPoint)
    {
        return true;
    }

    protected Object rejectRequest(
        Object caller,
        Subject subject,
```

Example 18-10. Applying delegation using the ProxyPattern aspect (continued)

```
    JoinPoint joinPoint)
{
    return null;
}

protected Object delegateRequest(
    Object caller,
    Subject subject,
    JoinPoint joinPoint)
{
    Object[] args = joinPoint.getArgs();
    if (args != null)
    {
        AnotherRealSubject.write((String) args[0]);
    }
    else
    {
        AnotherRealSubject.write("");
    }
    return null;
}
}
```

Figure 18-15 shows the effects when the DelegationProxy aspect is applied to the RealSubject class.

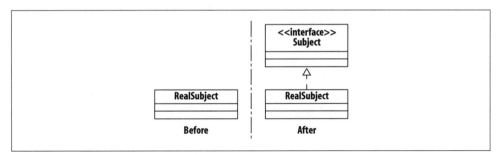

Figure 18-15. The effects of applying the proxy pattern to the RealSubject class

Figure 18-16 shows an example interaction with the aspect-oriented proxy pattern features.

See Also

For more information on defining abstract aspects and specializing them, see the recipes in Chapter 16; the call(Signature) pointcut is covered in Recipe 4.1; exposing join point context is examined in Recipe 13.2; the args(Type or Identifier) pointcut is described in Recipe 11.3; Recipe 11.1 describes the this(Type or Identifier)

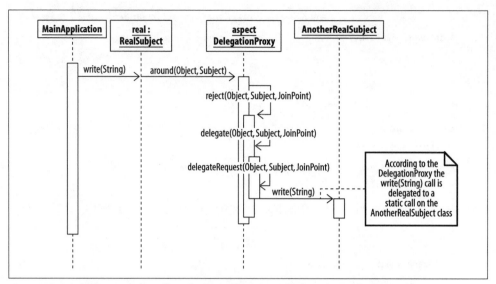

Figure 18-16. Delegating the call to the write(String) method on the RealSubject class

pointcut in more detail; the target(Type or Identifier) pointcut is examined in Recipe 11.2; Recipe 13.4 provides more detail on the proceed( ) call and its usage within around( ) advice; the Director aspect-oriented design pattern is explained in Recipe 23.3.

CHAPTER 19

Implementing Behavioral Object-Oriented Design Patterns

19.0 Introduction

The final category in this trio of design pattern chapters investigates how behavioral patterns can benefit from an aspect-oriented implementation.

Behavioral patterns are generic guidelines for structuring interactions and locating behavior throughout the participating classes. The recipes in this chapter show that these design patterns can gain considerable architectural advantages from using aspect orientation.

As with the structural patterns from the previous chapter, some GoF patterns simply don't seem to benefit significantly from aspects. In the case of behavioral aspects, this means that the Interpreter design pattern is not included in this chapter although the research, being completed by Jan Hanneman at *http://www.cs.ubc.ca/~jan/ AODPs/,* may uncover approaches that further refine the mechanisms presented in this chapter and perhaps lead to improvements that can be made to the interpreter patterns implementation using aspect orientation.

19.1 Implementing the Observer Pattern

Problem

You want to apply the observer pattern using AspectJ.

Solution

The *observer* pattern allows the designer to create dependencies between objects such that if one object's state changes the other objects will be notified and may act accordingly.

Example 19-1 uses the Director aspect-oriented design pattern (see Chapter 23) to provide a generic aspect implementation of the observer pattern.

Example 19-1. Defining the observer pattern using an abstract aspect

```
public abstract aspect ObserverPattern
{
    protected interface Subject
    {
        public void addObserver(Observer observer);
        public void removeObserver(Observer observer);
    }

    protected interface Observer
    {
        public void notifyOfChange(Subject subject);
    }

    private List Subject.observers = new LinkedList();

    public void Subject.addObserver(Observer observer)
    {
        this.observers.add(observer);
    }

    public void Subject.removeObserver(Observer observer)
    {
        this.observers.remove(observer);
    }

    private synchronized void Subject.notifyObservers()
    {
        Iterator iter = this.observers.iterator();
        while (iter.hasNext())
        {
            ((Observer)iter.next()).notifyOfChange(this);
        }
    }

    protected abstract pointcut subjectChange(Subject s);

    after(Subject subject) : subjectChange(subject)
    {
        subject.notifyObservers();
    }
}
```

Discussion

The ObserverPattern aspect defines the Subject and Observer roles as interfaces that can be applied to specific classes by inheriting subaspects. With these roles defined, the remainder of the ObserverPattern aspect implements the mechanism by which to notify the observers when a subject changes.

Figure 19-1 shows the structure of the ObserverPattern abstract aspect and the interfaces and behavior that it defines to support the observer design pattern.

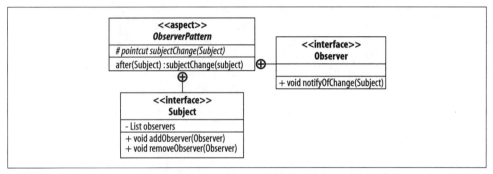

Figure 19-1. The ObserverPattern aspect and the interfaces it defines for the design pattern's roles

Example 19-2 shows how the abstract `ObserverPattern` aspect could be applied for a specific application.

Example 19-2. Applying the ObserverPattern to an application's classes

```
public aspect ConcreteClassAObserver extends ObserverPattern
{
    declare parents : ConcreteClassB implements Subject;

    declare parents : ConcreteClassA implements Observer;

    protected pointcut subjectChange(Subject s) :
        call(* ConcreteClassB.set*(..))
        && target(s);

    public void ConcreteClassA.notifyOfChange(Subject subject)
    {
        this.doSomething(
            "ConcreteClassA was notified of a change on " + subject);
    }
}
```

The `ConcreteClassAObserver` applies the `Observer` interface to the `ConcreteClassA` class and the `Subject` interface to the `ConcreteClassB` class. This means `ConcreteClassA` objects that are registered as observers are notified when a modifier is called on a `ConcreteClassB` object. The specifics of what methods are called when a notification is to be made are declared in the `notifyOfChange(Subject)` method added to the `ConcreteClassA` class.

Figure 19-2 shows an example set of application classes before the `ConcreteClassAOb-server` aspect is applied.

Figure 19-3 shows the effects after applying the `ConcreteClassAObserver` aspect to the `ConcreteClassA` and `ConcreteClassB` classes.

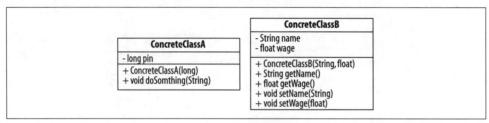

Figure 19-2. The ConcreteClassA and ConcreteClassB classes

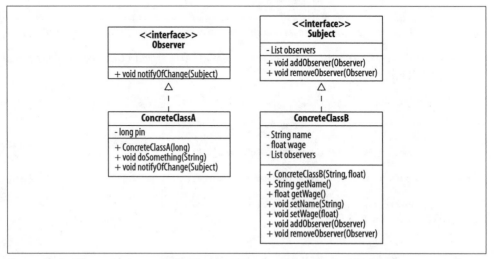

Figure 19-3. The static structure after the observer pattern has been applied to the ConcreteClassA and ConcreteClassB classes

See Also

The recipes in Chapter 16 contain more details on the mechanisms by which existing classes can be extended using aspects and the declare keyword; the call(Signature) pointcut is covered in Recipe 4.1; the execution(Signature) pointcut is described in Recipe 4.4; exposing join point context is examined in Recipe 13.2; the target(Type or Identifier) pointcut is examined in Recipe 11.2; the Director aspect-oriented design pattern is explained in Recipe 23.3.

Figure 19-4 shows how the new observer behavior of the ConcreteClassA class and the subject behavior of the ConcreteClassB class is interacted within an example application.

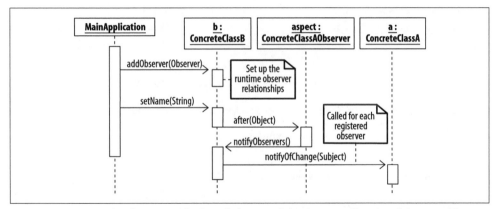

Figure 19-4. Using the observer and subject behavior of the ConcreteClassA and ConcreteClassB classes

19.2 Implementing the Command Pattern

Problem

You want to apply the command pattern using AspectJ.

Solution

The *command* design pattern supports the encapsulation of requests as objects within their own right. Single or multiple operations can be combined into a request or transaction depending on their purpose. Once the request object has been constructed, it can be managed as a separate entity from the originating object.

Example 19-3 uses the Director aspect-oriented design pattern (see Chapter 23) to provide an abstract aspect that can be used to apply the command pattern.

Example 19-3. Defining the command pattern using aspects

```
public abstract aspect CommandPattern
{
    public interface Command
    {
        public void executeCommand(CommandReceiver receiver);

        public boolean isExecutable();
    }

    public interface CommandInvoker
    {
    }
```

Example 19-3. Defining the command pattern using aspects (continued)

```
public interface CommandReceiver
{
}

private WeakHashMap mappingInvokerToCommand = new WeakHashMap( );

public Object setCommand(CommandInvoker invoker, Command command)
{
   return mappingInvokerToCommand.put(invoker, command);
}

public Object removeCommand(CommandInvoker invoker)
{
   return setCommand(invoker, null);
}

public Command getCommand(CommandInvoker invoker)
{
   return (Command) mappingInvokerToCommand.get(invoker);
}

private WeakHashMap mappingCommandToReceiver = new WeakHashMap( );

public Object setReceiver(Command command, CommandReceiver receiver)
{
   return mappingCommandToReceiver.put(command, receiver);
}

public CommandReceiver getReceiver(Command command)
{
   return (CommandReceiver) mappingCommandToReceiver.get(command);
}

protected abstract pointcut commandTrigger(CommandInvoker invoker);

after(CommandInvoker invoker) : commandTrigger(invoker)
{
   Command command = getCommand(invoker);
   if (command != null)
   {
      CommandReceiver receiver = getReceiver(command);
      command.executeCommand(receiver);
   } else
   {
      // Do nothing: This Invoker has no associated command
   }
}

protected pointcut setCommandTrigger(CommandInvoker invoker, Command command);

after(CommandInvoker invoker, Command command) : setCommandTrigger(invoker, command)
{
```

Example 19-3. Defining the command pattern using aspects (continued)

```
        if (invoker != null)
            setCommand(invoker, command);
    }

    protected pointcut removeCommandTrigger(CommandInvoker invoker);

    after(CommandInvoker invoker) : removeCommandTrigger(invoker)
    {
        if (invoker != null)
            removeCommand(invoker);
    }

    public boolean Command.isExecutable( )
    {
        return true;
    }
}
```

Discussion

The CommandPattern abstract aspect defines the mechanisms by which the roles of a CommandInvoker, a Command, and a CommandReceiver can be set up and interact with each other. These abstract roles are assigned to application specific classes by specialized subaspects.

Figure 19-5 shows the structure of the CommandPattern abstract aspect and the interfaces and behavior that it defines to support the command design pattern.

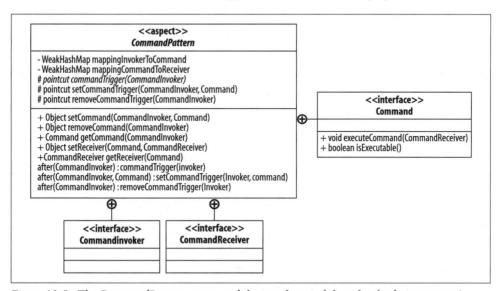

Figure 19-5. The CommandPattern aspect and the interfaces it defines for the design pattern's roles

Example 19-4 shows how the abstract CommandPattern aspect could be applied for a specific application.

Example 19-4. Applying the CommandPattern aspect to an application's classes

```
public aspect ConcreteCommand extends CommandPattern
{
    declare parents : TimedEvent implements CommandInvoker;
    declare parents : Printer implements CommandReceiver;
    declare parents : VCardPrinter implements CommandReceiver;
    declare parents : BusinessCard implements Command;

    public void BusinessCard.executeCommand(CommandReceiver receiver)
    {
        if (receiver instanceof Printer)
        {
            ((Printer) receiver).println(this.toString());
        } else
        {
            ((VCardPrinter) receiver).printVCard(this);
        }
    }

    public void executeCommand(CommandReceiver receiver)
    {
        ((Printer) receiver).println("Command triggered on printer receiver");
    }

    protected pointcut commandTrigger(CommandInvoker invoker) :
        call(void TimedEvent.timedOut())
        && target(invoker);
}
```

Figure 19-6 shows an example set of application classes before the ConcreteCommand aspect is applied. The TimerTask class is used from the Java standard libraries and supports the TimedEvent class in executing at timed intervals.

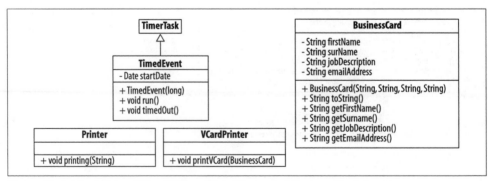

Figure 19-6. The Printer, VCardPrinter, TimedEvent, and BusinessCard classes

Figure 19-7 shows the effects of applying the ConcreteCommand aspect to the TimedEvent, Printer, VCardPrinter, and BusinessCard classes.

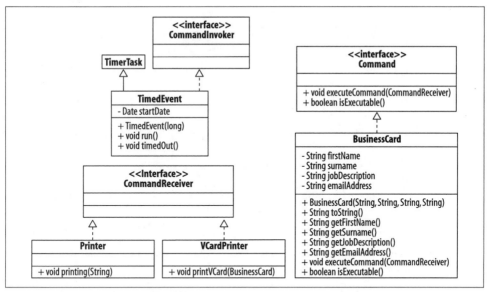

Figure 19-7. The static structure after the command pattern has been applied to the TimedEvent, Printer, VCardPrinter, and BusinessCard classes

Figure 19-8 shows how the new command pattern behavior of the application's classes interact with in an example application.

See Also

The recipes in Chapter 16 contain more details on the mechanisms by which existing classes can be extended using aspects and the declare keyword; aspects and inheritance are covered in Recipe 15.1; the after( ) form of advice is examined in Recipe 13.5; the Director aspect-oriented design pattern is explained in Recipe 23.3.

19.3   Implementing the Iterator Pattern

Problem

You want to apply the iterator pattern using AspectJ.

Solution

The *iterator* pattern provides a mechanism by which to separate the implementation of a collection of objects or an aggregate, as it is sometimes called, from the mechanisms by which the collection is sequentially accessed. The *iterator*, or cursor, is moved along

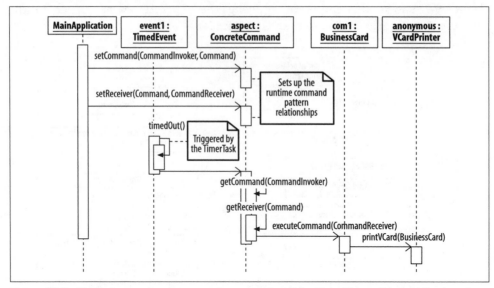

Figure 19-8. Using the command pattern characteristics of the TimedEvent, BusinessCard, and VCardPrinter classes

the aggregate of the objects providing each while hiding the ordering and access implementation details from the users of the aggregate.

Example 19-5 uses the Director aspect-oriented design pattern (see Chapter 23) to provide an abstract aspect that can be used to apply the iterator pattern.

Example 19-5. Using aspects to define the iterator pattern

```
public abstract aspect IteratorPattern
{
    public interface Aggregate
    {
        public Iterator createIterator( );

        public Iterator createReverseIterator( );
    }
}
```

Discussion

The abstract IteratorPattern aspect declares the Aggregate role by defining the interface that an aggregate, meaning any collection of objects that can be iterated over, must fulfill. This interface includes two operations to create a normal or reverse *iterator*. The Java standard libraries make things less complicated here as the generic aspect can use the Iterator interface from the java.util package to meet the iterator role of the pattern.

Figure 19-9 shows the structure of the IteratorPattern abstract aspect and the interfaces and behavior that it defines to support the iterator design pattern.

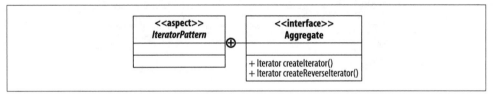

Figure 19-9. The IteratorPattern aspect and the interfaces it defines for the design pattern's roles

Example 19-6 shows how the abstract IteratorPattern aspect could be applied for a specific application.

Example 19-6. Specializing the abstract IteratorPattern aspect for a particular set of classes

```
public aspect EmployeeIteration extends IteratorPattern
{
    declare parents : EmployeeCollection implements Aggregate;

    public Iterator EmployeeCollection.createIterator( )
    {
        return new EmployeeIterator(this, true);
    }

    public Iterator EmployeeCollection.createReverseIterator( )
    {
        return new EmployeeIterator(this, false);
    }
}
```

The EmployeeIteration aspect, along with the supporting EmployeeIterator, declares that the EmployeeCollection is an aggregate and then implements the iterator creation methods for the collection.

Figure 19-10 shows the EmployeeCollection class before and after the EmployeeIteration aspect is applied.

Figure 19-11 shows how the new iterator pattern behavior of the EmployeeCollection class is interacted within an example application.

See Also

For more information on defining abstract aspects and specializing them, see Chapter 15; Chapter 16 contains more details on the mechanisms by which existing classes can be extended using aspects and the declare keyword; the Director aspect-oriented design pattern is explained in Recipe 23.3.

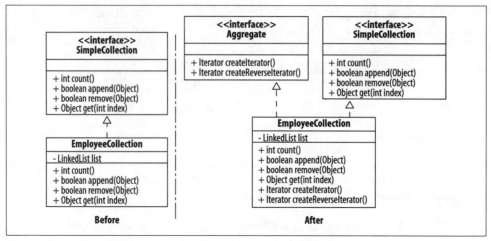

Figure 19-10. The static structure after the iterator pattern has been applied to the EmployeeCollection class

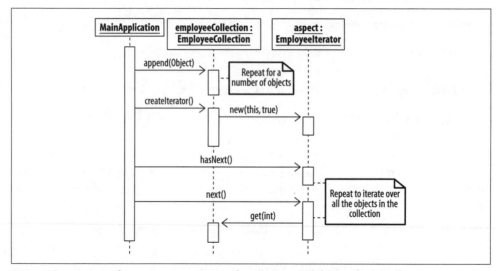

Figure 19-11. Using the new iterator pattern characteristics of the EmployeeCollection class

19.4   Implementing the Mediator Pattern

Problem

You want to apply the mediator pattern using AspectJ.

Solution

The *mediator* pattern allows the separation of potentially a large number of classes, that fit the colleague role, from each other by providing a single point of dependency in the mediator role. The class playing the mediator role minimizes dependencies between the colleague classes by providing a common point to control the different events that are initiated by the colleagues. The mediator accepts the events itself, and then encapsulates the logic that notifies the appropriate colleagues of the original event.

The abstract aspect in Example 19-7 uses the Director aspect-oriented design pattern (see Chapter 23) to provide the mechanisms by which the mediator pattern can be applied to an application.

Example 19-7. Defining the mediator pattern using aspects

```
public abstract aspect MediatorPattern
{
    protected interface Colleague
    {
    }

    protected interface Mediator
    {
    }

    private WeakHashMap mappingColleagueToMediator = new WeakHashMap( );

    private Mediator getMediator(Colleague colleague)
    {
        Mediator mediator =
            (Mediator) mappingColleagueToMediator.get(colleague);
        return mediator;
    }

    public void setMediator(Colleague c, Mediator m)
    {
        mappingColleagueToMediator.put(c, m);
    }

    protected abstract pointcut change(Colleague c);

    after(Colleague c) : change(c)
    {
        notifyMediator(c, getMediator(c));
    }

    protected abstract void notifyMediator(Colleague c, Mediator m);
}
```

Discussion

The `MediatorPattern` abstract aspect defines the `Colleague` and `Mediator` roles as interfaces that can be applied to application specific classes by inheriting subaspects. The aspect defines the `mappingColleagueToMediator` lookup which can be manipulated to assign colleague objects to mediator objects using the `setMediator(Colleague,Mediator)` method.

The `MediatorPattern` aspect provides the `change(..)` abstract pointcut that can be implemented by subaspects to trigger notifications on mediators when changes occur to colleagues by calling the `notifyMediator(Colleague,Mediator)` method that is also implemented by subaspects.

Figure 19-12 shows the structure of the `MediatorPattern` abstract aspect and the interfaces and behavior that it defines to support the mediator design pattern.

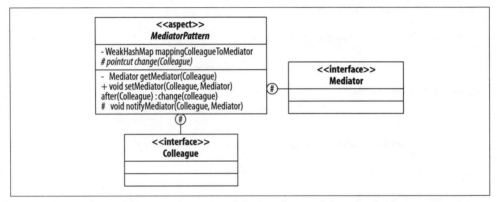

Figure 19-12. The MediatorPattern aspect and the interfaces it defines for the design pattern's roles

Example 19-8 shows how the abstract `MediatorPattern` aspect could be applied for a specific application.

Example 19-8. Applying the MediatorPattern aspect to an application's classes

```
public aspect DialogMediator extends MediatorPattern
{
    declare parents : ListBox implements Colleague;
    declare parents : EntryField implements Mediator;

    protected pointcut change(Colleague c) : (
            execution(void ListBox.setSelection(..)) && this(c));

    protected void notifyMediator(Colleague c, Mediator m)
    {
        ListBox listBox = (ListBox) c;
```

Example 19-8. Applying the MediatorPattern aspect to an application's classes (continued)

```
        EntryField entryField = (EntryField) m;
        entryField.setText(listBox.getSelection( ));
    }
}
```

Figure 19-13 shows the `ListBox` and `EntryField` classes before and after the `DialogMediator` aspect is applied.

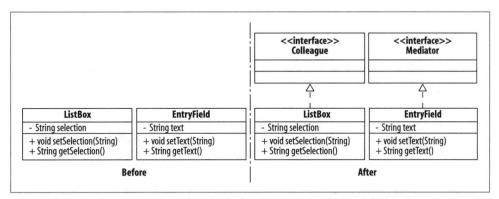

Figure 19-13. The static structure after the mediator pattern has been applied to the ListBox and EntryField classes

Figure 19-14 shows how the mediator pattern characteristics of the `ListBox` and `EntryField` classes interact together within an example application.

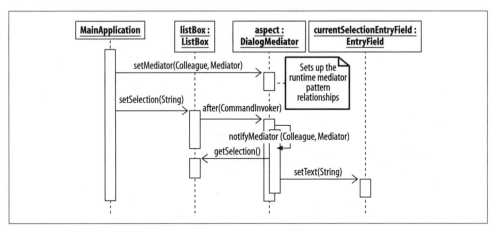

Figure 19-14. Using the new mediator pattern behavior of the ListBox and EntryField classes

See Also

The Observer Pattern works in a more hierarchical manner than the Mediator pattern, but its implementation can be useful when comparing the two in terms of their appropriateness to a particular design problem. The Observer pattern as implemented using aspects is shown in Recipe 17.1; more information on the extension of existing classes using aspects can be found in Recipe 16.1; the Director aspect-oriented design pattern is explained in Recipe 23.3.

19.5   Implementing the Chain of Responsibility Pattern

Problem

You want to apply the chain of responsibility pattern using AspectJ.

Solution

The *chain of responsibility* pattern allows the separation of the source of a request from deciding which of the potentially large number of handlers for the request should action it. The class representing the chain role channels the requests from the source along the list of handlers until a handler accepts the request and actions it.

The abstract aspect in Example 19-9 uses the Director aspect-oriented design pattern (see Chapter 23) to provide the generic mechanisms by which the chain of responsibility pattern can be applied to an application. The decision as to what occurs if none of the available handlers in the chain accept the request is an application-specific decision; although a default behavior is implemented in the abstract aspect, this can be overridden by extending implementations.

Example 19-9. Defining the chain of responsibility pattern using aspects

```
public abstract aspect ChainOfResponsibilityPattern
{
    protected interface Handler
    {
    }

    public WeakHashMap successors = new WeakHashMap( );

    protected void receiveRequest(Handler handler, Object request)
    {
        if (handler.acceptRequest(request))
        {
            handler.handleRequest(request);
        }
        else
        {
            // The handler will not accept the request
            Handler successor = getSuccessor(handler);
            if (successor == null)
            {
```

```
                // Last handler in the chain so must deal with the request
                // This is a rudimentary implementation and more complex
                // logic could be applied here or perhaps in the concrete
                // aspects that extend this abstract one
                handler.handleRequest(request);
            }
            else
            {

                // Hand the request on to the next successor in the chain
                receiveRequest(successor, request);
            }
        }
    }

    public boolean Handler.acceptRequest(Object request)
    {
        // The default as defined here is to reject the request
        // This is implemented by the application specific
        // concrete aspects
        return false;
    }

    public void Handler.handleRequest(Object request)
    {
        // A default empty implementation that is overridden
        // if required by the application specific concrete aspects
    }

    protected abstract pointcut eventTrigger(Handler handler, Object request);

    after(Handler handler, Object request) : eventTrigger(handler, request)
    {
        receiveRequest(handler, request);
    }

    public void setSuccessor(Handler handler, Handler successor)
    {
        successors.put(handler, successor);
    }

    public Handler getSuccessor(Handler handler)
    {
        return ((Handler) successors.get(handler));
    }
}
```

Discussion

The ChainOfResponsibilityPattern abstract aspect defines the Handler interface that can then be applied by specialized subaspect to all classes within a specific application that are to participate in the chain. The aspect maintains the chain and asks the specifics of how a request is to be handled by specific subaspects.

Figure 19-15 shows the structure of the ChainOfResponsibilityPattern abstract aspect and the interfaces and behavior that it defines to support the chain of responsibility design pattern.

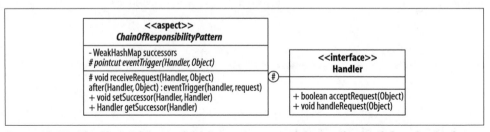

Figure 19-15. The ChainOfResponsibilityPattern aspect and the interfaces it defines for the design pattern's roles

Example 19-10 shows how the abstract ChainOfResponsibility aspect could be applied for a specific application.

Example 19-10. Applying the ChainOfResponsibility aspect to an application's classes

```
public aspect HelpChain extends ChainOfResponsibilityPattern
{
    declare parents : PrintButton implements Handler;
    declare parents : PrintDialog implements Handler;
    declare parents : Manager implements Handler;

    protected pointcut eventTrigger(Handler handler, Object event) :
        call(void PrintButton.doClick(..))
        && target(handler)
        && args(event);

    private boolean Handler.alreadyHandledRequest = false;

    public boolean Handler.acceptRequest(Object event)
    {
        return !this.alreadyHandledRequest;
    }

    public void PrintButton.handleRequest(Object event)
    {
        if (!this.acceptRequest(event))
        {
            System.out.println(
                "PrintButton Forced to handle Request" +
                "due to being last in the chain (Implementation Decision)");
        }
        System.out.println("PrintButton handling request: " + event);
        this.alreadyHandledRequest = true;
    }
```

Example 19-10. Applying the ChainOfResponsibility aspect to an application's classes (continued)

```
   public void PrintDialog.handleRequest(Object event)
   {
      if (!this.acceptRequest(event))
      {
         System.out.println(
            "PrintDialog Forced to handle Request" +
            "due to being last in the chain (Implementation Decision)");
      }
      System.out.println("PrintDialog handling request: " + event);
      this.alreadyHandledRequest = true;
   }

   public void Manager.handleRequest(Object event)
   {
      if (!this.acceptRequest(event))
      {
         System.out.println(
            "Manager Forced to handle Request due to being" +
            "last in the chain (Implementation Decision)");
      }
      System.out.println("Manager handling request: " + event);
      this.alreadyHandledRequest = true;
   }
}
```

The `HelpChain` aspect in Example 19-10, as its title suggests, implements a help chain where the request for help information is passed to the classes that are registered handlers until one accepts the request or it is the last in the chain.

Figure 19-16 shows the `PrintButton`, `PrintDialog`, and `Manager` classes before the `HelpChain` aspect is applied.

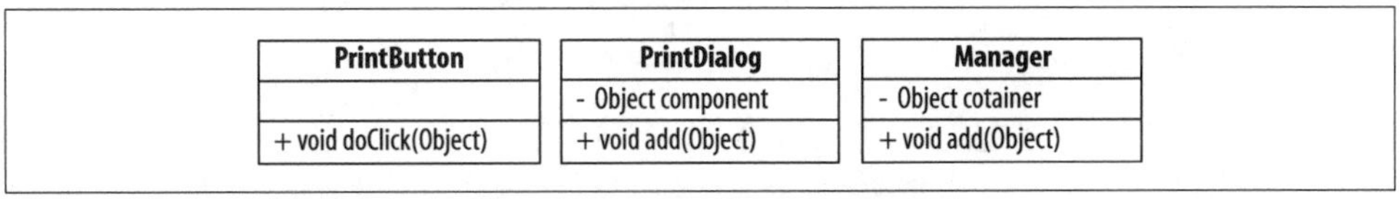
PrintButton
+ void doClick(Object)
PrintDialog
- Object component
+ void add(Object)
Manager
- Object cotainer
+ void add(Object)

Figure 19-16. The PrintButton, PrintDialog, and Manager classes

Figure 19-17 shows the effects of applying the `HelpChain` aspect to the `PrintButton`, `PrintDialog`, and `Manager` classes.

Figure 19-18 shows an example interaction with the classes in Figure 19-17, using the aspect introduced chain of responsibility pattern features.

See Also

The Mediator pattern, as shown in Recipe 19.4, is often combined with the Chain Of Responsibility pattern where a common mediator is required to work with the many objects of the application using the chain of responsibility to pass requests throughout

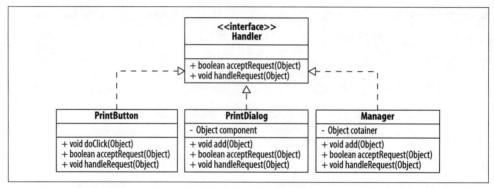

Figure 19-17. *The static structure after the chain of responsibility pattern has been applied to the PrintButton, PrintDialog, and EntryField classes*

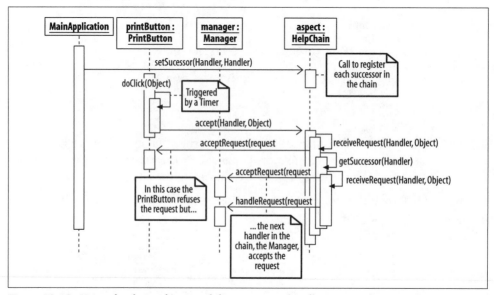

Figure 19-18. *Using the chain of responsibility pattern to handle a request between the PrintButton and Manager classes*

the application; more information on the extension of existing classes using aspects can be found in Recipe 16.1; the Director aspect-oriented design pattern is explained in Recipe 23.3.

19.6 Implementing the Memento Pattern

Problem

You want to apply the memento pattern using AspectJ.

Solution

The *memento* pattern provides a mechanism by which an object's original state can be reinstated at a later time without coupling the exact mechanisms with which the state of the object is rolled back to the object. The memento encapsulates all of the information needed to restore a prior internal state of an object at a later date. This capability can be used to provide a form of undo feature to the state of objects within a particular application.

The abstract aspect and support classes in Example 19-11 use the Director aspect-oriented design pattern (see Chapter 23) to specify the mechanisms by which the memento pattern can be applied to an application using AspectJ.

Example 19-11. Defining the memento pattern using aspects

```
public abstract aspect MementoPattern
{
    public interface Memento
    {
        public void setState(Originator originator);
        public Object getState();
    }

    public interface Originator
    {
        public void setMemento(Memento memento);
        public Memento createMemento();
        public Object getState();
    }
```

Discussion

The MementoPattern aspect defines the roles and behavior of memento and originator objects according to the design pattern. Those roles can be applied to the application specific classes by specialized subaspects.

Figure 19-19 shows the structure of the MementoPattern abstract aspect and the interfaces and behavior that it defines to support the memento design pattern.

Example 19-12 shows how the abstract MementoPattern aspect could be applied for a specific application.

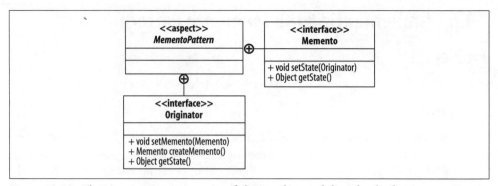

Figure 19-19. The MementoPattern aspect and the interfaces it defines for the design pattern's roles

Example 19-12. Applying the MementoPattern aspect to an application's classes

```
public aspect EmployeeMemento extends MementoPattern
{
    declare parents : Employee implements Originator;

    public void Employee.setMemento(Memento memento)
    {
        Object object = memento.getState();
        Employee stateToRestore = (Employee) object;
        this.setName(stateToRestore.getName());
        this.setSalary(stateToRestore.getSalary());
    }

    public Memento Employee.createMemento()
    {
        Memento memento = new DefaultMemento();
        memento.setState(this);
        return memento;
    }

    public Object Employee.getState() throws MementoException
    {
        Employee employee = new Employee(this.getName(), this.getSalary());
        return employee;
    }
}
```

The EmployeeMemento specifies that the Employee class is an originator and so supports mementos of its state being created. To completely support this new role, the Employee class is extended with the createMemento(), setMemento(Memento), and getState() methods.

The createMemento() method allows a client to get a memento for an Employee object, the setMemento(Memento) method will restore an Employee object to the state stored in a memento, and the getState( ) method is used by a memento when it is being created to access and store the state of the Employee originator object.

Figure 19-20 shows the effects before and after applying the EmployeeMemento aspect to the Employee class.

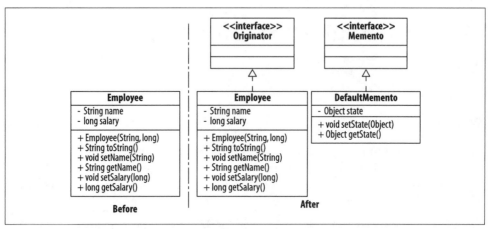

Figure 19-20. The static structure before and after the memento pattern has been applied to the Employee class

Figure 19-21 shows an example interaction with the Employee class using the aspect introduced memento pattern features.

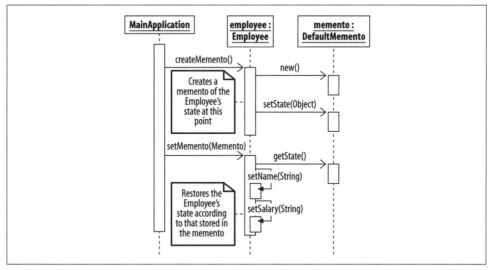

Figure 19-21. Using the new memento pattern characteristics of the Employee class

See Also

The recipes in Chapter 16 contain more details on the mechanisms by which existing classes can be extended using aspects and the declare keyword; the Director aspect-oriented design pattern is explained in Recipe 23.3.

19.7 Implementing the Strategy Pattern

Problem

You want to apply the strategy pattern using AspectJ.

Solution

The *strategy* pattern provides a mechanism to separate client classes from the actual implementation details of a particular algorithm or strategy. Traditionally, all of the separate classes, which implement the strategy, implemented a distinct interface to allow the client to be decoupled from the different implementations.

The abstract aspect in Example 19-13 uses the Director aspect-oriented design pattern (see Chapter 23) to provide a generic implementation of the strategy pattern that can be applied to your application.

Example 19-13. Defining the strategy pattern using aspects

```
public abstract aspect StrategyPattern
{
    Hashtable strategyPerContext = new Hashtable( );

    protected interface Strategy
    {
    }

    protected interface Context
    {
    }

    private Strategy Context.strategy = null;

    public void setConcreteStrategy(Context c, Strategy s)
    {
        strategyPerContext.put(c, s);
    }

    public Strategy getConcreteStrategy(Context c)
    {
        return (Strategy) strategyPerContext.get(c);
    }
}
```

Discussion

The StrategyPattern abstract provides definitions of the Strategy and Context roles as interfaces. A hash table is used to look up the specific concrete strategy to be used.

Figure 19-22 shows the structure of the StrategyPattern abstract aspect and the interfaces and behavior that it defines to support the strategy design pattern.

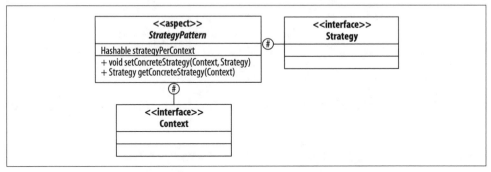

Figure 19-22. The StrategyPattern aspect and the interfaces it defines for the design pattern's roles

Example 19-14 shows how the abstract StrategyPattern aspect could be applied for a specific application. The SortingStrategy aspect defines the mapping of the strategy role to two types of sorter implementation and the overall context to be that of a Sorter class. The advice is applied to override the sort method on the Sorter context to apply the appropriate sorting strategy.

Example 19-14. Applying the StrategyPattern aspect to an application

```
public aspect SortingStrategy extends StrategyPattern
{
    declare parents : Sorter implements Context;
    declare parents : LinearSorter implements Strategy;
    declare parents : BubbleSorter implements Strategy;

    int[] around(Sorter s, int[] numbers) : call(int[] Sorter.sort(int[]))
        && target(s)
        && args(numbers)
    {
        Strategy strategy = getConcreteStrategy(s);
        if (strategy instanceof BubbleSorter)
            ((BubbleSorter) strategy).sort(numbers);
        else if (strategy instanceof LinearSorter)
            ((LinearSorter) strategy).sort(numbers);
        return numbers;
    }
}
```

The SortingStrategy aspect declares two different sorting strategies for a particular context, which is sorting. The actual strategy that is to be executed depends on the type of strategy that has been declared at runtime for a particular context.

Figure 19-23 shows the Sorter, LinearSorter, and BubbleSorter classes before the SortingStrategy aspect is applied.

Sorter	LinearSorter	BubbleSorter
- int[] numbers		
+ void setData(int[]) + int[] sort(int[])	- void exchange(int[], int, int) + void sort(int[])	- void exchange(int[], int, int) + void sort(int[])

Figure 19-23. The Sorter, LinearSorter, and BubbleSorter classes

Figure 19-24 shows the effects of applying the SortingStrategy aspect to the classes from Figure 19-23.

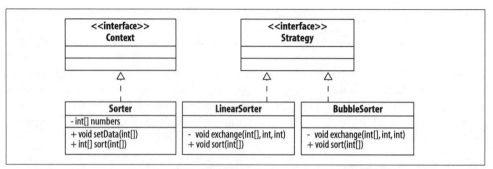

Figure 19-24. The static structure after the strategy pattern has been applied to the Sorter, LinearSorter, and BubbleSorter classes

Figure 19-25 shows an example interaction with the Sorter, LinearSorter, and BubbleSorter classes using the aspect introduced strategy pattern features.

See Also

The recipes in Chapter 16 contain more details on the mechanisms by which existing classes can be extended using aspects and the declare keyword; declaring and using abstract aspects are examined in Chapter 15; the args(Type or Identifier) pointcut is described in Recipe 11.3; the target(Type or Identifier) pointcut is examined in Recipe 11.2; the call(Signature) pointcut is covered in Recipe 4.1; exposing join point context is examined in Recipe 13.2; the Director aspect-oriented design pattern is explained in Recipe 23.3.

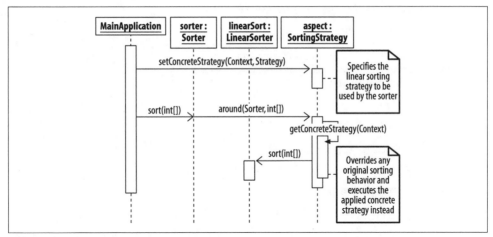

Figure 19-25. Using the new strategy pattern characteristics of the Sorter and LinearSorter classes

19.8   Implementing the Visitor Pattern

Problem

You want to apply the visitor pattern using AspectJ.

Solution

The *visitor* pattern encapsulates a request that can be executed by a hierarchy of objects as it is passed throughout the structure. The abstract aspect in Example 19-15 uses the Director aspect-oriented design pattern (see Chapter 23) to define the roles that take part in the Visitor pattern.

Example 19-15. Defining the visitor pattern using aspects

```
public abstract aspect VisitorPattern
{
   public interface Element
   {
      public void accept(Visitor visitor);
   }

   public interface CompositeElement extends Element
   {
      public Element[] getElements();
   }

   public interface Result
   {
   }
```

Example 19-15. Defining the visitor pattern using aspects (continued)

```
public interface Visitor
{
    public void visitElement(Element element);
    public void visitComposite(CompositeElement element);
    public Result getResult( );
}

public void CompositeElement.accept(Visitor visitor)
{
    visitor.visitComposite(this);
}

public void Element.accept(Visitor visitor)
{
    visitor.visitElement(this);
}
}
```

Discussion

The VisitorPattern abstract aspect defines the CompositeElement and Element roles as parts of the object structure that is to be visited. The Visitor role describes how the Visitor is notified of which type of element it is visiting. This role is applied to objects that may be passed to the different parts of the structure, be they composite or simple elements. The CompositeElement and Element roles are then extended to provide the methods by which the Visitor is passed.

Figure 19-26 shows the structure of the VisitorPattern abstract aspect and the interfaces and behavior that it defines to support the visitor design pattern.

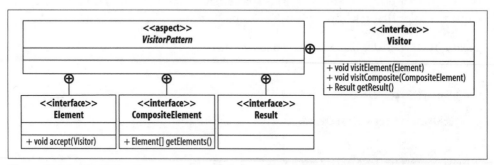

Figure 19-26. The VisitorPattern aspect and the interfaces it defines for the design pattern's roles

Example 19-16 shows how the abstract VisitorPattern aspect could be applied to a specific application.

Example 19-16. Applying the VisitorPattern aspect to an application

```
public aspect InventoryVisitor extends VisitorPattern
{
```

```
declare parents : FloppyDisk implements Element;
declare parents : HardDisk implements Element;
declare parents : Processor implements Element;
declare parents : Computer implements CompositeElement;
declare parents : Motherboard implements CompositeElement;
declare parents : InventoryReport implements Result;

public Element[] Computer.getElements( )
{
    Element[] elements = new Element[3];
    elements[0] = this.getMotherboard( );
    elements[1] = this.getHardDisk( );
    elements[2] = this.getFloppyDisk( );
    return elements;
}

public Element[] Motherboard.getElements( )
{
    Element[] elements = new Element[1];
    elements[0] = this.getProcessor( );
    return elements;
}
}
```

Figure 19-27 shows an example set of application classes before the `InventoryVisitor` aspect is applied.

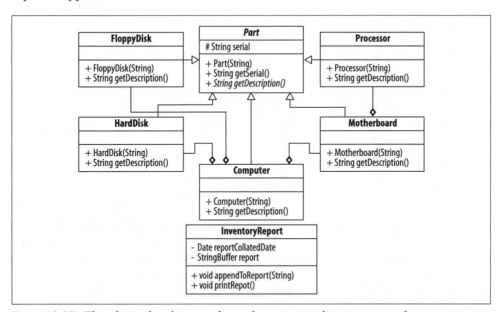

Figure 19-27. The relationships between classes that represent the components of a computer

Figure 19-28 shows the effects of applying the InventoryVisitor aspect to the application classes shown in Figure 19-27.

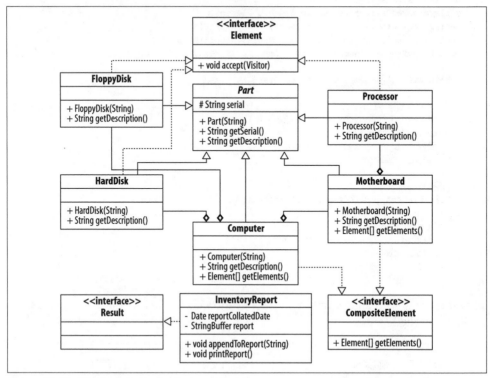

Figure 19-28. The computer part classes with the new visitor pattern interfaces applied

Figure 19-29 shows a partial example interaction with some of the classes in Figure 19-28 using the aspect introduced visitor pattern features. The interactions recursively continue throughout all of the composite elements and individual elements, calling accept(Visitor) and then getDescription( ) on each, that make up the top-level Computer object.

See Also

The visitor pattern is often used together with the composite pattern shown in Recipe 18.1; For more information on defining abstract aspects and specializing them, please refer to the recipes in Chapter 15; the recipes in Chapter 16 contain more details on the mechanisms by which existing classes can be extended using aspects and the declare keyword; the Director aspect-oriented design pattern is explained in Recipe 23.3.

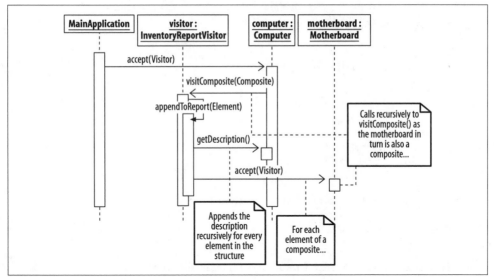

Figure 19-29. A partial interaction with the visitor pattern characteristics of the Computer, Motherboard, and InventoryReportVisitor classes

19.9 Implementing the Template Method Pattern

Problem

You want to apply the template pattern using AspectJ.

Solution

The *template method* pattern provides you with a mechanism by which to declare abstract methods within a generic work flow. These abstract steps or methods are implemented by specialized classes.

Example 19-17 shows how to apply the template method pattern using aspects.

Example 19-17. Defining the template method pattern using aspects

```
public interface AlgorithmDefinition
{
    public String runAlgorithm( );

    public StringBuffer stepOne( );

    public void stepTwo(StringBuffer data);

    public void stepThree(StringBuffer data);
```

```
    public String stepFour(StringBuffer data);
}

public aspect DefaultAlgorithmImplementation
{
    public String AlgorithmDefinition.runAlgorithm( )
    {
        StringBuffer dataInProcess = this.stepOne( );
        this.stepTwo(dataInProcess);
        this.stepThree(dataInProcess);
        return this.stepFour(dataInProcess);
    }

    public StringBuffer AlgorithmDefinition.stepOne( )
    {
        return new StringBuffer( );
    }

    public String AlgorithmDefinition.stepFour(StringBuffer data)
    {
        return data.toString( );
    }
}
```

Discussion

The DefaultAlgorithmImplementation aspect specifies the order of the steps for the algorithm and a default implementation for a couple of steps. By using aspect-oriented techniques, the algorithm template can be declared in an interface rather than an abstract class. Then, relying on static cross-cutting techniques, a default implementation of the appropriate generic steps, including the method to invoke the steps in the right order, can be specified in a concrete aspect. The more specific steps can be completed by the classes that implement the algorithm interface, automatically picking up on the default behavior where appropriate.

An aspect-oriented implementation advantage for this pattern is that it removes the constraint that the top-level class in the pattern must be an abstract class by moving the partial abstract implementation into the aspect and using static cross-cutting methods to provide that partial implementation by default on the interface. This leaves the design more flexible in that the concrete classes now implement the interface rather than using up their one inheritance relationship as allowed within Java to incorporate the pattern.

See Also

The recipes in Chapter 16 contain more details on the mechanisms by which existing classes can be extended using aspects.

19.10 Implementing the State Pattern

Problem

You want to apply the state pattern using AspectJ.

Solution

The *state* pattern provides a mechanism by which an object can vary its behavior based upon its state. The state is encapsulated in its own object that is then contained by the invoked object. The invoked object passes all method requests affected by its state to the state object, which varies its response based on its class at that point in time.

Example 19-18 shows how the state of a pseudo TCPConnection class could be declared using aspects including how those states are transitioned between as methods are invoked.

Example 19-18. Implementing the State pattern for a specific application's classes using aspects

```
public aspect TCPConnectionState
{
    protected TCPState listening = new TCPListen( );

    protected TCPState acknowledged = new TCPAcknowledged( );

    protected TCPState closed = new TCPClosed( );

    after(TCPConnection connection) : initialization(new ())
        && target(connection)
    {
        listening.setConnection(new SocketConnection( ));
        connection.setState(listening);
    }

    after(TCPConnection connection, TCPState state) : call(
        void TCPState +.acknowledge( ))
        && target(state)
        && this(connection)
    {
        if (connection.getState( ) == listening)
        {
            acknowledged.setConnection(listening.getConnection( ));
            connection.setState(acknowledged);
        }
    }

    after(TCPConnection connection, TCPState state) : call(
        void TCPState +.close( ))
        && target(state)
```

```
        && this(connection)
    {
        if ((connection.getState( ) == listening)
            || (connection.getState( ) == acknowledged))
        {
            connection.setState(closed);
        }
    }
}
```

Discussion

The `TCPConnectionState` aspect specifies that the `TCPConnection` classes state will be *listening* when it is created, *acknowledged* when the acknowledge( ) method is invoked, and *closed* when the close( ) call is invoked. It also specifies what to do if these methods are invoked depending on their order. This is all achieved without affecting the `TCPConnection` class.

Aspects are used in this solution to modularize the rules for changing from one state to another. By modularizing these rules, analyzing the rules for the change of state becomes easier as they are in one place and become more flexible to future changes such as the incorporation of new or changed states without affecting the original class. This provides distinct advantages over a more traditional object-oriented approach where the logic for deciding the state changes must be embedded in the methods and, therefore, may confuse the business logic.

Figure 19-30 shows how the state of the `TCPConnection` is affected by the sequence of methods called on the class as managed by the `TCPConnectionState` aspect.

See Also

The call(`Signature`) pointcut is covered in Recipe 4.1; the after( ) form of advice is discussed in Recipe 13.5; the this(`Type or Identifier`) pointcut is described in Recipe 11.3; the target(`Type or Identifier`) pointcut is examined in Recipe 11.2; exposing join point context is examined in Recipe 13.2; the initialization(`Signature`) pointcut is examined in Recipe 7.3.

19.11 Implementing the Interpreter Pattern

Problem

You want to harness the benefits of implementing the façade and interpreter patterns using AspectJ.

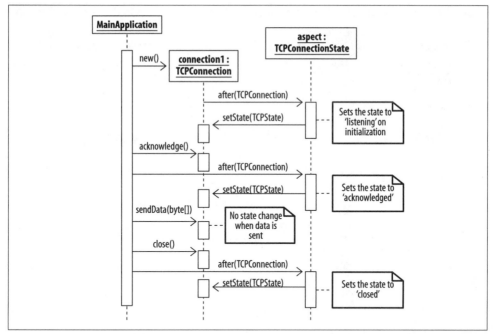

Figure 19-30. Managing the state of a TCPConnection object using the TCPConnectionState aspect

Solution

Unfortunately, the interpreter pattern by definition does not appear at this point to gain any design or implementation benefits from using aspect-oriented methods with AspectJ. The interpreter pattern's implementation is tied explicitly to the specific classes of the structure being interpreted; therefore, although the concept is generic, the implementation is specific and does not appear to benefit from aspect-oriented methods.

Discussion

In stating that the interpreter and the façade patterns do not benefit from AspectJ begs the question, why have they been included at all? First, it would seem odd to include some statement on all of the other GoF design patterns and just exclude these two. Second, an aspect-oriented façade in particular may prove useful. These situations are a gray area, and they benefit directly from AspectJ's ability to code weave against libraries (*.jar* files) and compiled code (*.class* files).

AspectJ can and does weave against the Java source and compiled byte code. This is useful when you wish to keep the decision whether an application contains specific aspects for a later point in a legitimate build process. However, an added feature is that you can potentially weave against legacy and third-party libraries where the source code is unavailable. This is a particularly gray area due to the legal and technical implications of changing a third party's proprietary libraries. AspectJ does provide the means by which this can be achieved if all other technical and nontechnical hurdles are overcome, although a great deal of care must be taken when this route is opted for.

See Also

Using the ajc command to compile and weave aspects into *.jar* libraries is shown in Recipe 2.4.

CHAPTER 20

Applying Class and Component Scale Aspects

20.0 Introduction

Aspects seem to be easily categorized as system or enterprise-wide concerns because those contexts gain the most visible benefits from aspect-oriented methods. However, any cross-cutting behavior is a good candidate for implementation using AspectJ whether that behavior is across the enterprise, system, or a single class or component.

The next three chapters will look at the different types of aspects that can be applied within these three different software development contexts: enterprise, system, and component. This chapter focuses on micro-scale aspects that are apparent in class or component-wide cross-cutting concerns.

You'd be forgiven for thinking that little could be described as cross-cutting within a single class or component. Take a closer look though and you'll discover that any behavior that affects the characteristics of a class can be a strong candidate for an aspect, especially if those characteristics are not core to the business logic of the class.

Examples of these micro-scale cross-cutting concerns examined in this chapter range from validating the parameters passed to a method, to controlling the instantiation of a class. These areas benefit from modularization and separation from the core business concerns of a class and show how using AspectJ can improve your design and implementation, even at the class and component level.

20.1 Validating Parameters Passed to a Method

Problem

You want to validate the parameters passed to a method.

Solution

Create an aspect that modularizes the parameter checking logic. Declare a pointcut to capture the execution of the method where the parameters are to be checked. The pointcut should expose the parameters to the corresponding advice so it can perform the checks.

Depending on the result of the parameter checking, the advice will proceed with the methods execution or safely override the method whenever the parameters are not suitable.

Discussion

Validation of method parameters is a chore every developer has to be concerned with whenever he has no control over how his clients will use a component. Even when the developer is writing the clients that will use a particular component, a useful practice would be to the values passed to a method are acceptable before working with those values.

This checking often confuses the logic within a method by introducing initial checking code that has little relationship to the job that the method is to complete. By using AspectJ, you can check a method's parameters separately from the core business logic of a method to make the solution cleaner.

The main method on a Java application is a common place where the parameters being supplied cannot be controlled and have to be checked before the application can continue execution. The normal means of achieving these checks is to code the test logic using an if statement into the main method and to produce an error message if the parameters provided on the command line do not meet the requirements of the application.

Example 20-1 shows a typical main method with the traditional parameter validation and checking support code highlighted.

Example 20-1. Interleaving traditional command-line argument checking with the business logic of the main method

```
package com.oreilly.aspectjcookbook;

import java.net.URL;
import java.net.MalformedURLException;

public class TraditionalMainApplication
{
    private static final String COMMAND_LINE_USAGE =
        "TraditionalMainAppliction usage :\n\n" +
        "\tjava TraditionalMainApplication <url>";

    public static void main(String[] args)
    {
```

```
    if (args.length == 1)
    {
        try
        {
            // Assuming that the first argument supplied is a url
            // Concentrating on the business logic, not validation which
            // is handled by the aspect.
            URL url = new URL(args[0]);

            System.out.println("Application Started, doing stuff with " + url);
        }
        catch (MalformedURLException mue)
        {
            System.err.println(COMMAND_LINE_USAGE);
            System.err.println("Please enter a valid URL for <url>");
        }
    }
    else
    {
        System.err.println(COMMAND_LINE_USAGE);
    }
  }
}
```

First, the TraditionalMainApplication class declares the COMMAND_LINE_USAGE constant that contains a message that will be displayed to the user if a problem occurs with the arguments passed to the main method. Then an if statement within the main method checks that the right number of arguments have been supplied; if not, the error message is displayed. Finally, one of the parameters is a URL, and since this could be invalid, this is checked by a try/catch block. All of this occurs before the main method can do anything useful such as starting the application.

Refactoring the checking logic into a separate method moves the problem to another part of the same class and doesn't offer a satisfactory solution. AspectJ can remove these messy beginnings to your application by creating an aspect such as the one shown in Example 20-2.

Example 20-2. Parameter checking using an aspect

```
package com.oreilly.aspectjcookbook;

import java.net.URL;
import java.net.MalformedURLException;

public aspect VerifyMethodArgsAspect
{
    private static final String COMMAND_LINE_USAGE =
        "MyAppliction usage :\n\n" +
        "\tjava MainApplication <url>";
```

Example 20-2. Parameter checking using an aspect (continued)

```
public pointcut captureMain(String[] arguments) :
    execution(void MainApplication.main(String[])) &&
    args(arguments);

public pointcut createURLCalledinMainMethod( ) :
    call(java.net.URL.new(..)) &&
    withincode(public void MainApplication.main(String[]));

void around(String[] arguments) : captureMain(arguments)
{
    if (arguments.length == 1)
    {
    // Test that the host and port are valid
        try
        {
            URL url = new URL(arguments[0]);
            proceed(arguments);
        }
        catch(MalformedURLException mfe)
        {
            System.err.println(COMMAND_LINE_USAGE);
            System.err.println("Please enter a valid URL for <url>");
        }
    }
    else
    {
        System.err.println(COMMAND_LINE_USAGE);
    }
}

// If necessary soften the exception that would normally have been raised
// if the url parameter was badly formed, but only in the validated main method
declare soft : MalformedURLException : createURLCalledinMainMethod( );

}
```

The VerifyMethodArgsAspect aspect declares the captureMain(String[]) pointcut that interrupts the execution of the main method and provides the arguments to the corresponding advice. The around( ) advice then checks the number of parameters and that the URL parameter is valid before calling proceed( ) with the original arguments if everything checks out. If any problems occur with the arguments then the error messages are displayed in the same way as before.

Using an aspect to modularize the parameter checking logic leaves your main method looking much neater without losing any of that important checking behavior, as shown in Example 20-3.

Example 20-3. Providing the parameter checking logic via an aspect leaves the main method to focus on its job

```
package com.oreilly.aspectjcookbook;

import java.net.URL;

public class MainApplication
{

    public static void main(String[] args)
    {
        // Assuming that the first argument supplied is a url
        // Concentrating on the business logic, not validation which
        // is handled by the aspect.
        URL url = new URL(args[0]);

        System.out.println("Application Started, doing stuff with " + url);
    }
}
```

The main method logic still uses the URL argument as before, but because the aspect has provided the necessary checking to ensure a problem will not occur, it is reasonably safe to use the declare soft statement to save the main method from having to explicitly handle the MalformedURLException.

The createURLCalledinMainMethod( ) pointcut captures where the exception would normally be raised—i.e., when a java.net.URL instance is created and within the main method—and this is the only join point where the MalformedURLException is to be softened. Without this softening of the exception, the main method would have to handle the possibility of a MalformedURLException being thrown even with the aspect based checking.

See Also

The execution(Signature) pointcut is described in Recipe 4.4; The args([TypePatterns || Identifiers]) pointcut is covered in Recipe 11.3; the around( ) form of advice is shown in Recipe 13.4; softening exceptions is discussed in Recipe 16.5.

20.2 Overriding the Class Instantiated on a Call to a Constructor

Problem

You want to be able to control the actual classes that are instantiated on a constructor call.

Solution

Use the Cuckoo's Egg aspect-oriented design pattern to create an aspect that modularizes the override of a constructor call to be able to vary the implementation returned at runtime. Use the call(Signature) pointcut to capture calls to a classes constructor and then use around() advice to return a different object.

Discussion

It can be useful to be able to migrate to different implementations of an interface or specialization of a base class without affecting the code that uses that interface or base class. Traditionally, deciding the class selection is performed at object construction time, as shown in Example 20-4.

Example 20-4. Hardcoding the selection of the MyClass implementation of MyInterface

```
public static void traditionalObjectOrientedImplementationSelection()
{
    MyInterface myObject = new MyClass(); // Specifies the MyClass implementation
                                          // of the MyInterface interface

    System.out.println(myObject);
    myObject.foo(); // Calls the MyClass implementation of the foo() method
}
```

This code produces the following output:

```
com.oreilly.aspectjcookbook.MyClass@cf8583
foo() called on MyClass
```

To change the implementation of MyInterface, the code would need to be changed to:

```
public static void traditionalObjectOrientedImplementationSelection()
{
    MyInterface myObject = new AnotherClass();  // Specifies the AnotherClass
                                                // implementation  of the
                                                // MyInterface interface

    System.out.println(myObject);
    myObject.foo(); // Calls the AnotherClass implementation of the foo() method
}
```

This will produce the following output:

```
com.oreilly.aspectjcookbook.AnotherClass@dbe178
foo() called on AnotherClass
```

The client code doesn't care what the implementation of the MyInterface interface is when making calls to the foo() method since, in Java, the method is called dynamically at runtime based on the object type. The disadvantage of this approach is that the implementation class (MyClass or AnotherClass) is exposed when it is instantiated. Anywhere this interface is used, at least one line of implementation-specific code can occur and if you wanted to change the implementation, this would result in an error-prone ripple of changes across your application to migrate to the new class.

A common way around this problem is to use a factory method or an abstract factory design pattern. Aspect-oriented techniques offer advantages to both of these approaches, as shown in Recipes 13.3 and 13.4 respectively. However, things can be made simpler and neater by using AspectJ's call(Signature) pointcut and around( ) advice, as shown in Example 20-5.

Example 20-5. Using an aspect to override instantiation of a class

```
package com.oreilly.aspectjcookbook;

public aspect ControlClassSelectionAspect
{
    public pointcut myClassConstructor() : call(MyClass.new());

    Object around() : myClassConstructor()
    {
        return new AnotherClass();
    }
}
```

The ControlClassSelectionAspect declares the myClassConstructor( ) pointcut that intercepts calls to instantiate a MyClass object. The corresponding around( ) advice then returns a new instance of the overriding AnotherClass class.

> The class that is instantiated and returned from your around( ) advice must be a subtype of the type expected on the overridden constructor call. For instance, in Example 20-5, AnotherClass must extend MyClass as the constructor call being overridden specified that it is creating a new MyClass( ). If the around( ) advice returned an object that was not a subtype of MyClass, you'd get ClassCastException errors at runtime wherever the around( ) advice was applied.

Using this technique, the code in Example 20-4 does not need to be changed at all to use the AnotherClass implementation of the MyInterface interface. If the ControlClassSelectionAspect is woven into the application, the AnotherClass implementation automatically overrides the MyClass implementation.

You could refine the myClassConstructor( ) pointcut further so the MyClass constructor could be overridden in certain circumstances. You could, for example, add within(TypePattern) or withincode(Signature) pointcut definitions to declare the overriding should only occur within a designated scope.

You could examine a user-defined runtime parameter to vary the implementation that is instantiated within the around( ) advice:

```
Object around() : myClassConstructor() &&
                    if (System.getProperty("select_class").equals("AnotherClass"))
{
    return new AnotherClass();
}
```

This variation would allow you to change the class instantiated at runtime by changing the value of your application's `select_class` runtime parameter without being forced to recompile your application.

 Looking ahead, Recipe 23.1 shows a typical use of the Cuckoo's Egg aspect-oriented design pattern. This pattern provides a common solution to the problem of overriding a call to a constructor to return a different object than expected.

See Also

The `call(Signature)` pointcut when used to capture calls on constructors is described in Recipe 7.1; the `around()` form of advice is discussed in Recipe 13.4; the `within(TypePattern)` and `withincode(Signature)` pointcuts are described in Recipes 9.1 and 9.3 respectively; the Cuckoo's Egg aspect-oriented design pattern is discussed in Recipe 23.1.

20.3   Adding Persistence to a Class

Problem

You want to add persistence to a class so it can be saved and restored.

Solution

Apply the Director aspect-oriented design pattern and create an abstract aspect that defines the roles and behavior required to manage object persistence, as shown in Example 20-6.

This abstract aspect can be extended into specialized subaspects that will implement an appropriate persistence mechanism for each collection of persisted objects within your application.

Example 20-6. Defining the generic roles and behavior of persistence in an abstract aspect

```
public abstract aspect PersistenceAspect
{
   public interface ObjectStore
   {
      public void persist( );
      public void restore( );
   }

   protected abstract pointcut restoreStorage(ObjectStore store);

   after(ObjectStore store) : restoreStorage(store)
   {
```

```
        store.restore( );
    }

    protected abstract pointcut persistStorage(ObjectStore store);

    after(ObjectStore store) : persistStorage(store)
    {
        store.persist( );
    }
}
```

Discussion

The abstract PersistenceAspect aspect defines the ObjectStore role as an interface that can be applied to any class that will manage the persistence of a collection of objects. The restoreStorage(ObjectStore) and persistStorage(ObjectStore) abstract pointcuts are implemented by specialized subaspects to trigger the corresponding after( ) advice blocks that will restore or persist the specified ObjectStore.

The restore( ) and persist( ) methods specified in the ObjectStore interface are implemented according to the specific persistence strategy for a collection of objects within your application so you can vary the persistence strategy on a per ObjectStore basis.

Example 20-7 shows how the abstract PersistenceAspect can be implemented to provide persistence to an Employee class managed as a collection within the EmployeeCollection class.

Example 20-7. Applying the abstract Persistence aspect to the Employee and EmployeeCollection classes

```
public aspect EmployeePersistenceAspect extends PersistenceAspect
{
    declare parents : EmployeeCollection implements ObjectStore;

    protected pointcut restoreStorage(ObjectStore store) :
        execution(EmployeeCollection.new(..)) &&
        target(store);

    protected pointcut persistStorage(ObjectStore store) :
        call(* java.util.List.add(..)) &&
        target(EmployeeCollection) &&
        target(store);

    declare parents : Employee extends Serializable;
```

```
    private File EmployeeCollection.employeesFile = new File("employees.ser");

    public void EmployeeCollection.persist()
    {
        try
        {
            ObjectOutput out = new ObjectOutputStream(
                new FileOutputStream(this.employeesFile));

            Object[] objectsToStore = this.toArray();
            out.writeObject(objectsToStore);
            out.flush();
            out.close();
        }
        catch (Exception e)
        {
            System.err.println("Couldn't store employees to " + this.employeesFile);
        }
    }

    public void EmployeeCollection.restore()
    {
        if (this.employeesFile.exists() && this.employeesFile.canRead())
        {
            try
            {
                ObjectInput input = new ObjectInputStream(
                    new FileInputStream(this.employeesFile));

                Object[] objectsToRestore = (Object[]) input.readObject();
                for(int x = 0; x < objectsToRestore.length; x++)
                {
                    this.add(objectsToRestore[x]);
                }

                input.close();
            }
            catch (Exception e)
            {
                System.err.println(
                    "Couldn't restore employees due to a corrupt " +
                     this.employeesFile +
                    " file");
                e.printStackTrace();
            }
        }
    }
}
```

The EmployeePersistenceAspect applies the ObjectStore interface to the EmployeeCollection class. The restoreStorage(ObjectStore) aspect is then implemented to capture when the EmployeeCollection is constructed and uses the target(TypePattern || Identifier) pointcut to expose the EmployeeCollection as the ObjectStore to be restored.

The persistStorage(ObjectStore) pointcut is implemented to capture whenever the EmployeeCollection is changed and to persist the contents of the ObjectStore at this point. The EmployeeCollection is a specialization of java.util.ArrayList; to avoid weaving directly into the Java standard libraries, a call(Signature) pointcut is used to capture when the add(..) method is called on java.util.List.

However, the call(Signature) pointcut definition on its own is too general, so you must restrict the join points captured by the persistStorage(ObjectStore) pointcut to only capturing when add(..) is called on an EmployeeCollection. To apply this restriction, the first target(TypePattern || Identifier) pointcut uses a TypePattern to specify you are only interested in join points where the target of the join point is an EmployeeCollection class. The second target(TypePattern || Identifier) pointcut uses an Identifier to pass the current ObjectStore to the advice block as the persistStorage(ObjectStore) pointcut's single parameter.

Finally, a straightforward object serialization persistence strategy is applied to the EmployeeCollection. Each object within the EmployeeCollection is an instance of the Employee class, and this class is extended to implement the Serializable interface so it can be subjected to standard Java object serialization techniques. The serialized Employee objects are to be stored in a file; therefore, this file information is added to the EmployeeCollection class in the form of an employeesFile attribute.

To complete the picture, the persist() and restore() method implementations are added to the EmployeeCollection class so it can meet the behavior required of the ObjectStore interface. These methods execute the serialization and restoration of the Employee objects to and from the file indicated by the employeesFile attribute.

In Example 20-7, the EmployeeCollection was persisted every time it was changed. This could be overkill for your application, but you can change the join points captured by the persistStorage(ObjectStore) pointcut to persist an ObjectStore more applicable to your own application.

Example 20-8 shows part of an alternative implementation of the abstract PersistenceAspect that only persists its corresponding ObjectStore when the application is shutting down.

Example 20-8. Declaring that an ObjectStore should be persisted when an application is shut down

```
public privileged aspect AccountPersistenceAspect extends PersistenceAspect
{
    declare parents : MainApplication implements ObjectStore, Runnable;
```

```
    protected pointcut restoreStorage(ObjectStore store) :
        execution(MainApplication.new(..)) &&
        target(store);

    protected pointcut persistStorage(ObjectStore store) :
        execution(public void MainApplication.run()) &&
        this(store);

    declare parents : Account extends Serializable;

    private File MainApplication.accountsFile = new File("accounts.ser");

    public void MainApplication.persist()
    {
        // ... Code to persist the Accounts ...
    }

    public void MainApplication.restore()
    {
        // ... Code to restore the Accounts ...
    }

    after(MainApplication mainApplication) :
        restoreStorage(ObjectStore) &&
        target(mainApplication)
    {
        // Register a shutdown hook
        Thread shutdownThread = new Thread(mainApplication);
        Runtime.getRuntime().addShutdownHook(shutdownThread);
    }

    public void MainApplication.run()
    {
        // Do nothing, merely provides the trigger that the shutdown hook has been
        // executed so as to persist the store on shutdown.
    }
}
```

The AccountPersistenceAspect declares that the MainApplication class is to fulfill the ObjectStore interface and adds the Runnable interface as well. The Runnable interface, from java.lang, is used in Java as the interface to all objects that can be executed in their own thread. The public void run() method is required by the Runnable interface to provide the entry point for the Java Virtual Machine (JVM) to execute the class in its own thread.

In this example, the persistStorage(ObjectStore) pointcut is amended to capture the execution of the Runnable enforced public void run() method on the MyApplication class. The AccountPersistenceAspect then adds the necessary run() method implementation to the MainApplication class to meet the needs of the Runnable interface, but this merely provides a marker and does not need any implementation.

The addition of the Runnable interface and the stub run( ) method on the MainApplication class means that the MainApplication can be registered with the JVM as a shutdown hook so the MainApplicatin.run( ) method will be called when the overall application finishes normally. Registering the MainApplication class as a shutdown hook is completed by the around(MainApplication) advice block executed when an ObjectStore that is a MainApplication class is restored.

By using the MainApplication as a shutdown hook, the persistStorage(ObjectStore) pointcut will trigger the persisting of the MainApplication's objects when the shutdown hook is triggered. Therefore, the collection of Account classes stored within the MainApplication will be persisted once the application is shut down cleanly.

See Also

The call(Signature) pointcut is discussed in Recipe 4.1; the execution(Signature) pointcut is explained in Recipe 4.4; the this(TypePattern | Identifier) pointcut is explained in Recipe 9.1; the target(TypePattern | Identifier) pointcut is described in Recipe 9.2; the after( ) form of advice is described in Recipe 13.5; specializing abstract aspects is discussed in detail in Recipe 15.2; extending an existing class using the declare parents statement is explained in Recipe 16.2; the Director aspect-oriented design pattern is described in Recipe 23.2.

20.4 Applying Mock Components to Support Unit Testing

Problem

You want to unit test your own component in isolation by providing a test harness implementation of a component that your component uses.

Solution

Create a mock implementation of the external component that your component depends on. Create an aspect that applies the mock component implementation in place of the real component.

When unit testing is complete, use a separate AspectJ build configuration file to switch out the testing aspect so the real implementation can be used again.

Discussion

When you are creating your software components, unit test those components in isolation to ensure that the component works as it should. However, when your component relies on other components, it can be tricky and error prone to manually unhook all of the dependencies to the external components for the unit testing and to restore those hooks when unit testing is complete.

Example 20-9 shows a typical situation where MyComponent is the component to be tested, and it has dependencies on an external implementation of ThirdPartyComponentInterface. The real implementation of ThirdPartyComponentInterface is retrieved by making a call to the factory method ThirdPartyFactory.getThirdPartyComponent( ).

Example 20-9. Creating and using an external component

```
package com.ourcompany;

import com.thirdparty.ThirdPartyComponentFactory;
import com.thirdparty.ThirdPartyComponentInterface;

public class MyComponent implements MyComponentInterface
{
    private ThirdPartyComponentInterface thirdPartyComponent;

    public MyComponent( )
    {
        this.thirdPartyComponent = ThirdPartyComponentFactory.getThirdPartyComponent( );
        System.out.println("Component found " + thirdPartyComponent);
    }

    public void foo( )
    {
        System.out.println("Inside MyComponent.foo( )");
        this.thirdPartyComponent.bar( );
    }
}
```

 Example 20-9 shows the use of a factory class, but this is not a mandatory feature of this recipes solution. Overriding the instantiation of a third-party component directly is possible using the same techniques as shown in Recipe 20.2 without the need for a factory.

To run a unit test against MyComponent in isolation, you will need to override the ThirdPartyComponent implementation so you will not confuse the test results by including the real external component in the test. One strategy is to apply a mock component that overrides the real component implementation manually, as shown in Example 20-10.

Example 20-10. Creating a mock class and then manually amending your component to use the new mock object

```
package test.com.ourcompany;

import com.thirdparty.ThirdPartyComponentInterface;
```

Example 20-10. Creating a mock class and then manually amending your component to use the new mock object (continued)

```java
public class MockThirdPartyComponent implements ThirdPartyComponentInterface
{
    public void bar()
    {
        System.out.println("Inside MockThirdPartyComponent.bar()");
    }
}


package com.ourcompany;

import com.thirdparty.ThirdPartyComponentFactory;
import com.thirdparty.ThirdPartyComponentInterface;
import test.com.ourcompany.MockThirdPartyComponent;

public class MyComponent implements MyComponentInterface
{
    private ThirdPartyComponentInterface thirdPartyComponent;

    public MyComponent()
    {
        // Manually commented out for unit testing purposes
        // this.thirdPartyComponent =
        //     ThirdPartyComponentFactory.getThirdPartyComponent();

        // Replaced with mock object
        this.thirdPartyComponent = new MockThirdPartyComponent();

        System.out.println("Component found " + thirdPartyComponent);
    }

    public void foo()
    {
        System.out.println("Inside MyComponent.foo()");

        this.thirdPartyComponent.bar();
    }
}
```

The MockThirdPartyComponent is under your control, unlike the real implementation of the ThirdPartyComponentInterface, so you can tailor the component to test your MyComponent correctly. The MyComponent is no longer reliant on the real implementation of the ThirdPartyComponentInterface, so you can safely conclude that any problems that occur when it is tested are your problems.

After your unit testing is complete and you are satisfied that MyComponent is working correctly, the mock component can be removed and the original code uncommented. Using this method, switching back to the real implementation of ThirdPartyComponentInterface is another manual and potentially error-prone task.

Though the solution in Example 20-10 works fine, it can be a difficult approach to manage if your component uses more than a few interfaces. Using an aspect-oriented alternative, an aspect can be created that intercepts the creation of the ThirdPartyComponent and overrides the returned object with your mock object implementation, as shown in Example 20-11.

Example 20-11. Using an aspect to apply a mock object for isolation unit testing purposes

```
package test.com.ourcompany;

import com.thirdparty.*;

public aspect MockThirdPartyComponentAspect
{
    public pointcut catchThirdPartyConstructor() :
        call(ThirdPartyComponentInterface ThirdPartyComponentFactory.
            getThirdPartyComponent());

    Object around() : catchThirdPartyConstructor()
    {
        return new MockThirdPartyComponent();
    }
}
```

The catchThirdPartyConstructor() pointcut catches calls to the ThirdPartyFactory. getThirdPartyComponent() method and uses the associated around() advice to return your MockThirdPartyComponent object rather than the real implementation of the ThirdPartyComponentInterface. By using aspects rather than manual code changes, your component is prepared for isolation unit testing automatically after the aspect is woven into your application.

Similar to Recipe 6.3, this recipe shows another typical application of the Cuckoo's Egg aspect-oriented design pattern, which is discussed in Recipe 23.1.

You can switch between using the real or mock implementation of the external component at compile time by creating two different AspectJ build configuration files. A build configuration file that includes the mock object testing aspect will result in a build that will be all set for isolation unit testing of your component, and a build configuration file that excludes the mock object testing aspect will result in a deployment build that uses the real implementation of the external component.

AspectJ makes the task of applying mock objects for testing purposes less intrusive to your code, much more scalable and much less of a headache when it comes to switching between testing and deployment builds.

See Also

Using different build configurations to vary the aspects applied to an application is explained in Recipe 2.5; the call(Signature) pointcut is described in Recipe 4.1; the around( ) form of advice is covered in Recipe 13.4; how to implement the Abstract Factory and Factory Method design patterns using AspectJ is shown in Recipes 17.3 and 17.4, respectively; the Cuckoo's Egg aspect-oriented design pattern is discussed in Recipe 23.1.

CHAPTER 21

Applying Application Scale Aspects

21.0   Introduction

Application scale aspects affect significant areas of your software and are often characteristics of your software that affect many, even all, of the classes within your application. This chapter focuses on a set of these system scale cross-cutting concerns where AspectJ can be used to implement their characteristics better. The recipes in this chapter can be split into two categories: passive and active aspects.

Passive aspects are interceptors, or observers, or your application's logic and do not affect or feedback into this logic in an obvious way. One of the key characteristics of a passive aspect is that it will usually only contain before( ) and after( ) advice, and if around( ) advice is used, it will still always call the proceed( ) method.

Active aspects affect the application to which they are applied in ways such as changing logical paths through the software. Although both aspects affect your application's code when they are compiled and woven, active aspects will change the behavior of your application. Active aspects often contain around( ) advice that may not call the proceed( ) method and can override the triggering join point that was part of the original business logic.

This chapter begins by showing two passive application scale aspects that implement tracing and logging. Tracing and logging are almost the "Hello World" use cases for AspectJ, partially because they are good examples of flexible and modularized application-wide cross-cutting behavior. Although tracing and logging are not the most interesting of aspects, they are powerful examples of passive aspect implementation in AspectJ.

In the category of more active aspects, this chapter ends by showing how an application's properties can be managed better by modularizing how they are stored and how they are applied and updated using aspects. A property management aspect interacts directly with any classes that use those properties and can monitor the internals of those classes to register when a property has been updated.

21.1   Applying Aspect-Oriented Tracing

Problem

You want to apply tracing to areas of your application using AspectJ.

Solution

Create an abstract base aspect, as shown in Example 21-1, to encapsulate the generic tracing logic. Extend the generic tracing aspect using specialized subaspects to include or exclude areas of your application from the tracing.

Example 21-1. An abstract tracing aspect that defines the generic tracing logic to be specialized for your application

```
import org.aspectj.lang.JoinPoint;

public abstract aspect TracingAspect
{
    public abstract pointcut pointsToBeTraced();

    public abstract pointcut pointsToBeExcluded();

    public pointcut filteredPointsToBeTraced(Object caller) :
        pointsToBeTraced() &&
        !pointsToBeExcluded() &&
        !within(com.oreilly.aspectjcookbook.tracing.TracingAspect+) &&
        this(caller);

    public pointcut catchStaticCallers() :
        pointsToBeTraced() &&
        !pointsToBeExcluded() &&
        !within(com.oreilly.aspectjcookbook.tracing.TracingAspect+) &&
        !filteredPointsToBeTraced(Object);

    before(Object caller) : filteredPointsToBeTraced(caller)
    {
        traceBefore(thisJoinPoint, caller);
    }

    before() : catchStaticCallers()
    {
        traceStaticBefore(thisJoinPoint);
    }

    after(Object caller) : filteredPointsToBeTraced(caller)
    {
        traceAfter(thisJoinPoint, caller);
    }

    after() : catchStaticCallers()
    {
```

```
        traceStaticAfter(thisJoinPoint);
    }

    protected void traceBefore(JoinPoint joinPoint, Object caller)
    {
        System.out.println(caller + " calling " +
            joinPoint.getSignature() + " @ " +
            joinPoint.getSourceLocation());
    }

    protected void traceStaticBefore(JoinPoint joinPoint)
    {
        System.out.println("Static code calling " +
            joinPoint.getSignature() + " @ " +
            joinPoint.getSourceLocation());
    }

    protected void traceAfter(JoinPoint joinPoint, Object caller)
    {
        System.out.println("Returning from call to" +
            joinPoint.getSignature() + " @ " +
            joinPoint.getSourceLocation());
    }

    protected void traceStaticAfter(JoinPoint joinPoint)
    {
        System.out.println("Returning from static call to " +
            joinPoint.getSignature() + " @ " +
            joinPoint.getSourceLocation());
    }

    private static aspect FormatCallDepthAspect
    {
        private static int callDepth;

        private pointcut captureTraceBefore() :
            call(protected void TracingAspect.trace*Before(..));

        private pointcut captureTraceAfter() :
            call(protected void TracingAspect.trace*After(..));

        after() : captureTraceBefore()
        {
            callDepth++;
        }

        before() : captureTraceAfter()
        {
            callDepth--;
        }
```

Example 21-1. An abstract tracing aspect that defines the generic tracing logic to be specialized for your application (continued)

```
    private pointcut captureMessageOutput(String message) :
        call(* *.println(String)) &&
        args(message) &&
        within(TracingAspect) &&
        !within(FormatCallDepthAspect);

    Object around(String originalMessage) : captureMessageOutput(originalMessage)
    {
        StringBuffer buffer = new StringBuffer( );
        for (int x = 0; x < callDepth; x++)
        {
            buffer.append("  ");
        }
        buffer.append(originalMessage);

        return proceed(buffer.toString( ));
    }
  }
}
```

Discussion

The TracingAspect has a couple of abstract pointcuts, pointsToBeTraced( ) and pointsToBeExcluded( ), to allow specialized subaspects to specify the areas of the target application to be subjected to the tracing.

The filteredPointsToBeTraced(Object) pointcut then combines the pointsToBeTraced( ) and pointsToBeExcluded( ) pointcuts along with logic for excluding the TracingAspect itself and exposure of the calling object that triggered the tracing. This combined pointcut captures all of the join points to be traced within the target application that have a calling object. Unfortunately, the filteredPointsToBeTraced(Object) pointcut will exclude those join points that occur in a static code block because of the use of the this(TypePattern | Identifier) pointcut.

The catchStaticCallers( ) pointcut solves this problem by capturing all of the join points to be included in the tracing but not caught by the filteredPointsToBeTraced(Object) pointcut.

Two sets of before( ) and after( ) advice output the tracing messages to System.out. One set performs the message output for when the calling object is available; the other set does the same thing for when the calling object is not available.

If the TracingAspect was left at that, the tracing messages would be a little hard to read. It would be useful to format the tracing messages appropriately by indenting each message according to the current call depth. This turns out to be an aspect-wide cross-cutting concern because all of the advice blocks in the aspect will need to be affected with the appropriate formatting logic.

The FormatCallDepth inner aspect meets the formatting needs for all of the tracing messages across the TracingAspect aspect. The FormatCallDepth aspect keeps an internal count on the current call depth by monitoring when the TracingAspect performs before and after tracing. When the TracingAspect makes a tracing call to System.out, the FormatCallDepth aspect amends the tracing message according to the current call depth.

Example 21-2 shows how the TracingAspect aspect can be applied to an example application.

Example 21-2. Applying the TracingAspect to a specific example application

```
public aspect ApplicationSpecificTracingAspect extends TracingAspect
{
    public pointcut pointsToBeTraced() : call(* *.*(..));

    public pointcut pointsToBeExcluded() : call(void java.io.PrintStream.*(..));
}
```

See Also

The call(Signature) pointcut is described in Recipe 4.1; the within(TypePattern) pointcut is described in Recipe 9.1; the this(TypePattern | Identifier) pointcut is explained in Recipe 7.1; the args([TypePatterns || Identifiers]) pointcut is covered in Recipe 7.3; the AND (&&) operator and the OR (||) operator are described in Recipes 12.2 and 12.3 respectively; the before( ) form of advice is explained in Recipe 13.3; the around( ) form of advice, including using the proceed( ) method, is discussed in Recipe 13.4; the after( ) form of advice is explained in Recipe 13.5; using inheritance to implement abstract aspects is explained in Recipe 15.2; defining and using inner aspects is explained in Recipe 15.4.

21.2   Applying Aspect-Oriented Logging

Problem

You want to apply logging in a modular and application independent way.

Solution

Create an abstract Logging aspect that extends the generic TracingAspect from Recipe 21.1. Extend the TracingAspect with abstract pointcut definitions and advice for exception logging to complete the logging aspect, as shown in Example 21-3. The new exception logging abstract pointcut definitions allow specialized subaspects to capture areas of the target application where exception logging needs to take place.

Example 21-3. An abstract logging aspect that defines the generic logging logic to be specialized for your application

```
public abstract aspect LoggingAspect extends TracingAspect
{
    protected abstract pointcut exceptionsToBeLogged();

    private pointcut filteredExceptionCapture() :
        exceptionsToBeLogged() &&
        !pointsToBeExcluded();

    before() : filteredExceptionCapture()
    {
        logException(thisJoinPoint);
    }

    public abstract void logException(JoinPoint joinPoint);
}
```

Discussion

The LoggingAspect aspect inherits all of the behavior from the TracingAspect shown in Recipe 21.1 but adds some new capabilities specific to logging. The exceptionsToBeLogged() abstract pointcut is provided so specialized subaspects can specify the join points where exception information is to be logged. The logException(JoinPoint) abstract method allows subaspects to implement the exact behavior that will occur when exceptions are logged.

 The handler(TypePattern) pointcut is the most appropriate pointcut declaration to use in the specialized subaspects when implementing the abstract exceptionsToBeLogged() pointcut. However, no way exists to restrict the exceptionsToBeLogged() pointcut to just handler(TypePattern) pointcut definitions.

The filteredExceptionCapture() pointcut then combines the exceptionsToBeLogged() pointcut with the pointcutsToBeExcluded() pointcut inherited from the TracingAspect so any join points that have been declared as excluded continue to be excluded from the logging.

Example 21-4 shows how the abstract LoggingAspect in Example 21-3 can be applied to an example application.

Example 21-4. Implementing logging for an example application

```
public aspect ApplicationLoggingAspect extends LoggingAspect
{
    public pointcut pointsToBeTraced() : call(* *.*(..));

    public pointcut pointsToBeExcluded() :  call(* java.io.*.*(..));
```

Example 21-4. Implementing logging for an example application (continued)

```
public pointcut exceptionsToBeLogged( ) :
    handler(com.oreilly.aspectjcookbook.PackageA.BusinessException);

protected void traceBefore(JoinPoint joinPoint, Object caller)
{
    System.out.println("Log Message: Called " + joinPoint.getSignature( ));
}

protected void traceStaticBefore(JoinPoint joinPoint)
{
    System.out.println("Log Message: Statically Called " + joinPoint.getSignature( ));
}

protected void traceAfter(JoinPoint joinPoint, Object object)
{
    System.out.println("Log Message: Returned from " + joinPoint.getSignature( ));
}

protected void traceStaticAfter(JoinPoint joinPoint)
{
    System.out.println("Log Message: Returned from static call to " +
        joinPoint.getSignature( ));
}

protected void logException(JoinPoint joinPoint)
{
    System.out.println("Log Message: " + joinPoint.getArgs( )[0] + " exception thrown");
}

private static aspect FormatCallDepthAspect
{
    private static int callDepth;

    private pointcut captureTraceBefore( ) :
        call(protected void TracingAspect.trace*Before(..));

    private pointcut captureTraceAfter( ) :
        call(protected void TracingAspect.trace*After(..));

    after() : captureTraceBefore( )
    {
        callDepth++;
    }

    before() : captureTraceAfter( )
    {
        callDepth--;
    }

    private pointcut captureMessageOutput(String message) :
        call(* *.println(String)) &&
        args(message) &&
```

Example 21-4. Implementing logging for an example application (continued)

```
        within(ApplicationLoggingAspect) &&
        !within(FormatCallDepthAspect);

    Object around(String originalMessage) : captureMessageOutput(originalMessage)
    {
        StringBuffer buffer = new StringBuffer( );
        for (int x = 0; x < callDepth; x++)
        {
            buffer.append("  ");
        }
        buffer.append(originalMessage);

        return proceed(buffer.toString( ));
    }
  }
}
```

The `ApplicationLoggingAspect` aspect provides an implementation of the
`pointsToBeTraced( )` and `pointsToBeExcluded( )` pointcuts to specify the areas of the
target application to be logged and excluded from logging. The new exception logging pointcut, `exceptionsToBeLogged( )`, is implemented to meet the requirements of
the `LoggingAspect`.

The `FormatCallDepth` inner aspect is included in the `ApplicationLoggingAspect` for
convenience to make the logging messages easy to read when they are output
through `System.out`. If you were using a full logging solution, this inner aspect would
most likely not be required as the logging API would probably provide formatting
options of its own.

 You can plug in any logging API you want to use by placing the code
that initializes and invokes your logging API in the specialized subaspects of the `LoggingAspect` aspect.

The abstract `LoggingAspect` aspect supports multiple subaspects potentially logging
parts of your application in different ways at the same time. The code sample in
Example 21-5 shows how an additional aspect could be added to logs calls to targets
within a specific package using an XML format for the message output.

Example 21-5. Applying multiple logging solutions to the same application

```
public aspect PackageSpecificLoggingAspect extends LoggingAspect
{
    declare precedence : ApplicationLoggingAspect, PackageSpecificLoggingAspect;

    public pointcut pointsToBeTraced( ) :
        call(* com.oreilly.aspectjcookbook.PackageA.*.*(..));

    public pointcut pointsToBeExcluded( ) : call(void java.io.PrintStream.*(..));
```

```
    public pointcut exceptionsToBeLogged( ) : handler(PackageA.*);

    protected void traceBefore(JoinPoint joinPoint, Object object)
    {
        System.out.println("<before>" + joinPoint.getSignature( ) + "</before>");
    }

    protected void traceStaticBefore(JoinPoint joinPoint)
    {
        System.out.println("<before type=\"static\">" +
            joinPoint.getSignature( ) + "</before>");
    }

    protected void traceAfter(JoinPoint joinPoint, Object object)
    {
        System.out.println("<after>" + joinPoint.getSignature( ) + "</after>");
    }

    protected void traceStaticAfter(JoinPoint joinPoint)
    {
        System.out.println("<after type=\"static\">" +
            joinPoint.getSignature( ) + "</after>");
    }

    protected void logException(JoinPoint joinPoint)
    {
        System.out.println("<exception>" + joinPoint.getSignature( ) + "</exception>");
    }
```

See Also

The call(Signature) pointcut is described in Recipe 4.1; the handler(TypePattern) pointcut is shown in Recipe 5.1; the AND (&&) operator and the OR (||) operator are described in Recipes 12.2 and 12.3 respectively; the before( ) form of advice is explained in Recipe 13.3; the around( ) form of advice, including using the proceed( ) method, is discussed in Recipe 13.4; the after( ) form of advice is explained in Recipe 13.5; using inheritance to implement abstract aspects is explained in Recipe 15.2; defining and using inner aspects is explained in Recipe 15.4.

21.3 Applying Lazy Loading

Problem

You want to apply lazy loading techniques to a component of your application.

Solution

Use the Director aspect-oriented design pattern to set up the roles involved in lazy loading as interfaces inside an abstract aspect, as shown in Example 21-6.

Example 21-6. Using the Director aspect-oriented pattern to define the roles that take part in lazy loading

```
public abstract aspect LazyLoading extends DelegatingProxyPattern
{
   public interface RealComponent extends Subject
   {
   }

   public interface LazyProxy extends RealComponent
   {
      public RealComponent getRealComponent( ) throws LazyLoadingException;
   }

   public abstract LazyProxy initializeComponent(Object configuration);
}
```

The LazyLoading aspect in turn inherits from an implementation of the Proxy pattern, as shown in Recipe 14.6, that focuses on the delegation characteristics of the Proxy pattern, as shown in Example 21-7.

Example 21-7. Specializing the ProxyPattern behavior to focus on delegation

```
public abstract aspect DelegatingProxyPattern extends ProxyPattern
{
   protected boolean reject(
      Object caller,
      Subject subject,
      JoinPoint joinPoint)
   {
      return false;
   }

   protected boolean delegate(
      Object caller,
      Subject subject,
      JoinPoint joinPoint)
   {
      return true;
   }

   protected Object rejectRequest(
      Object caller,
      Subject subject,
      JoinPoint joinPoint)
   {
      return null;
   }
}
```

Finally, create specialized subaspects of the `LazyLoading` aspect that will implement the lazy loading behavior for specific components of your target application.

Discussion

Lazy loading involves the loading and instantiation of a class being delayed until the point just before the instance is used. The goal of lazy loading is to dedicate memory resources when necessary by loading and instantiating an object at the point when it is needed.

The `LazyLoading` aspect in Example 21-6 builds in the `DelegatingProxyPattern` in Example 21-7 to intercept calls to classes that it is to lazily load on demand. The `DelegationProxyPattern` in turn specializes the `ProxyPattern` aspect from Recipe 14.6 to limit the scope to a delegation form of proxy.

The `RealComponent` interface declared in the `LazyLoading` aspect is applied by specialized subaspects to any classes within the target application to be lazily loaded. You need a proxy object to store the information by which the real class can be instantiated when needed and this role is provided by the `LazyProxy` interface.

The `LazyProxy` interface offers enough functionality to work with the real components without having to load them. The `LazyProxy` defines a single method which is called to load the real component when needed.

Finally, the `LazyLoading` abstract aspect defines the abstract `initializeComponent(Object)` method which is implemented by subaspects to instantiate lazy proxies in place of the real components.

Example 21-8 shows how the abstract `LazyLoading` aspect can be applied to an example application.

Example 21-8. Applying the LazyLoading abstract aspect to an application's classes

```
package com.oreilly.aspectjcookbook.feature_management;

import org.aspectj.lang.JoinPoint;
import com.oreilly.aspectjcookbook.lazyloading.LazyLoading;
import com.oreilly.aspectjcookbook.lazyloading.LazyLoadingException;
import com.oreilly.aspectjcookbook.features.Feature;

public aspect LazyFeatureLoading extends LazyLoading
{
    declare parents : Feature implements RealComponent;

    declare parents : LazyProxy implements Feature;

    public LazyProxy initializeComponent(Object object)
    {
        LazyProxy proxy =
            new LazyFeatureProxy((String) object);
        return proxy;
    }
}
```

```
protected pointcut requestTriggered() :
    call(* com.oreilly.aspectjcookbook.features.Feature.* (..)) &&
    !within(com.oreilly.aspectjcookbook.oopatterns.ProxyPattern+);

protected Object delegateRequest(
    Object caller,
    Subject subject,
    JoinPoint joinPoint)
{
    if (subject instanceof LazyFeatureProxy)
    {
        LazyFeatureProxy feature =
            (LazyFeatureProxy) subject;

        try
        {
            Feature implementedFeature =
                (Feature) feature.getRealComponent();

            implementedFeature.doSomething(
                    (String) joinPoint.getArgs()[0]);

        }
        catch (LazyLoadingException lle)
        {
            lle.printStackTrace();
            lle.getOriginalException().printStackTrace();
            System.out.println(
                    "Exception when attempting to "
                + "lazy load"
                + " a particular class,"
                + " aborting the call");
        }
    }
    else
    {
        ((Feature) subject).doSomething(
                (String) joinPoint.getArgs()[0]);
    }
    return null;
}

private class LazyFeatureProxy implements Feature, LazyProxy
{
    private Object configuration;
    private Feature delegate;

    public LazyFeatureProxy(Object configuration)
    {
        this.configuration = configuration;
    }
```

```
    public synchronized RealComponent getRealComponent( )
        throws LazyLoadingException
    {
        if (this.configuration instanceof String)
        {
            try
            {
                if (this.delegate == null)
                {
                    return this.delegate =
                        (Feature) Class
                        .forName((String) this.configuration)
                        .newInstance( );
                }
                else
                {
                    return this.delegate;
                }
            }
            catch (Exception e)
            {
                throw new LazyLoadingException(
                    "Exception raised when loading real component", e);
            }
        }
        else
        {
            throw new LazyLoadingException("Error in configuration");
        }
    }

    public void doSomething(String message)
    {
    }
  }
}
```

The LazyFeatureLoading aspect encapsulates how to lazily load the category of classes that implement the Feature interface. The two declare parent statements specify that any class implementing the Feature interface meets the RealComponent role and that the LazyProxy can replace a Feature to fulfill its role of providing a proxy for any Feature objects.

The initializeComponent(Object) method returns a LazyProxy instance set up with the necessary configuration to load the real component. The initializeComponent(Object) method is called whenever the target application decides that a particular instance is to be lazily loaded.

The requestTriggered(..) pointcut and the delegateRequest(..) method are required by the abstract DelegatingProxyPattern. The requestTriggered(..) pointcut is used to capture all calls to methods on classes that implement the Feature interface. Additional protection is provided to stop the LazyFeatureLoading aspect advising itself when the method being called on a LazyProxy is called by the aspect.

The delegateRequest(..) method examines the subject being called to see if it is an instance of the LazyfeatureProxy class. If the subject is an instance of LazyFeatureProxy, the getRealComponent( ) method is called to load the real component. The method call is then forwarded to the real component.

Finally, the LazyFeatureLoading aspect defines the LazyFeatureProxy class. This class contains all of the information necessary to load the corresponding real Feature implementation should a method be called. The loading of the real Feature implementation is performed by the getRealComponent( ) method required by the LazyProxy interface.

Example 21-9 shows how the LazyFeatureLoading aspect is used by an example application to support the lazy loading of the FeatureA and FeatureB classes. In this example, both of these classes implement the Feature interface.

Example 21-9. Using the LazyFeatureLoading aspect in an example application

```
public class MainApplication
{
    private Feature[] features;

    public MainApplication( )
    {
        features = new Feature[2];

        features[0] =
            LazyFeatureLoading
                .aspectOf( )
                .initializeComponent(
                "com.oreilly.aspectjcookbook.features.FeatureA");

        features[1] =
            LazyFeatureLoading
                .aspectOf( )
                .initializeComponent(
                "com.oreilly.aspectjcookbook.features.FeatureB");

        features[0].doSomething("Hello there");
        features[0].doSomething("Hello again");

        features[1].doSomething("Hi to you too");
        features[1].doSomething("Hi again");
    }

    public static void main(String[] args)
    {
```

Example 21-9. Using the LazyFeatureLoading aspect in an example application (continued)

```
        MainApplication mainApplication =
            new MainApplication( );
    }
}
```

See Also

The call(Signature) pointcut is described in Recipe 4.1; the within(TypePattern) pointcut is described in Recipe 9.1; the AND (&&) operator and the OR (||) operator are described in Recipes 12.2 and 12.3 respectively; using inheritance to implement abstract aspects is explained in Recipe 15.2; creating a delegating proxy pattern using aspects is shown in Recipe 18.6; the Director aspect-oriented design pattern is explained in Recipe 23.2.

21.4 Managing Application Properties

Problem

You want to manage your applications configuration properties transparently to your applications classes.

Solution

Create an aspect that loads, supplies, monitors, and stores your applications properties.

Discussion

Java application properties are traditionally loaded from and managed by a singleton class. An example of this is the System.getProperty( ) method, which returns a property supplied to the application from the command line with the –D option.

Unfortunately, singletons tend to be a brittle solution resulting in many areas of your application depending on the interface to the singleton. If the singleton's interface were to change, it is likely that the many dependent areas of your application would have to change to incorporate the new interface. This is the sort of cross-cutting concern that aspects can solve.

In traditional approaches to property management, the singleton property manager is a passive participant in your application and responds to requests for property information from the various parts of your application. The property manager doesn't have any knowledge of what is done with the property information it provides, or where it goes, and is dependent on notifications when any property is updated.

With an aspect-oriented approach to system properties, the perspective is switched around. The mechanisms provided by AspectJ allow you to design your property manager so it will actively apply the properties to those areas of your application where they are needed. All of the information about where a property is deployed is contained within the aspect, so if new properties are required then only the aspect will change.

The property managing aspect decouples the rest of the application from any considerations about how a property is loaded, stored, and supplied. You are no longer tied to a simplistic name/value form of interface to properties because that interface no longer exists. The aspect loads the properties, applies them where they are needed, and stores them away when the application closes.

One final advantage to managing properties using aspects is that, because a property management aspect is likely to be a privileged aspect to set the variables in the application that correspond to the properties that it manages, it can monitor any changes to those variables if necessary to reflect those changes back into its properties. This means that the aspect loads, supplies, and stores the properties and can monitor the properties for changes removing any need for the application to notify the properties manager when a property has changed.

Example 21-10 shows a property manager aspect for a simple example application.

Example 21-10. Loading, applying, monitoring, and storing an application's properties using aspects

```
package com.oreilly.aspectjcookbook;

import java.util.Properties;
import java.io.File;
import java.io.FileInputStream;
import java.io.FileOutputStream;

public privileged aspect MyApplicationProperties
{
    // Property names

    private static final String MYCLASS_PROPERTY_NAME =
        "com.oreilly.aspectjcookbook.MyClass.property";

    private static final String MAINAPPLICATION_PROPERTY_NAME =
        "com.oreilly.aspectjcookbook.MainApplication.property";

    // Default property values

    private static final int DEFAULT_MAINAPPLICATION_PROPERTY = 1;

    private static final String DEFAULT_MYCLASS_PROPERTY = "Property Initialized:";

    // Property Storage

    private static final String PROPERTY_FILE_SYSTEM_PROPERTY = "props";
```

Example 21-10. Loading, applying, monitoring, and storing an application's properties using aspects (continued)

```
   private static final String DEFAULT_PROPERTIES_FILENAME =
      "myapplication.properties";

   Properties applicationProperties = new Properties();

   File propertiesFile;

   // Load Properties

   public MyApplicationProperties()
   {
      try
      {
         String propertyFilename = System.getProperty(PROPERTY_FILE_SYSTEM_PROPERTY);
         if (propertyFilename != null)
         {
            propertiesFile = new File(propertyFilename);
         }
         else
         {
            propertiesFile = new File(DEFAULT_PROPERTIES_FILENAME);
         }
         FileInputStream inputStream = new FileInputStream(propertiesFile);
         applicationProperties.load(inputStream);
         inputStream.close();
      }
      catch (Exception e)
      {
         // Just using default properties instead.
         System.err.println("Unable to load properties file, reverting to default
values");
      }

   }

   // Supply Properties

   public pointcut mainApplicationInitialization() :
      staticinitialization(MainApplication);

   after() : mainApplicationInitialization()
   {
      try
      {
         int mainApplicationProperty =
            new Integer(
               applicationProperties.getProperty(
                  MAINAPPLICATION_PROPERTY_NAME)).intValue();

         MainApplication.property = mainApplicationProperty;
      }
```

```
      catch (Exception e)
      {
          MainApplication.property = DEFAULT_MAINAPPLICATION_PROPERTY;

          applicationProperties.setProperty(
            MAINAPPLICATION_PROPERTY_NAME,
            new Integer(DEFAULT_MAINAPPLICATION_PROPERTY).toString( ));
      }
  }

  public pointcut myClassObjectCreation(MyClass myObject) :
    execution(public MyClass.new(..)) &&
    this(myObject);

  before(MyClass myObject) : myClassObjectCreation(myObject)
  {
      String myClassProperty = applicationProperties.
        getProperty(MYCLASS_PROPERTY_NAME);
      if (myClassProperty != null)
      {
          myObject.property = myClassProperty;
      }
      else
      {
          myObject.property = DEFAULT_MYCLASS_PROPERTY;
          applicationProperties.setProperty(
            MYCLASS_PROPERTY_NAME, DEFAULT_MYCLASS_PROPERTY);
      }
  }

  // Monitoring properties

  public pointcut monitorMainApplicationProperty(int newValue) :
    set(int MainApplication.property) &&
    args(newValue);

  after(int newValue) : monitorMainApplicationProperty(newValue) &&
    !within(MyApplicationProperties)
  {
      applicationProperties.setProperty(
        MAINAPPLICATION_PROPERTY_NAME,
        new Integer(newValue).toString( ));
  }

  public pointcut monitorMyClassProperty(String newValue) :
    set(String MyClass.property) &&
    args(newValue);

  after(String newValue) : monitorMyClassProperty(newValue) &&
    !within(MyApplicationProperties)
  {
```

```
        applicationProperties.setProperty(MYCLASS_PROPERTY_NAME, newValue);
    }

    // Store properties on application close

    class ShutdownMonitor implements Runnable
    {
        public ShutdownMonitor()
        {
            Thread shutdownThread = new Thread(this);
            Runtime.getRuntime().addShutdownHook(shutdownThread);

        }

        public void run()
        {
            try
            {
                FileOutputStream outputStream = new FileOutputStream(propertiesFile);

                applicationProperties.store(
                outputStream);
                outputStream.close();
            }
            catch (Exception e)
            {
                System.err.println(
                    "Unable to save properties file, will use default on next run");
            }
        }
    }

    private ShutdownMonitor shutdownMonitor = new ShutdownMonitor();
}
```

First, the MyApplicationProperties aspect needs to be declared as privileged because it is going to affect the internal private areas of the application's class to apply and monitor the property values to the areas where they are needed.

The names of the two application properties are then declared as constants. In this case, two properties are being managed, an int in the com.oreilly.aspectjcookbook. MainApplication class and a String in the com.oreilly.aspectjcookbook.MyClass class. Some default values for these two properties will be defined in case any problems occur when loading the properties.

The properties are loaded from a file and stored as java.util.Properties within the aspect as specified by the java.util.File attribute, propertiesFile, and applicationProperties attribute. Aspects in AspectJ are initialized before the class containing the public void main(String[]) method entry point for a Java application, so the MyApplicationProperties constructor can load the applications properties from the specified file and then apply those properties before the application starts running.

The mainApplicationInitialization() and myClassObjectCreation() pointcuts capture when the classes that need the properties are initialized so as to apply the properties before instances of the classes access those properties. The monitorMainApplicationProperty() and monitorMyClassProperty() pointcuts then watch the properties in the classes that need them to detect when any class changes the properties' value. If a change occurs, the after() advice will be triggered and the master value of the property updated. Other objects that use the property are not notified when the master value is changed because this is not how properties traditionally work. If one object changes a properties value, another object will not be informed of that change. You could implement notification of all dependent objects when a property value changes by using the Observer pattern from Recipe 15.1.

Finally, to handle storage of the applications properties when the application closes, the ShutdownMonitor class is created and instantiated as an attribute of the aspect. The ShutdownMonitor class registers itself as a shutdown hook in its constructor, and when its run() method is called as the application closes, the ShutdownMonitor stores the applications properties back to the indicated file.

See Also

The execution(Signature) pointcut is described in Recipe 4.4; the set(Signature) pointcut is examined in Recipe 8.3; the staticinitialization(TypePattern) pointcut is described in Recipe 7.5; the within(TypePattern) pointcut is described in Recipe 9.1; the this(TypePattern | Identifier) pointcut is explained in Recipe 11.1; The args([TypePatterns || Identifiers]) pointcut is covered in Recipe 11.3; the AND (&&) operator and the OR (||) operator are described in Recipes 12.2 and 12.3 respectively; the before() form of advice is explained in Recipe 13.3; the after() form of advice is explained in Recipe 13.5; Recipe 19.1 shows how to implement the Observer object-oriented design pattern using aspects.

CHAPTER 22
Applying Enterprise Scale Aspects

22.0   Introduction

An enterprise-scale application often has to consider factors that are above and beyond the scope of more traditional desktop software. Those concerns can be good candidates for an aspect-oriented approach because they are rarely closely coupled to the core business logic of the software.

Concerns such as transactional behavior, distributed communications, and security implications are the mainstays of any serious enterprise system. Even tasks such as providing and enforcing development guidelines, often a headache for large systems development, are shown to benefit from AspectJ's capability to advise the compiler.

Because so much of an enterprise system is not core to an application's business logic, these systems are seen as one of the areas where aspect orientation comes into its own. Enterprise systems are the fastest growing area for aspect orientation, and the aspects in this chapter represent a small selection of some of the concerns within those systems that benefit from an aspect-oriented approach.

 Evidence of the rapid adoption of aspect-oriented techniques in enterprise systems appears in the work within the leading J2EE communities. In particular, the open source Spring Framework (*http://www.springframework.org*) and JBoss (*http://www.jboss.org*) communities incorporate fairly mature implementations of aspect orientation and, with commercial companies, notably IBM, staunchly backing the approach, aspect-oriented facilities may soon become a regular and important part of the enterprise developer's tool suite.

22.1   Applying Development Guidelines and Rules

Problem

You want to control what programmatic constructs are allowed in your application by providing a policy that is enforced at compile time.

Solution

Use the Border Controller aspect-oriented design pattern to declare a set of regions within your code. Reuse those regions when declaring any top-level rules for your project in an aspect according to the Policy pattern. Optionally extend your projects' top-level policies to specialize them for particular regions of your application.

Discussion

This solution gives you a sneak preview of two of the aspect-oriented design patterns coming in Chapter 23. Providing the foundation for this recipe's solution, the Border Controller design pattern allows you to capture your application's architecture as a set of reusable pointcuts that declare important regions within your code. Those regions can be referenced throughout the rest of the aspects in your application.

The BorderControllerAspect shown in Example 22-1 declares four regions within an example application: the withinTestingRegion( ) region incorporates the packages where testing code is located, withinMyApp( ) specifies the packages and subpackages that make up your application, withinThirdParty( ) specifies any areas where you may be using third-party source code, and withinMyAppMainMethod( ) conveniently declares the location of the main(..) method for your application.

Example 22-1. Providing a foundation for your project and application's policies by declaring the important regions within your code

```
package com.oreilly.aspectjcookbook;

public aspect BorderControllerAspect
{
   /**
    * Specifies the testing region.
    */
   public pointcut withinTestingRegion() :
     within(com.oreilly.aspectjcookbook.testing.+);

   /**
    * Specifies My Applications region.
    */
   public pointcut withinMyApp() : within(com.oreilly.aspectjcookbook.myapp.+);
```

```
/**
 * Specifies a third party source code region.
 */
public pointcut withinThirdParty() :
    within(com.oreilly.aspectjcookbook.thirdpartylibrary.+);


/**
 * Specifies the applications main method.
 */
public pointcut withinMyAppMainMethod() :
    withincode(public void com.oreilly.aspectjcookbook.myapp.MyClass.main(..));
}
```

Example 22-1 shows only some of the areas that could be defined in an application. Other good candidates are areas where special logging is to take place, areas that are subjected to lazy loading logic, and anywhere you find it useful to formally bound parts of your architecture so that further pointcut definitions can reuse and work safely within those borders. The idea is that if those borders were to change, you would only change the Border Controller so the rest of your application's pointcut logic would immediately pick up on any relevant changes to their scope.

The Border Controller provides a useful library of reusable pointcut definitions incorporated into the Policy aspect-oriented design pattern. This pattern is used to solve this recipe's problem by declaring the different policies for your project's areas, as shown in Example 22-2.

Example 22-2. Defining a project-wide policy

```
package com.oreilly.aspectjcookbook;

public abstract aspect ProjectPolicyAspect
{
    protected abstract pointcut allowedSystemOuts();

    declare warning :
        call(* *.println(..)) &&
        !allowedSystemOuts() &&
        !BorderControllerAspect.withinTestingRegion()
    : "System.out usage detected. Suggest using logging?";
}
```

The ProjectPolicyAspect in Example 22-2 defines the project-wide rule that messages being output to the System.out stream are to be warned against at compile time. The aspect leaves an abstract pointcut so specialized aspects can define areas where using System.out is acceptable. The specialized MyAppPolicyAspect in Example 22-3 extends the abstract ProjectPolicyAspect to declare that the testing and the thirdpartylibrary source directories are allowed to use System.out.

Example 22-3. Specializing the project-wide policy for the specifics of your application's area

```
package com.oreilly.aspectjcookbook.myapp;

import com.oreilly.aspectjcookbook.ProjectPolicyAspect;
import com.oreilly.aspectjcookbook.BorderControllerAspect;

public aspect MyAppPolicyAspect extends ProjectPolicyAspect
{
    /**
     * Specifies regions within the application where messages
     * to System.out are allowed.
     */
    protected pointcut allowedSystemOuts() :
        BorderControllerAspect.withinMyAppMainMethod() ||
        BorderControllerAspect.withinThirdParty() ||
        BorderControllerAspect.withinTestingRegion();
}
```

Using the Policy and Border Controller aspect-oriented patterns, you can formalize the structure of your architecture and apply consistent project, application, package, class, and method scope policies.

See Also

The call(Signature) pointcut is described in Recipe 4.1; the within(TypePattern) pointcut is described in Recipe 9.1; the withincode(Signature) pointcut is described in Recipe 9.3; the AND (&&) operator and the OR (||) operator are described in Recipes 12.2 and 12.3 respectively; the unary NOT (!) operator is shown in Recipe 12.4; defining reusable libraries of pointcut definitions is covered in Recipe 12.6; extending the compiler with new warnings and errors is shown in Recipe 16.6; the Border Controller aspect-oriented design pattern is explained in Recipe 23.3; the Policy aspect-oriented design pattern is described in Recipe 23.4.

22.2   Applying Transactions

Problem

You want to introduce transactional behavior to a method in your application.

Solution

Use the Director aspect-oriented design pattern to declare an abstract aspect that captures the generic behavior of controlling a transaction, as shown in Example 22-4. Extending the abstract transaction aspect, declare specialized subaspects for each transaction within your application.

Example 22-4. Declaring the generic behavior of a transaction in a reusable abstract aspect

```
public abstract aspect TransactionAspect
{
    protected abstract pointcut transactionalCall();

    protected pointcut transactionBoundary() :
        transactionalCall() && !cflowbelow(transactionalCall());

    protected interface Transaction
    {
        public void commit();
        public void rollback();
    }

    protected Transaction transaction;

    before() : transactionBoundary()
    {
        setupTransaction(thisJoinPoint.getArgs());
    }

    after() returning: transactionBoundary()
    {
        transaction.commit();
    }

    after() throwing: transactionBoundary()
    {
        transaction.rollback();
    }

    protected abstract void setupTransaction(Object[] args);
}
```

Discussion

Transactions are used to group a selection of operations into a cohesive unit that either completes or, in the case where one step in the process fails, reverts back to its original state.

In Example 22-4, the TransactionAspect first specifies the transactionCall() abstract pointcut. This pointcut is used by specialized subaspects to specify the methods within the target application that are to be treated as transactional.

The transactionBoundary() pointcut then builds on the transactionCall() pointcut to specify where the transaction starts and ends. The cflowbelow() pointcut is used to ignore any join points that may occur within the life of the transaction.

The TransactionAspect needs to store and interact with transactions generically so the Transaction interface is defined. The Transaction interface provides a base for subaspects to implement their own transaction classes. A single transaction attribute is then used to indicate the current transaction being managed by the aspect.

Finally, three pieces of advice work with the transaction attribute at the different points within a transaction's lifecycle. The before( ) advice calls the abstract setupTransaction(Object[]) method so the transaction attribute can be correctly initialized with the appropriate Transaction implementation. The after( ) returning advice will be executed if the join points selected by the transactionCall( ) pointcut return without raising an exception; this is a good time for the transaction to be committed. The after( ) throwing advice caters to the situation where a join point returns with an exception, so the transaction needs to be rolled back.

Example 22-5 shows how to specialize the TransactionAspect for an example application where the transfer(..) method is selected by the implementation of the transactionalCall( ) pointcut to mark the beginning of a transaction.

Example 22-5. Implementing transactional behavior where a transfer occurs between two bank accounts within an example application

```
import com.oreilly.aspectjcookbook.Account;
import com.oreilly.aspectjcookbook.InsufficientFundsException;

public aspect TransferTransactionAspect extends TransactionAspect
{
    protected pointcut transactionalCall() :
        call(public void com.oreilly.aspectjcookbook.Bank.transfer(..));

    private class TransferTransaction extends ThreadLocal implements Transaction
    {
        private Account from;
        private Account to;
        private float value;

        public TransferTransaction(Account from, Account to, float value)
        {
            this.from = from;
            this.to = to;
            this.value = value;
        }

        public void commit()
        {
            System.out.println("Committing");
            // Nothing to actually commit here, all the changes have been accepted ok
        }

        public void rollback()
        {
            System.out.println("Rolling back");
            try
            {
                to.debit(value);
```

Example 22-5. Implementing transactional behavior where a transfer occurs between two bank accounts within an example application (continued)

```
        }
        catch(InsufficientFundsException ife)
        {
            System.err.println("Could not complete rollback!");
            ife.printStackTrace();
        }
    }
}

protected void setupTransaction(Object[] args)
{
    this.transaction =
        new TransferTransaction(
            (Account) args[0],
            (Account) args[1],
            ((Float)args[2]).floatValue());
}
}
```

See Also

This example was adapted from the presentation given by Ron Bodkin, New Aspects of Security, available at *http://newaspects.com/presentations/*; *Java Enterprise in a Nutshell* by William Crawford, Jim Farley and David Flanagan (O'Reilly) covers transactions in the enterprise Java application; the call(Signature) pointcut is covered in Recipe 4.1; the cflowbelow(Pointcut) pointcut is described in Recipe 10.2; the before() form of advice is covered in Recipe 13.3; the after() returning form of advice is covered in Recipe 13.6; the after() throwing form of advice is covered in Recipe 13.7; defining abstract aspects and pointcuts is explained in Recipe 15.4; the Director aspect-oriented design pattern is discussed in Recipe 23.3.

22.3   Applying Resource Pooling

Problem

You want to optimize the access to a commonly used resource by creating a reusable pool of those resources without affecting the existing operation of your application.

Solution

Using the Director aspect-oriented design pattern, create an abstract aspect that defines the roles of the Resource and Resource Pool as interfaces and the generic reusable behavior of resource pooling, as shown in Example 22-6. The abstract resource pooling aspect can then be specialized for each resource to be pooled within your target application.

Example 22-6. Defining the generic resource pooling behavior in an abstract aspect

```
public abstract aspect ResourcePoolingAspect
{
   public interface Resource
   {

   }

   public interface ResourcePool
   {
      public void add(Resource resource);
      public Resource remove( );
   }

   protected class ResourcePoolsCollection
   {
      WeakHashMap pools = new WeakHashMap( );

      public void putResourcePool(ResourcePool pool, Class resourceClass)
      {
         pools.put(resourceClass, pool);
      }

      public ResourcePool getResourcePool(Class resourceClass)
      {
         return (ResourcePool) pools.get(resourceClass);
      }
   }

   protected ResourcePoolsCollection resourcePools = new ResourcePoolsCollection( );

   public ResourcePoolingAspect( )
   {
      initializeSpecificPool( );
   }

   protected abstract void initializeSpecificPool( );

   private pointcut excludeAspects( ) : !within(ResourcePoolingAspect+);

   public abstract pointcut catchResourceConstruction( );

   public abstract pointcut catchResourceDestruction(Resource resource);

   Object around( ) : catchResourceConstruction( ) && excludeAspects( )
   {
      ResourcePool resources =
         resourcePools.getResourcePool(
            thisJoinPoint.getSignature().getDeclaringType( ));
      return resources.remove( );
   }
```

```
Object around(Resource resource) :
    catchResourceDestruction(resource) && excludeAspects( )
{
    ResourcePool resources =
        resourcePools.getResourcePool(
            thisJoinPoint.getSignature().getDeclaringType( ));
    Object returnValue = resourceReturnedToPool(resource);
    System.out.println("Resource added back into pool: " + resource);
    resources.add(resource);
    return returnValue;
}

protected abstract Object resourceReturnedToPool(Resource resource);

// A resource must use and resort to a simple default constructor for initialization
// As protected by the warning declared below
declare warning : call(public Resource+.new(*,..))
    : "Use a default constructor when using classes declared as pooled resources";
}
```

Discussion

Example 22-6 shows how a reusable abstract aspect can be defined that will provide resource pooling within an application that originally did not support it. The Resource and ResourcePool interfaces are declared so the generic resource pooling behavior can be defined against those interfaces separately from how those interfaces may be implemented.

The behavior declared within the abstract ResourcePoolingAspect is shared across all of the resource pools declared as subaspects. The ResourcePoolCollection class provides a common repository for all the resource pools throughout your application so the generic code can look up a specific resource pool based on the class of the resource it contains.

When the ResourcePoolingAspect is initialized, a call is made to the abstract initializeSpecificPool( ) method. This method is implemented by subaspects of the ResourcePoolingAspect to initialize their own pool implementations and add them to the ResourcePoolCollection.

The abstract catchResourceConstruction( ) and catchResourceDestruction(Resource) pointcuts are provided so subaspects can specify the join points where a resource is first accessed and released. The pointcuts are then applied to the two sets of around( ) advice that override when a resource is created or destroyed so the resources that exist in the corresponding resource pool can be used instead. The abstract resourceReturnedToPool( ) method is called when a resource is released and placed back in its corresponding pool to give the subaspects an opportunity to do any applicable post-processing.

Example 22-7 shows how the abstract ResourcePoolingAspect can be applied to an example application. Once the aspect is applied, objects of the BusinessResource class are obtained and released back into a resource pool transparently to the rest of the application.

Example 22-7. Applying resource pooling to a resource within a simple example application

```java
import java.util.List;
import java.util.ArrayList;

import com.oreilly.aspectjcookbook.BusinessResource;

public aspect BusinessResourcePoolingAspect extends ResourcePoolingAspect
{
    declare parents : BusinessResource implements Resource;

    public pointcut catchResourceConstruction() : call(public BusinessResource.new());

    public pointcut catchResourceDestruction(Resource resource) :
        call(public void BusinessResource.close()) && target(resource);

    private class BusinessResourcePool implements ResourcePool
    {
        private static final int RESOURCE_POOL_SIZE = 10;

        List resources = new ArrayList();

        public BusinessResourcePool()
        {
            for (int x = 0; x < RESOURCE_POOL_SIZE; x++)
            {
                this.add(new BusinessResource());
            }
        }

        public synchronized void add(Resource resource)
        {
            resources.add(resource);
        }

        public synchronized Resource remove()
        {
            if (resources.size() == 0)
            {
                resources.add(new BusinessResource());
            }
            return (Resource) resources.remove(resources.size() - 1);
        }
    }

    protected void initializeSpecificPool()
    {
        try
```

Example 22-7. Applying resource pooling to a resource within a simple example application (continued)

```
        {
            this.resourcePools.putResourcePool(new BusinessResourcePool( ),
                Class.forName("com.oreilly.aspectjcookbook.BusinessResource"));
        }
        catch (ClassNotFoundException cnfe)
        {
            System.err.println("Couldn't find resource class to pool");
        }
    }

    protected Object resourceReturnedToPool(Resource resource)
    {
        // Do any resource specific tudying up if necessary
        // None to do in this example
        return null;
    }
}
```

The BusinessResourcePoolingAspect applies the Resource role to the example application's BusinessResource class. The catchResourceConstruction( ) and catchResourceDestruction(Resource) pointcuts are implemented to specify when a BusinessResource is constructed and when it is released by a call to its close( ) method.

The ResourcePool role is implemented by the BusinessResourcePool class, which contains a list of BusinessResource objects. If the application needed it, this resource pool could be implemented in more efficient ways depending on the situation and the requirements.

Finally, the initializeSpecificPool( ) method is implemented to construct the single instance of the BusinessResourcePool. This BusinessResourcePool will be added to the ResourcePoolCollection managed by the parent ResourcePoolingAspect. The BusinessResource objects do not require anything special to be done when they are released back into the pool so the resourceReturnedToPool(Resource) method does nothing extra in this case.

See Also

The call(Signature) pointcut is described in Recipe 4.1; using the call(Signature) pointcut to capture and override a call to a constructor is examined in Recipes 7.1 and 20.1; using the target( ) pointcut is described in Recipe 4.3; the around( ) form of advice is covered in Recipe 13.4; defining abstract aspects and pointcuts is explained in Recipe 15.4; the Director aspect-oriented design pattern is explained in Recipe 23.3.

22.4   Remoting a Class Transparently Using RMI

Problem

You want to use Java Remote Method Invocation (RMI) to remote calls on a local object to an instance on another machine without making changes to how the original local object is used.

Solution

Create an RMI server application that contains an instance of the class, as shown in Example 22-8.

Example 22-8. Declaring an instance of BusinessClass that is contained within an RMI Server implementation

```java
import java.rmi.RemoteException;
import java.rmi.server.UnicastRemoteObject;

public class ThisOrThatServerImpl extends UnicastRemoteObject
    implements ThisOrThatServer
{
    BusinessClass businessClass = new BusinessClass();

    public ThisOrThatServerImpl() throws RemoteException
    {

    }

    public void foo() throws RemoteException
    {
        this.businessClass.foo();
    }
}
```

Within the client application, create an aspect that intercepts the calls to a specific instance of the class that has been remoted and route those calls to the corresponding RMI server, as shown in Example 22-9.

Example 22-9. Intercepting calls to a local instance and channeling those calls to the remotely managed instance

```java
import java.rmi.*;

public aspect RemoteBusinessClassAspect
{
    public pointcut callBusinessClassFooInMain() :
        call(public void BusinessClass.foo()) &&
        withincode(public void MainApplication.main(String[]));
```

Example 22-9. Intercepting calls to a local instance and channeling those calls to the remotely managed instance (continued)

```
void around() : callBusinessClassFooInMain()
{
    try
    {
        ThisOrThatServer rmtServer =
            (ThisOrThatServer) Naming.lookup("rmi://localhost/TTServer");
        rmtServer.foo();
    }
    catch (Exception e)
    {
        System.err.println("Problems occured when attempting " +
        "to use remote object, default to local");
        proceed();
    }
}
}
```

Discussion

Using Java RMI can intrude on your application's classes in terms of new interfaces, new exceptions, and new code that must be incorporated. Traditionally, the object-oriented façade design pattern could be used to hide these complexities, but by using aspects, you are given the ability to use RMI to remote areas of your application transparently to your existing code and without the addition of a complex façade.

The RemoteBusinessClass aspect in Example 22-9 captures when the foo() method is called on the BusinessClass instance within the execution of the application's main(..) method. The corresponding around() advice overrides that call and attempts to pass the message to the remote instance of BusinessClass as managed by the RMI Server and identified as TTServer in this case. If any exceptions occur when attempting to use the remote object, then the aspect reverts to using the original local instance by making the call to proceed().

RMI has some peculiarities that you need to know about to use the example code that accompanies this recipe, available at *http://www.aspectjcookbook.com*. The *readme.txt* file that is provided with the example code contains useful information on how to get RMI and the example working properly.

See Also

The foundation of this example was supplied by *Java Enterprise in a Nutshell* by William Crawford, Jim Farley, and David Flanagan (O'Reilly); the call(Signature) pointcut is described in Recipe 4.1; the withincode(Signature) pointcut is described in Recipe 9.3; the around() form of advice is covered in Recipe 13.4.

22.5   Applying a Security Policy

Problem

You want to add security considerations to areas of an existing application.

Solution

Define an aspect that specifies join points within your application that need to be subjected to additional security. When those join points are encountered, store and authenticate against a specific security implementation within the aspect, as shown in Example 22-10.

Example 22-10. Applying authentication to calls on a specific class

```
public aspect SecureClassAAspect
{
    private boolean authenticated;

    public pointcut secureClassAMethods() :
        call(* com.oreilly.aspectjcookbook.ClassA.*(..));

    Object around() : secureClassAMethods()
    {
        if (authenticated)
        {
            return proceed();
        }
        else
        {
            LoginScreen loginScreen = new LoginScreen();
            loginScreen.setVisible(true);

            // Use the authentication procedure of your choice here
            // In this simple example we are just going to check that
            // it is the one person we know of
            if ((loginScreen.getUsername().equals("Kim")) &&
                (new String(loginScreen.getPassword()).equals("password")))
            {
                authenticated = true;
                loginScreen.dispose();
                return proceed();
            }
            loginScreen.dispose();
            return null;
        }
    }
}
```

Discussion

Security is an ideal example of a cross-cutting concern. Security characteristics rarely have anything to do with the simple business logic of an application. They are often intrusive and, unfortunately, the last thing to be applied to a piece of software.

In Example 22-10, the aspect captures when any method on the ClassA class is called and checks to see if the current user is authenticated to run those methods. In this example, authentication takes the form of displaying a login dialog comparing the username and password with some internally stored constants. Once the user has been recognized, the aspect's authenticated attribute is set to remember that no future checks are necessary as the application calls other methods on instances of ClassA.

 Example 22-10 uses a simple authentication mechanism to keep this recipe focused on the aspect-oriented characteristics of applying a security policy rather than on the particulars of a specific authentication technology. In practice, consider using a more formal authentication procedure such as JAAS.

By applying security with aspects, you can modularize your security code in one place, apply the security policies transparently to a large degree, and apply security to an application where the concern was not originally part of the design.

See Also

Java Security by Scott Oaks (O'Reilly) goes into more detail on how to use JAAS and Java's other security features in your applications; the call(Signature) pointcut is described in Recipe 4.1; the around( ) form of advice is covered in Recipe 13.4.

CHAPTER 23

Applying Aspect-Oriented
Design Patterns

23.0 Introduction

You've already seen how AspectJ can provide enhancements to existing object-oriented design patterns in Chapters 17 through 19. This books finishes by giving you an overview of some of the emerging best practices in AspectJ software development by focusing on some of the new aspect-oriented design patterns and how those patterns are implemented using AspectJ.

Aspect-oriented design patterns are common, best practice aspect-oriented solutions to common aspect-oriented design problems. AspectJ idioms are common uses of the AspectJ language syntax and tool usage. Although aspect-orientation is a fairly new discipline and AspectJ an even younger implementation of that discipline, the active AspectJ community has discovered some design patterns and idioms.

As adoption of the aspect-oriented approach continues to increase in momentum, new best practices will be discovered and captured as design patterns. In time these discoveries could lead to as rich and useful a collection of patterns as those that the object-oriented development community enjoys.

For more information and examples of AspectJ language and tool usage idioms check out Ron Bodkin's work on the aTrack project, which has a wealth of reusable aspect and pointcut libraries, available at *http://atrack.dev.java.net* Check out Mik Kersten's standard pointcut idioms, which are available by going to *http://www.eclipse.org/ aspectj* and clicking on Documentation → standard pointcut idioms. These two experts have provided some of the pioneering work on AspectJ language and tool idioms.

23.1   Applying the Cuckoo's Egg Design Pattern

Problem

You want to override the type of object instantiated on a constructor call to return an object of a different class transparently to the original business logic.

Solution

Apply the Cuckoo's Egg aspect-oriented design pattern. Figure 23-1 shows the key components of the Cuckoo's Egg pattern.

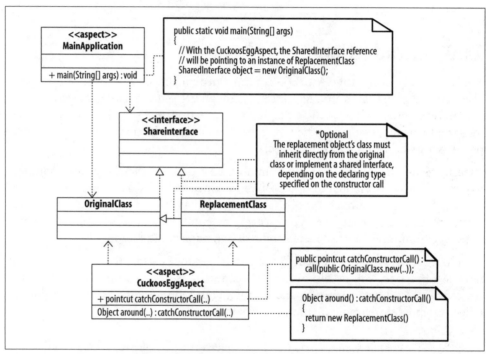

Figure 23-1. The structure of the Cuckoo's Egg pattern

The key roles in the Cuckoo's Egg pattern shown in Figure 23-1 are:

CuckoosEggAspect

   The aspect at the center of the design pattern that intercepts the creation of the OriginalClass class and instead returns an instance of ReplacementClass.

SharedInterface

   Optional component of the pattern. According to the AspectJ rules for overriding around( ), the ReplacementClass must inherit from the type expected on the constructor call. In this example, that type is the SharedInstance interface.

`OriginalClass`
> The class originally being constructed when that constructor call is overridden by the `CuckoosEggAspect`.

`ReplacementClass`
> The class instantiated when the constructor call to `OriginalClass` is overridden.

`MainApplication`
> Represents an example area within your application where the constructor call to `OriginalClass` is to be overridden.

Discussion

As simple as the Cuckoo's Egg pattern is, it is one of the more powerful capabilities of aspect orientation as implemented in AspectJ. It is reasonably common to want to control and change an object instantiated on a constructor call or on a factory method when an aspect is applied. The Cuckoo's Egg design pattern formalizes this common AspectJ use case.

Example 23-1 is modified from Recipe 20.2 and shows how the Cuckoo's Egg pattern can be implemented in AspectJ to return an instance of `AnotherClass` when a `MyClass` constructor is called.

Example 23-1. An example of the Cuckoo's Egg design pattern

```
public aspect ControlClassSelectionAspect // Cuckoo's Egg Aspect
{
    public pointcut myClassConstructor() : call(MyClass.new());

    Object around() : myClassConstructor()
    {
        return new AnotherClass();
    }
}
```

The key characteristics of the Cuckoo's Egg pattern are:

- It provides a suitable pointcut declaration to capture the construction of a class to be overridden.
- You can obtain any arguments supplied on the original constructor call by using the args([Types | Identifiers]) pointcut to pass the identifiers to the corresponding advice if applicable.

The Cuckoo's Egg pattern is useful in circumstances where you do the following:

- Implement mock objects for testing purposes
- Provide a proxy object in place of real instance of the class

The Cuckoo's Egg pattern can collaborate with the Border Controller design pattern, which can be used to limit the constructor calls to a particular class overridden by the Cuckoo's Egg pattern.

See Also

The article at *http://www.onjava.com/pub/a/onjava/2004/10/20springaop2.html* shows how to implement the Cuckoo's Egg Pattern using the Spring Framework; using the call(Signature) pointcut to capture and override a call to a constructor is described in Recipes 7.1 and 20.1; the around( ) form of advice is covered in Recipe 13.4; the AspectJ rules on how overriding around( ) advice can be applied are covered in more detail in Recipe 20.2.

23.2   Applying the Director Design Pattern

Problem

You want to define a set of roles to be implemented by unknown sets of application classes so they can be interacted with generically by an abstract aspect.

Solution

Apply the Director aspect-oriented design pattern. Figure 23-2 shows the key components of the Director pattern.

The key roles in the Director pattern shown in Figure 23-2 are:

DirectorAspect
> The abstract aspect at the center of the design pattern that specifies the roles to be directed using Java interfaces and optionally specifies interactions that can occur between those roles.

Role1 *and* Role2
> A pair of example roles defined as nested interfaces within the abstract DirectorAspect.

BusinessClassA *and* BusinessClassB
> A pair of business classes within the target application that are candidates for the roles defined by the DirectorAspect.

SpecializedAspect
> Applies the roles to specific classes within the target application. In this example, Role1 is applied to BusinessClassA and Role2 is applied to BusinessClassB. When BusinessClassB does not implement the bar( ) method necessary for the Role2 interface, this can be supplied using static cross-cutting techniques by the SpecializedAspect.

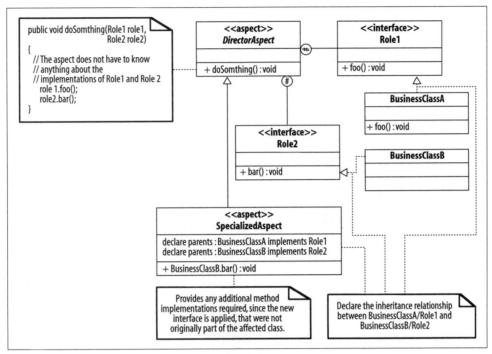

Figure 23-2. The structure of the Director pattern

Discussion

The Director pattern decouples the generic and reusable aspect behavior from the implementation classes of a specific application, allowing the aspect's logic to direct the abstract roles rather than the implementations.

Example 23-2 is modified from Recipe 19.1 and shows how the Director pattern can be implemented in AspectJ to specify the Subject and Observer roles along with some default implementation details for the Subject role.

Example 23-2. An example of the Director pattern

```
public abstract aspect ObserverPattern
{
    protected interface Subject
    {
        public void addObserver(Observer observer);
        public void removeObserver(Observer observer);
    }

    protected interface Observer
    {
        public void notifyOfChange(Subject subject);
    }
```

Example 23-2. An example of the Director pattern (continued)

```
    private List Subject.observers = new LinkedList( );

    public void Subject.addObserver(Observer observer)
    {
        this.observers.add(observer);
    }

    public void Subject.removeObserver(Observer observer)
    {
        this.observers.remove(observer);
    }

    private synchronized void Subject.notifyObservers( )
    {
        Iterator iter = this.observers.iterator( );
        while (iter.hasNext( ))
        {
            ((Observer)iter.next( )).notifyOfChange(this);
        }
    }

    protected abstract pointcut subjectChange(Subject s);

    after(Subject subject) : subjectChange(subject)
    {
        subject.notifyObservers( );
    }
}
```

Example 23-3, modified from Recipe 19.1, shows how the abstract `ObserverPattern` aspect uses the Director pattern to apply the `Observer` and `Subject` roles to the `ConcreteClassA` and `ConcreteClassB` target application classes.

Example 23-3. Applying the Director patterns roles to the target application's classes

```
public aspect ConcreteClassAObserver extends ObserverPattern
{
    declare parents : ConcreteClassB implements Subject;

    declare parents : ConcreteClassA implements Observer;

    protected pointcut subjectChange(Subject s) :
        call(* ConcreteClassB.set*(..))
        && target(s);

    public void ConcreteClassA.notifyOfChange(Subject subject)
    {
        this.doSomething(
            "ConcreteClassA was notified of a change on " + subject);
    }
}
```

Here are the key characteristics of the Director pattern:

- Provides a mechanism for declaring reusable aspect logic, including advice, and how it can interact with a set of abstract roles without having to know what target implementation classes will be coupled to those roles
- Supports the encapsulation of the roles and the logic that works upon those roles in one place: the Director aspect
- Allows you to declare logic that can be applied to entire families of target application classes

The Director pattern is useful in circumstances where you want to:

- Define an abstract aspect without knowing what target application classes the aspect's logic will be applied to
- Implement a set of relationships between abstract entities within your application, such as the implementation of an object-oriented design pattern

 Since the release of AspectJ 1.1, applying abstract roles as interfaces according to the Director pattern is the only way to introduce behavior across multiple classes as explained in the AspectJ documentation available at *http://dev.eclipse.org/viewcvs/indextech.cgi/~checkout~/aspectj-home/doc/README-11.html#SINGLE_INTERCLASS_TARGET*.

See Also

Using abstract aspects and pointcuts and declaring the inheritance between aspects is covered in Chapter 15; the Director pattern is most prominently used throughout Chapters 17 through 19 when implementing the traditional object-oriented design patterns using aspect-oriented techniques.

23.3   Applying the Border Control Design Pattern

Problem

You want to formally define important regions within your application so your aspects can reuse those definitions to ensure they are only applied in the correct areas.

Solution

Apply the Border Control aspect-oriented design pattern. Figure 23-3 shows the key components of the Border Control pattern.

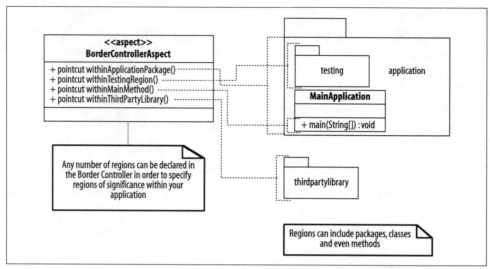

Figure 23-3. The structure of the Border Controller pattern

The key roles in the Border Control pattern shown in Figure 23-3 are:

BorderControllerAspect
>   The aspect at the center of the design pattern that specifies any important regions in your application that can be used by other aspects to limit their effects to the appropriate areas

The application, application.testing, *and* thirdpartylibrary *packages*
>   The example target application's important packages as they are selected by the BorderControllerAspect's reusable pointcut declarations

MainApplication
>   The main(String[]) method of this class provides an example of an important region inside a class

Discussion

The Border Controller declares important characteristic regions of your code that can be method, class, and package in scope. Example 23-4 is modified from Recipe 22.1 and shows how the Border Controller pattern can be implemented in AspectJ to specify a set of regions that include packages and methods within an example application.

Example 23-4. An example of the Border Controller pattern

```
public aspect BorderControllerAspect
{
    /**
     * Specifies the testing region.
     */
```

Example 23-4. An example of the Border Controller pattern (continued)

```
    public pointcut withinTestingRegion() :
        within(com.oreilly.aspectjcookbook.testing.+);

    /**
      * Specifies My Applications region.
      */
    public pointcut withinMyApp() : within(com.oreilly.aspectjcookbook.myapp.+);

    /**
      * Specifies a third party source code region.
      */
    public pointcut withinThirdParty() :
        within(com.oreilly.aspectjcookbook.thirdpartylibrary.+);

    /**
      * Specifies the applications main method.
      */
    public pointcut withinMyAppMainMethod() :
        withincode(public void com.oreilly.aspectjcookbook.myapp.MyClass.main(..));
}
```

In Example 23-4, the regions declared in the Border Controller aspect could then be reused within the target application's aspects:

```
    pointcut regionsOfInterest() :
        BorderControllerAspect.withinMyAppMainMethod() ||
        BorderControllerAspect.withinThirdParty() ||
        BorderControllerAspect.withinTestingRegion();
```

Here are the key characteristics of the Border Controller pattern:

- It provides a mechanism for declaring reusable pointcut logic that formalizes your application's architecture.

- The regions that are declared within a Border Controller aspect can be reused throughout your application's aspects whenever an aspect is to work within one or more specific application areas only.

- If the structure of your application were to change and the Border Controller pattern had been applied, then it is likely that only the Border Controller aspect would need to be updated to reflect these changes throughout all the aspects in your application.

- The Border Controller is usually best applied as a singleton in that one Border Controller is usually enough for a single application.

The Border Controller pattern is useful when you want to do the following:

- Have an application of reasonable complexity where there are defined internal areas to your application to which aspects must be constrained.

- Protect your application's aspects from future changes to overall application structure. To save yourself the headache of updating all your aspects when your application's structure changes, the Border Controller pattern provides a single point where those changes can be made and automatically reflected across your applications aspects.

The Border Controller design pattern can be used as a foundation to define an application's structure when using most design patterns and applications, including the Cuckoo's Egg and Policy aspect-oriented design patterns.

See Also

The programmatic scope based pointcuts are examined in Chapter 9; the Border Controller aspect is used in Recipe 22.1; the Cuckoo's Egg aspect-oriented design pattern is described in Recipe 23.1; the Policy aspect-oriented design pattern is described in Recipe 23.4.

23.4   Applying the Policy Design Pattern

Problem

You want to define a set of development rules within a policy that can be applied to your application's structure.

Solution

Apply the Policy aspect-oriented design pattern. Figure 23-4 shows the key components of the Policy pattern.

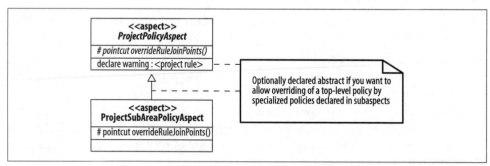

Figure 23-4. The structure of the Policy pattern

The key roles in the Policy pattern shown in Figure 23-4 are:

ProjectPolicyAspect

> The aspect that specifies project-wide or top-level policies for your application. This can optionally be declared abstract if it is to be extended by specialized subaspects.

ProjectSubAreaPolicyAspect

> In this case, the ProjectPolicyAspect has been declared abstract leaving an abstract pointcut that gives this subaspect the ability to override the top-level rules according to the specifics of a particular project subarea's policy.

Discussion

The Policy pattern can declare a set of rules for any area within your application. Those rules can vary from being compiler errors and warnings to overriding the use of certain classes and libraries.

Example 23-5 is modified from Recipe 22.1 and shows how the Policy pattern can be implemented in AspectJ to specify a top-level policy for an example application that contains one rule stating that if the Java System.out.println(..) method is called then a warning is to be issued at compilation time.

Example 23-5. An example of the policy pattern being applying top level rules to an application

```
public abstract aspect ProjectPolicyAspect
{
    protected abstract pointcut allowedSystemOuts();

    declare warning :
        call(* *.println(..)) &&
        !allowedSystemOuts() &&
        !BorderControllerAspect.withinTestingRegion()
    : "System.out usage detected. Suggest using logging?";
}
```

Because, in this example, the top-level policy aspect is abstract and declares an abstract pointcut that can be used to override the System.out.println(..) rule, it can then be specialized for different areas within the target application, as shown in Example 23-6.

Example 23-6. Extending an abstract top-level policy

```
public aspect MyAppPolicyAspect extends ProjectPolicyAspect
{
    /**
     * Specifies regions within the application where messages
     * to System.out are allowed.
     */
```

Example 23-6. Extending an abstract top-level policy (continued)

```
    protected pointcut allowedSystemOuts( ) :
       BorderControllerAspect.withinMyAppMainMethod( ) ||
       BorderControllerAspect.withinThirdParty( ) ||
       BorderControllerAspect.withinTestingRegion( );
}
```

Here are the key characteristics of the Policy pattern:

- Provides a mechanism for rules that can be applied a compilation and runtime
- Can be used to declare a hierarchy of complex rules for different areas of your application

The Policy pattern is useful in the following circumstances:

- When you are developing an application where many developers are involved, such as in an open source project, and you want to convey some rules and guidelines for development more actively than simply by providing documentation.
- The policies can be changed to facilitate migration of the application from one set of libraries and APIs to another. At first, the use of a set of libraries could be warned against in the policy; this could be increased to an error when the libraries must not be used. Finally, if the libraries are still being used for any reason, a proxy could be applied to move code away from the forbidden library to the policy preferred one.

The Policy pattern can collaborate with the following design patterns:

- It may use the Cuckoo's Egg design pattern to override the usage of a particular class or library.
- It may use the Proxy object-oriented design pattern to intercept calls to a particular class or library and either reject or delegate those calls to the right library or class according to the applications policy.

You may want to define specialized policies for different areas of your application building on the Border Controller design pattern.

See Also

Extending the compiler to include new warnings and errors is shown in Recipe 16.6; how to implement the Proxy object-oriented pattern using aspect-oriented techniques is shown in Recipe 18.6; the Cuckoo's Egg aspect-oriented design pattern is explained in Recipe 23.1; the Border Controller aspect-oriented design pattern is explained in Recipe 23.3.

The AspectJ Runtime API

It is sometimes useful to access information about the join points that trigger an advice in your aspects at runtime, and AspectJ provides a runtime API in the `org.aspectj.*` packages that can be used for just this purpose. Figure A-1 shows the package breakdown for the AspectJ runtime API.

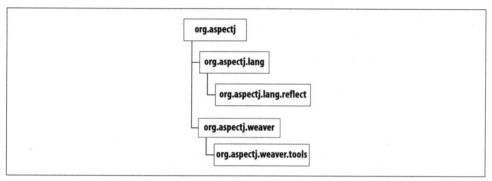

Figure A-1. The package structure of the AspectJ runtime API

The main packages of the AspectJ runtime API contain:

`org.aspectj.lang`
Provides interfaces and support classes for discovering runtime information about join points.

`org.aspectj.lang.reflect`
Contains interfaces that provide more specialized information concerning join point signatures.

`org.aspectj.weaver.tools`
Provides interfaces to support a JVM class loader in performing load-time weaving.

This appendix focuses on the contents of `org.aspectj.lang` and `org.aspectj.lang.reflect` and gives a brief overview of each of the main components in those packages.

If you want to delve into the API, then the full documentation is available within your AspectJ installation at *%ASPECTJ_INSTALLATION_DIR%/doc/api/index.html*.

org.aspectj.lang

Similar to the familiar `java.lang` package that conatins the most fundamental constructs for the Java language, the `org.aspectj.lang` package provides a set of classes for interacting with join points at the most basic and common level.

JoinPoint and JoinPoint.StaticPart

Figure A-2 shows the structure of the `JoinPoint` and `JoinPoint.StaticPart` interfaces.

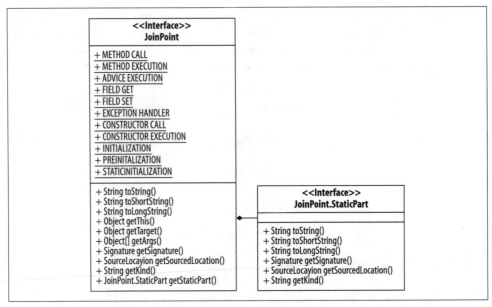

Figure A-2. The JoinPoint and JoinPoint.StaticPart interfaces

The JoinPoint interface

The `JoinPoint` interface is most commonly used by the `thisJoinPoint` reference that is made available to any advice block. The interface provides access to the dynamic and static information that is available about a specific join point.

`public String toString()`

Overrides the default `toString()` method on an object to return a string representation of the join point. An example of the string returned from the `toString()` method on a method call join point is:

```
call(void com.oreilly.aspectjcookbook.MyClass.foo(int, String))
```

```
public String toShortString()
```
Provides an alternative to the toString() method that returns an abbreviated version of the string representation of the join point. An example of the string returned from the toShortString() method on a method call join point is:

```
call(MyClass.foo(..))
```

```
public String toLongString()
```
Provides an alternative to the toString() method that returns an extended version of the string representation of the join point. An example of the string returned from the toLongString() method on a method call join point is:

```
call(public void com.oreilly.aspectjcookbook.MyClass.foo(int, java.lang.String))
```

```
public Object getThis()
```
Returns the object, if any, that is executing—i.e., the value of this reference—at the join point. Returns null if there is no reference at the corresponding join point, as is the case with static blocks of code.

```
public Object getTarget()
```
Returns the object, if any, that is the target of the join point. For example, the target of a method call join point is the object being called. Returns null if there is no target object at the corresponding join point.

```
public Object[] getArgs()
```
Returns an array containing the arguments, if any, available at a join point. For example, the getArgs() method returns the parameters being passed on a method call join point.

```
public Signature getSignature()
```
Returns the signature at the join point.

Note that the JoinPoint.StaticPart.getSignature() method returns the same value as this method.

```
public SourceLocation getSourceLocation()
```
Returns an object that contains all information available, if any, about the source location of the join point. A null will be returned if no source location information is available.

Note that the JoinPoint.StaticPart.getSourceLocation() method returns the same value as this method.

```
public String getKind()
```
Returns a string enumeration indicating the type of the join point. The JoinPoint interface declares the following constants that can be compared against the string that is returned from this method to determine the type of the join point:

METHOD_CALL

Indicates that the join point occurred on the call to a method. See Recipe 4.1 for the pointcut declaration that specifically captures this kind of pointcut.

METHOD_EXECUTION
> Indicates that the join point occurred during the execution of a method. See Recipe 4.2 for the pointcut declaration that specifically captures this kind of pointcut.

ADVICE_EXECUTION
> Indicates that the join point occurred during advice execution. See Recipe 4.3 for the pointcut declaration that specifically captures this kind of pointcut.

FIELD_GET
> Indicates that the join point occurred when an attribute was accessed. See Recipe 4.4 for the pointcut declaration that specifically captures this kind of pointcut.

FIELD_SET
> Indicates that the join point occurred when an attribute is modified. See Recipe 4.5 for the pointcut declaration that specifically captures this kind of pointcut.

EXCEPTION_HANDLER
> Indicates that the join point occurred when an exception was handled. See Recipe 4.6 for the pointcut declaration that specifically captures this kind of pointcut.

CONSTRUCTOR_CALL
> Indicates that the join point occurred on the call to a constructor. See Recipe 4.7 for the pointcut declaration that specifically captures this kind of join point.

CONSTRUCTOR_EXECUTION
> Indicates that the join point occurred during the execution of a constructor. See Recipe 4.8 for the pointcut declaration that specifically captures this kind of join point.

INITIALIZATION
> Indicates that the join point occurred during the initialization of an object. See Recipe 4.9 for the pointcut declaration that specifically captures this kind of join point.

PREINITIALIZATION
> Indicates that the join point occurred before the initialization of an object. See Recipe 4.10 for the pointcut declaration that specifically captures this kind of join point.

STATICINITIALIZATION
> Indicates that the join point occurred during the initialization of a class. See Recipe 4.11 for the pointcut declaration that specifically captures this kind of join point.

Note that the `JoinPoint.StaticPart.getKind()` method returns the same value as this method.

public `JoinPoint.StaticPart getStaticPart()`
> Returns an object that contains the information about a join point that can be statically determined. An alternative method for accessing the static information is to use the `thisJoinPointStaticPart` reference available to any advice block.

The JoinPoint.StaticPart interface

The `JoinPoint.StaticPart` interface is most commonly accessed using the `thisJoinPointStaticPart` reference available to all advice blocks. An alternative method is to use the `getStaticPart()` method on the `JoinPoint` interface that can be accessed using the `thisJoinPoint` reference.

public `String toString()`
> Overrides the default `toString()` method on an object to return a string representation of the join point.
>
> Note that the `JoinPoint.toString()` method returns the same value as this method.

public `String toShortString()`
> Provides an alternative to the `toString()` method that returns an abbreviated version of the string representation of the join point.
>
> Note that the `JoinPoint.toShortString()` method returns the same value as this method.

public `String toLongString()`
> Provides an alternative to the `toString()` method that returns an extended version of the string representation of the join point.
>
> Note that the `JoinPoint.toLongString()` method returns the same value as this method.

public `Signature getSignature()`
> Returns the signature at the join point.
>
> Note that the `JoinPoint.getSignature()` method returns the same value as this method.

public `SourceLocation getSourceLocation()`
> Returns an object that contains all information available, if any, about the source location of the join point. A `null` will be returned if no source location information is available.
>
> Note that the `JoinPoint.getSourceLocation()` method returns the same value as this method.

public `String getKind()`
> Returns a string enumeration indicating the type of the join point.

Note that the description of the `JoinPoint.getKind()` method shows the differ-ent enumerations that are supported by AspectJ.

Signature

A Signature interface is used to determine the signature of the code to which a join point is associated. The Signature interface provides access to the information avail-able at any join point, whereas its subinterfaces in the next section provide more information depending on the join point type. (See Figure A-3.)

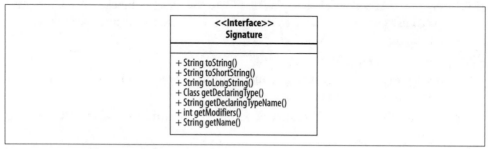

Figure A-3. The Signature interface

The Signature Interface

`public String toString()`
> Overrides the default `toString()` method on an object to return a string represen-tation of the signature. An example of the string returned from the `toString()` method on a method call join point is:
> ```
> void com.oreilly.aspectjcookbook.MyClass.foo(int, String)
> ```

`public String toShortString()`
> Provides an alternative to the `toString()` method that returns an abbreviated version of the string representation of the signature. An example of the string returned from the `toShortString()` method on a method call join point is:
> ```
> MyClass.foo(..)
> ```

`public String toLongString()`
> Provides an alternative to the `toString()` method that returns an extended ver-sion of the string representation of the signature. An example of the string returned from the `toLongString()` method on a method call join point is:
> ```
> public void com.oreilly.aspectjcookbook.MyClass.foo(int, java.lang.String)
> ```

`public Class getDeclaringType()`
> Returns the class that declared the member associated with the corresponding signature.

```
public String getDeclaringTypeName( )
```
Returns the fully qualified name of the member associated with the corresponding signature. An example of the string returned from the getDeclaringTypeName( )
method on a method call join point is:

```
com.oreilly.aspectjcookbook.MyClass
```
```
public int getModifiers( )
```
Returns the modifiers that are set on the corresponding signature.

Note that manipulating the int value that represents the modifiers using the
java.lang.reflect.Modifier class.

```
public String getName( )
```
Just returns the identifier section of the signature. An example of the string
returned from the getName( ) method on a method call join point is:

```
Foo
```

org.aspectj.lang.reflect

The org.aspectj.lang.reflect package contains a selection of more specialized
classes that represent specific types of join points and the additional information that
they may be able to provide at runtime.

The Specialized Subinterfaces of Signature

Depending on the join point, various specialized subinterfaces are available to access
the particulars of the signatures on different join points. Figure A-4 shows the relationships between the different interfaces that can be associated with join points.

The AdviceSignature interface

Represents the signature on an advice block:

```
public Class getReturnType( )
```
Returns the type of the object that a particular advice block returns, if any

The CatchClauseSignature interface

Represents the signature of a catch code block:

```
public String getParameterName( )
```
Returns object name being passed as the parameter to a particular catch block

```
public Class getParameterType( )
```
Returns object type that is being passed as the parameter to a particular
catch block

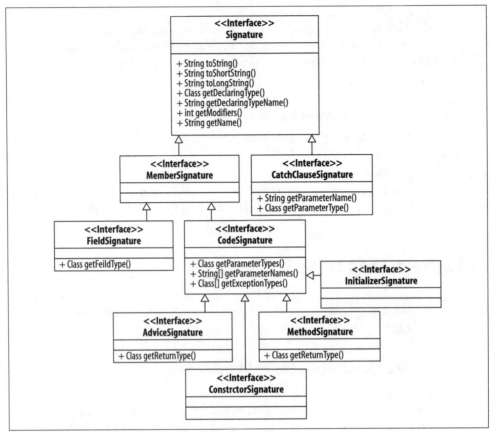

Figure A-4. The relationships between the Signature interface and its specialized subinterfaces

The CodeSignature interface

Represents the signature of a generic code block:

public Class[] getParameterTypes( )
> Returns the types of any available parameters on a signature

public String[] getParameterNames( )
> Returns the names of any available parameters on a signature

public Class[] getExceptionTypes( )
> Returns the types of any available exceptions that can be raised on a signature

The ConstructorSignature interface

Represents a constructor's signature.

The FieldSignature interface

Represents the signature of a field access or modification:

public Class getFieldType( )
> Returns field type being accessed or modified according to the signature and the associated join point

The InitializerSignature interface

Represents the signature of an object initialization.

The MemberSignature interface

Represents the signature of a join point that involves a class member.

The MethodSignature interface

Represents the signature on a method:

public Class getReturnType( )
> Returns the type of the object that a particular method returns, if any

SourceLocation

The SourceLocation interface defines the information that can potentially be accessed about the location within the source that a particular join point was encountered. (See Figure A-5.)

public String getFileName( )
> Returns the file name of the source file where the associated join point is located

public int getLine( )
> Returns the line in the source file where the associated join point is located

public Class getWithinType( )
> Returns the type that the join point is located within

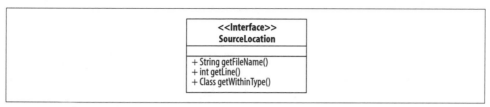

Figure A-5. The SourceLocation interface

The SoftException Class

The SoftException class is used when declaring exceptions that are thrown on a join point as softened into runtime exceptions.

Recipe 12.5 shows how exception softening is used.

The NoAspectBoundException Class

The NoAspectBoundException class is potentially used when an exception is thrown when the aspectOf(..) method is called to obtain access to a particular aspect and there are no aspects of the indicated type available.

Index

Symbols

&& (logical AND) operator
  combining pointcuts with, 118–120
  short-circuit behavior, 120
|| operator, 121
  short-circuiting behavior, 123
! (unary) operator, 123

A

abstract factory pattern, 183
accept(Visitor) class, 236
AccountPersistenceAspect aspect, 254
acknowledge( ) method, 240
adapter design pattern, 196
advice, 3, 29
  accessing attributes and methods from
    within, 129–131
  accessing join point context from
    within, 131–134
  advising same join point within same
    aspect, 145
  after( )
    change triggered, 279
    execute advice after, 139–140, 142
    outputing tracing messages, 263
    returning(<ReturnType>
      <Identifier>), 140–141
    returning(<ReturnValue>) form, 88
    throwing, 142
    throwing(<ExceptionType>
      <Identifier>), 142
    transactions, 285
  apply to other aspects, 146

around( )
  constructor calls on Singleton interface
    classes, 178
  join point triggers, executing advice
    around, 135
  overriding original logic with, 137
  return value required, 138
around(MainApplication) block, 255
aspects and pointcuts, relationship
    with, 4
before( )
  outputing tracing messages, 263
  transactions, 285
capturing join points on, 67–73
capturing value of field being
    accessed, 88–89
capturing when executing, 67, 68
executed
  after join point raised
    exception, 142–143
  after normally returned join
    point, 140–142
  after specific join point, 139
  all pointcut conditions true, 118
  around join point triggers, 135–138
  before join point triggers, 134
  excluding join points from within, 69
  one pointcut condition true, 120
exposing original join point while being
    advised, 72
javadoc tags, applying to, 18
join points, excluding execution, 69–72
JoinPoint implicit object passed to
    block, 73

We'd like to hear your suggestions for improving our indexes. Send email to *index@oreilly.com*.

compiler *(continued)*
    project forced rebuild, 22
    supplying files for, 13
    weaving, 6
        aspects into .jar files, 13
        load-time, 15–17
component scale aspects, 243–259
composite design pattern, 188–191
CompositeElement roles, 234
CompositePattern aspect, 190
ConcreteClassA class, 300
ConcreteClassAObserver aspect, 209
ConcreteClassB class, 300
Conditional pointcut logic, 115
configuration files
    .ajproperites file, 24
    excludeAspects.lst file, 26
    .lst files, 24
configuration properties, managing, 274
constructors
    calls to, capturing, 75
    no default, 176
ConstructorSignature interface, 314
ControlClassSelectionAspect aspect, 249
createMemento( ) method, 228
createNewFlyweight(...) abstract
        method, 194
createURLCalledinMainMethod( )
        pointcut, 247
cross-cutting, 2
    micro-scale, 243
Cuckoo's Egg design pattern, 296–298
    modularizing the override of a constructor
        call, 248
CuckoosEggAspect aspect, 296

D

declare error statement, 173
declare parents statement, 169
declare precedence statement, 143
declare soft statement, 172
declare warning statement, 173
DecoratedComponent interface, 200
decorator design pattern, 199–201
DecoratorPattern abstract aspect, 200
DefaultAlgorithmImplementation
        aspect, 238
delegateRequest(..) method, 272
DelegatingProxyPattern aspect, 270
DelegationProxy aspect, 204

deployment/lib directory, aspectjrt.jar
        within, 33
design patterns
    adapter, 196
    AspectJ
        abstract base class not needed, 175
        cleaner business logic, 175
        modularized code, less intrusive
          in, 175
    aspect-oriented, 295–306
    behavioral, 207–242
    Border Control, 301–304
    Border Controller
        Cuckoo's Egg pattern
          collaboration, 298
        declaring sets of regions, 281
        reusable pointcut definition
          library, 282
    bridge, 197–199
    chain of responsibility, 222–226
    command, 211–215
    composite, 188–191
    creational object-oriented, 175–187
    Cuckoo's Egg, 296–298
    decorator, 199–201
    Director, 176, 188, 216, 298–301
        BusinessClassA, 298
        BusinessClassB, 298
        chain of responsibility, 222
        classes, adding persistence to, 250
        DirectorAspect, 298
        resource pooling with, 286
        Role1 and Role2, 298
        roles for lazy loading, 269
        SpecializedAspect, 298
        transaction controlling with, 283
    façade, 241
    flyweight, 192–195
    Hannemann, Jan, 176
    interpreter, 240
        research by Jan Hanneman, 207
    iterator, 215–218
    Kiczales, Gregor, 176
    mediator, 218–222
    memento, 227–230
    observer, 207–211
        heirarchical manner of, 221
    policy, 304–306
        collaborates with, 306
        ProjectPolicyAspect, 305
        ProjectSubAreaPolicyAspect, 305
    proxy, 202–206

iterator design pattern, 215–218
IteratorPattern abstract aspect, 216

J

JAAS authentication procedure for security
    policies, 294
JAR files
    executable, 33–35
        deployment setup, 35
    weaving aspects into, 13
Java classes, pointcuts for initialization and
    construction stages, 74
Java Enterprise in a Nutshell (William
    Crawford, Jim Farley and David
    Flanagan), 286
Java in a Nutshell (David Flanagan), 33, 35
Java runtime requirements, 31
Java Security (Scott Oaks), 294
Java Server Pages (JSP), 41–45
Java Servlet & JSP Cookbook (Bruce W.
    Perry), 40, 45
Java Servlet executable, 35–40
    deployed structure, 39
javadoc generation, 17–20
java.util.Properties, 278
JBoss implementation, 280
join points, 3, 50, 99
    adding additional security to, 293
    advice execution, excluding from
        within, 69
    capturing
        advice, on, 67–73
        attributes, on, 85–92
        Boolean or combined, 115–128
        class and object construction
            stages, 74–84
        class initialization, 82–84
        constructor call matches
            signature, 74–76
        constructor execution, 77, 78
        control flow–based, 99–104
        exception handling, 61–66
        methods, 50–60
        object initialization, 79–81
        object preinitialization, 81, 82
        object type–based, 105–114
        within a class, 93–95
        within a method, 97–98
        within a package, 95
    code signature, determining, 312
    dynamic context information, 133

excluding result of advice
    execution, 69–72
getFileName() public String, 315
getLine() public int, 315
getWithinType() public Class, 315
ignoring during transaction life, 284
JoinPoint identifier, 72
JointPoint.StaticPart getStaticPart() public
    Joinpoint, 311
list of supported, 3
original join point, exposing while being
    advised, 72
originalJoinPoint identifier, 72
static context information, 133
(see also pointcuts)
JoinPoint class, 133
JoinPoint identifier, 72
JoinPoint interface, 308–312
    JoinPoint.StaticPart interface, 311
JoinPoint.StaticPart getStaticPart() public
    Joinpoint, 311

K

Kiczales, Gregor, 176
Krestein, Mik, 50, 295

L

LazyFeatureLoading aspect, 272
LazyFeatureProxy class, 273
LazyLoading aspect, 268–274
LazyProxy interface, 270
LinearSorter class, 232
logException(JoinPoint) abstract
    method, 265
logging
    API, plugging in, 267
    different ways concurrently, 267
    excluding from, 265
    passive aspects, 264–268
Logging abstract aspect, 264–265
logging and tracing passive aspects, 260
.lst files, 24

M

main(..) method, declaring location of, 281
MainApplicatin.run() method, 255
MainApplication aspect, 297
MainApplication class, 255
mainApplicationInitialization()
    pointcut, 279
main(String[]) method, 302

MalformedURLException, 247
Manager classes, 225
manifest file, 34
mappingColleagueToMediator lookup, 220
Measuring the Dynamic Behaviour of AspectJ
    Programs (Ganesh
    Sittampalam), 102
mediator design pattern, 218–222
    common mediator requirement, 225
mediator roles as interfaces, 220
MediatorPattern abstract aspect, 220
MemberSignature interface, 315
MementoPattern abstract aspect, 227
method calls, capturing, 50–54
    bar() call, 71
    on execution, 57
        "this" reference value, 59, 60
    parameter values, 54, 56
    targets, 56
methods
    acknowledge(), 240
    capturing all join points within, 97–98
    characteristic regions, declaring, 302
    close(), 290
    createMemento(), 228
    createNewFlyweight(...) abstract, 194
    declaring abstract with work flow, 238
    delegateRequest(..), 272
    extending behavior of, maintain public
        interface, 199
    getRealComponent(), 273
    getResult(), default implementation, 186
    getState(), 228
    getStaticPart(), 133
    initializeComponent(Object), 272
    initializeSpecificPool(), 288, 290
    Java System.out.println(..), 305
    logException(JoinPoint) abstract, 265
    main(..), declaring location of, 281
    MainApplicatin.run(), 255
    main(String[]), 302
    notifyMediator(Colleague,Mediator), 220
    notifyOfChange(Subject), 209
    overloading from mismatched
        parameters, 114
    parameters passed to,
        validating, 243–247
    resourceReturnedToPool(), 288
    resourceReturnedToPool(Resource), 290
    setMediator(Colleague, Mediator), 220
    setMemento(Memento), 228

setT(float), 130
setupTransaction(Object[ ]) abstract, 285
stub run(), 255
System.getProperty(), 274
ThirdPartyFactory.getThirdParty-
    Component() factory, 256
thisJoinPoint.getStaticPart(), 133
transactional behavior,
    introducing, 283–286
transactions, specifying treatment as, 284
MethodSignature interface, 315
mock component unit testing, 255–259
memento design pattern, 227–230
monitorMainApplicationProperty
    pointcut, 279
monitorMyClassProperty() pointcut, 279
MyAppPolicyAspect aspect, 282
myClassConstructor() pointcut, 249
myClassObjectCreation() pointcut, 279
myExceptionHandlerPointcut pointcut, 64

N

named pointcuts, 115
New Aspects of Security (Ron Bodkin), 286
NoAspectBoundException class, 316
NonSingleton interface, 177
notifyMediator(Colleague,Mediator)
    method, 220
notifyOfChange(Subject) method, 209

O

objects
    construction, capturing join points
        on, 74–84
    creating state change dependencies, 211
    duplicate supported by prototype
        pattern, 180
    getArgs() public Object[], 309
    getTarget() public Object, 309
    getThis() public Object, 309
    grouping together in a collection, 191
    incorporating fine-grained with flyweight
        patterns, 192
    overriding instantiation on constructor
        call, 296
    reinstating original state, 227
    request execution by heirarchy of, 236
    requests, encapsulation as, 211
    surrogate, 202
    XWindow, sharing, 198

pointcuts *(continued)*
    execution(Pointcuts)
        inherited or overridden methods, 54
        static and dynamic targets, 53, 54
    execution(Signature)
        capturing excuting methods, 57–59
        capturing "this" reference value, 59
        for constructors, 77
    filteredExceptionCapture( ), 265
    filteredPointsToBeTraced(Object), 263
    getConstrantPointcut( ), 87
    get(Signature), 85–92
        breaks encapsulation of private
            attributes, 88
        object's attribute, capturing when
            accessed, 85–88
        simple class, applied to, 86
    handler(TypePattern), 61–66, 265
        class hierarchy, simple, 63
        exceptions, 62, 64–65
    idioms, Mik Krestein's standard, 50, 295
    initialization(Signature), 79
        for constructors, 79–81
    for Java class and object initialization and
            construction stages, 74
    javadoc tags, applying to, 18
    join points
        on Java methods, 50
        picking with, 50
    mainApplicationInitialization( ), 279
    monitorMainApplicationProperty( ), 279
    monitorMyClassProperty( ), 279
    myClassConstructor( ), 249
    myClassObjectCreation( ), 279
    myExceptionHandlerPointcut, 64
    named, 115
    persistStorage(ObjectStore), 251
    pointcutadviceexecution( ), 67–68
        as parameter declaraion, 69
    pointsToBeExcluded( ), 263, 267
    pointsToBeTraced( ), 263, 267
    preinitialization(Signature), for
            constructors, 81–82
    regionsOfInterest( ), 303
    requestTriggered(..), 272
    restoreStorage(ObjectStore), 251
    reusable pointcut libraries, aTrack project
            (Ron Bodkin), 295
    reusable definition library, 282
    reusing, 115, 126–128
    selectSingletons( ) pointcut, 177

    set(Signature), 85–92
    solitary adviceexecution( ), 67
    staticinitialization(TypePattern), for
            constructors, 83–84
    target([Type | Identifier]), 108–110
    target(TypePattern | Identifier), 253
    this([Type | Identifier]), 59, 65, 106–108,
            130
    this(TypePattern | Identifier), 263
    traceCalls( ), 71
    tracedCalls( ), 71
    transactionBoundary( ), 284
    transactionCall( ), 284–285
    within( ), NOT (!) operator use, 69
    !within(CallRecipe+), 71
    withincode(Signature), 97
        class instantiation, overriding, 249
        key characteristics, 97
    within(TypePattern), 93–96
        capturing all join points within a
            package, 96
        class instantiation, overriding, 249
    (see also join points)
pointsToBeExcluded( ) pointcut, 263, 267
pointsToBeTraced( ) pointcut, 263, 267
policies
    issingleton( ) aspect instantiation, 148,
            178
    pertarget(Pointcut) aspect
            instantiation, 151
    perthis(..) aspect instantiation, 198
    perthis(Pointcut) aspect
            instantiation, 151
    scope, applying consistent, 283
    security, 293–294
policy design pattern, 304–306
    collaborates with, 306
    ProjectPolicyAspect, 305
    ProjectSubAreaPolicyAspect, 305
preinitialization(Signature) pointcut, for
            constructors, 81, 82
PrintableCharacter class, managed as
            flyweight, 194
PrintableCharacterFlyweight aspect, 194
PrintButton class, 225
PrintDialog class, 225
Printer class, 215
PrinterScreenAdapter aspect, 196
proceed( ) call, 137
programmatic constructs, controlling, 283

W

weaving
  aspects into .jar files, 13
  compile-time, 6
  load-time, 6, 15–17
Window class, capturing all methods of, 198
within() pointcut, NOT (!) operator use, 69
!within(CallRecipe+) pointcut, 71
withincode(Signature) pointcut, 97
  class instantiation, overriding, 249
withinMyApp() region, 281
withinMyAppMainMethod() region, 281

withinTestingRegion() region, 281
withinThirdParty() regions, 281
within(TypePattern) pointcut, 93–96
  capturing all join points within a
    package, 96
  class instantiation, overriding, 249

X

Xerox Parc, 2
XWindow object, sharing, 198
XWindowBridge aspect, 198

About the Author

Russ Miles is a developer with 10 years of programming experience in languages ranging from Basic on the Atari 800XL to Mono on Mac OS X. A confirmed Mac enthusiast, Russ has been focusing recently on complex distributed system development for multiplatform environments, including developments on various flavors of Windows, Linux, Unix, and Mac OS X. Russ is currently a Senior Technologist for General Dynamics UK Limited and is a consultant on projects ranging from internal tools development to international standards publications. Whenever possible, Russ likes to get back to the programming coal-face and is a contributor to various open source projects. He has also founded some of his own.

Russ "discovered" aspect-oriented programming when he accidentally attended the wrong meeting of the British Computer Society's Advanced Programming Specialist Group. Russ can't remember which meeting he was actually aiming for, but as luck would have it, the presentation he did attend, entitled "Aspect-Oriented Programming Using AspectJ," was given by Adrian Colyer of IBM. Impressed by the potential of aspect orientation and the maturity of AspectJ, Russ's perspective on software architecture was permanently changed. He immediately took advantage of this new approach, changing the way he and his team developed software. Fast-forward two years, and Russ is still developing and advocating the aspect-oriented approach. This book is the result of that experience triggered by that fortunate first meeting with the AspectJ folks.

Russ holds a first-class bachelor's degree in computer science from Greenwich University and is currently a member of Kellogg College at Oxford University, where he is finishing up his master's degree in computer science. He also writes articles for ONJava.com and java.net and is a technical advisor at O'Reilly.

Colophon

Our look is the result of reader comments, our own experimentation, and feedback from distribution channels. Distinctive covers complement our distinctive approach to technical topics, breathing personality and life into potentially dry subjects.

The animal on the cover of *AspectJ Cookbook* is a marmoset. Marmosets are small monkeys (usually no bigger than an oversized rat) that live in the tropical and subtropical forests of South America. They are arboreal and incredibly agile. Their powerful hind legs, dextrous claw-like hands, and extra-long tails make swinging from branch to branch a breeze.

Marmosets are not too picky about what they eat. They are partial to tree sap (the stickier the better), but they also enjoy lizards, frogs, snails, insects, fruit, and nectar.

A group of marmosets (a social group consists of 8–20 individuals) communicates with facial expressions, body movements, and occasional squeaks. They also rely heavily on smell to identify each other. A highly adaptable species, marmosets can endure blistering temperatures and sparse forest environments. Because of this tenacity, they are not under serious threat, unlike most other primates.

Matt Hutchinson was the production editor for *AspectJ Cookbook*. GEX, Inc. provided production services. Marlowe Shaeffer, Sarah Sherman, and Emily Quill provided quality control.

Emma Colby designed the cover of this book, based on a series design by Edie Freedman. The cover image is a 19th-century engraving from *Illustrated Natural History*. Clay Fernald produced the cover layout with QuarkXPress 4.1 using Adobe's ITC Garamond font.

Melanie Wang designed the interior layout, based on a series design by David Futato. This book was converted by Julie Hawks to FrameMaker 5.5.6 with a format conversion tool created by Erik Ray, Jason McIntosh, Neil Walls, and Mike Sierra that uses Perl and XML technologies. The text font is Linotype Birka; the heading font is Adobe Myriad Condensed; and the code font is LucasFont's TheSans Mono Condensed. The illustrations that appear in the book were produced by Robert Romano, Jessamyn Read, and Lesley Borash using Macromedia FreeHand MX and Adobe Photoshop CS. The tip and warning icons were drawn by Christopher Bing. This colophon was written by Matt Hutchinson.

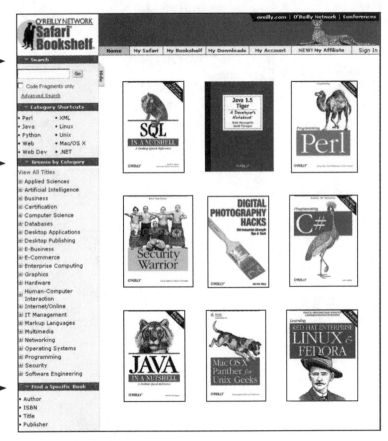

Related Titles Available from O'Reilly

Java

Ant: The Definitive Guide

Better, Faster, Lighter Java

Eclipse

Eclipse Cookbook

Enterprise JavaBeans,
4th Edition

Hardcore Java

Head First Java

Head First Servlets & JSP

Head First EJB

Hibernate:
A Developer's Notebook

J2EE Design Patterns

Java 1.5 Tiger:
A Developer's Notebook

Java & XML Data Binding

Java & XML

Java Cookbook, *2nd Edition*

Java Data Objects

Java Database Best Practices

Java Enterprise Best Practices

Java Enterprise in a Nutshell,
2nd Edition

Java Examples in a Nutshell,
3rd Edition

Java Extreme Programming
Cookbook

Java in a Nutshell, *4th Edition*

Java Management Extensions

Java Message Service

Java Network Programming,
2nd Edition

Java NIO

Java Performance Tuning,
2nd Edition

Java RMI

Java Security, *2nd Edition*

JavaServer Faces

Java ServerPages, *2nd Edition*

Java Servlet & JSP Cookbook

Java Servlet Programming,
2nd Edition

Java Swing, *2nd Edition*

Java Web Services in a Nutshell

Learning Java, *2nd Edition*

Mac OS X for Java Geeks

Programming Jakarta Struts
2nd Edition

Tomcat: The Definitive Guide

WebLogic:
The Definitive Guide

O'REILLY®

Our books are available at most retail and online bookstores.
To order direct: 1-800-998-9938 • *order@oreilly.com* • *www.oreilly.com*
Online editions of most O'Reilly titles are available by subscription at *safari.oreilly.com*

Keep in touch with O'Reilly

1. Download examples from our books

To find example files for a book, go to:

www.oreilly.com/catalog

select the book, and follow the "Examples" link.

2. Register your O'Reilly books

Register your book at *register.oreilly.com*

Why register your books?
Once you've registered your O'Reilly books you can:

- Win O'Reilly books, T-shirts or discount coupons in our monthly drawing.
- Get special offers available only to registered O'Reilly customers.
- Get catalogs announcing new books (US and UK only).
- Get email notification of new editions of the O'Reilly books you own.

3. Join our email lists

Sign up to get topic-specific email announcements of new books and conferences, special offers, and O'Reilly Network technology newsletters at:

elists.oreilly.com

It's easy to customize your free elists subscription so you'll get exactly the O'Reilly news you want.

4. Get the latest news, tips, and tools

www.oreilly.com

- "Top 100 Sites on the Web"—PC Magazine
- CIO Magazine's Web Business 50 Awards

Our web site contains a library of comprehensive product information (including book excerpts and tables of contents), downloadable software, background articles, interviews with technology leaders, links to relevant sites, book cover art, and more.

5. Work for O'Reilly

Check out our web site for current employment opportunities:

jobs.oreilly.com

6. Contact us

O'Reilly & Associates
1005 Gravenstein Hwy North
Sebastopol, CA 95472 USA

TEL: 707-827-7000 or 800-998-9938
(6am to 5pm PST)

FAX: 707-829-0104

order@oreilly.com
For answers to problems regarding your order or our products. To place a book order online, visit:

www.oreilly.com/order_new

catalog@oreilly.com
To request a copy of our latest catalog.

booktech@oreilly.com
For book content technical questions or corrections.

corporate@oreilly.com
For educational, library, government, and corporate sales.

proposals@oreilly.com
To submit new book proposals to our editors and product managers.

international@oreilly.com
For information about our international distributors or translation queries. For a list of our distributors outside of North America check out:

international.oreilly.com/distributors.html

adoption@oreilly.com
For information about academic use of O'Reilly books, visit:

academic.oreilly.com

O'REILLY®

Our books are available at most retail and online bookstores.
To order direct: 1-800-998-9938 • *order@oreilly.com* • *www.oreilly.com*
Online editions of most O'Reilly titles are available by subscription at *safari.oreilly.com*